LANDSCAPE
CONSTRUCTION

LANDSCAPE CONSTRUCTION

PROCEDURES, TECHNIQUES, AND DESIGN

FLOYD GILES
UNIVERSITY OF ILLINOIS

ISBN 0-87563-884-8

PUBLISHED BY

STIPES PUBLISHING L.L.C.
204 WEST UNIVERSITY AVENUE
CHAMPAIGN, ILLINOIS 61820

Preface

This book was written in an attempt to improve the home landscape. It is not a collection of plans intended only to explain how to build; rather, its purpose is to provide reasons why and how to design and build. Often, in the rush to install a landscape in order to beat either the weather or a construction deadline, time is not taken to determine how to build—and how to avoid some of the pitfalls of building. Most of the construction items discussed herein are the result of experiences gained during twenty-five years as a landscape contractor, vocational agriculture teacher, extension specialist, and professor of horticulture. I have either built or taken part in the designing and building of most of the projects described. Construction projects are grouped for easy location; the first part of the book is developed in sequence as the landscape would be implemented.

Whether they will do the work themselves or have it done, homeowners should know the how and what of a good landscape installation. An attractive, functional landscape that requires less maintenance will result from knowledge of sound installation practices and how to achieve them.

I would like to thank the many landscape contractors who have taken my classes over the years and shared their experiences with me, in particular Leo Kelly of the KellyGreen Company in Palatine, Illinois, a former student of mine at the University of Illinois. The decks and gazebos illustrated in this book were built by the KellyGreen Company.

The person most responsible for this book is my wife, Mary.

Table of Contents

Landscape Plan Implementation

Plan interpretation is the first skill necessary for implementing a landscape. Whether the plan is installed by a firm or an individual, it is important to be able to transfer measurements from the plan to the ground. Do this job very carefully. The smaller the scale, the more attention that must be given to measurements. In a plan drawn 1″ = 20′ for example, the width of a pencil is about 2′. Most residential drawings, however, are done at a scale of ⅛″ = 1′ or ¼″ = 1′ (fig. 1). Home landscape plans are most often drawn ⅛″ = 1′, small enough to be handled on a sheet of blueprint paper, but at the

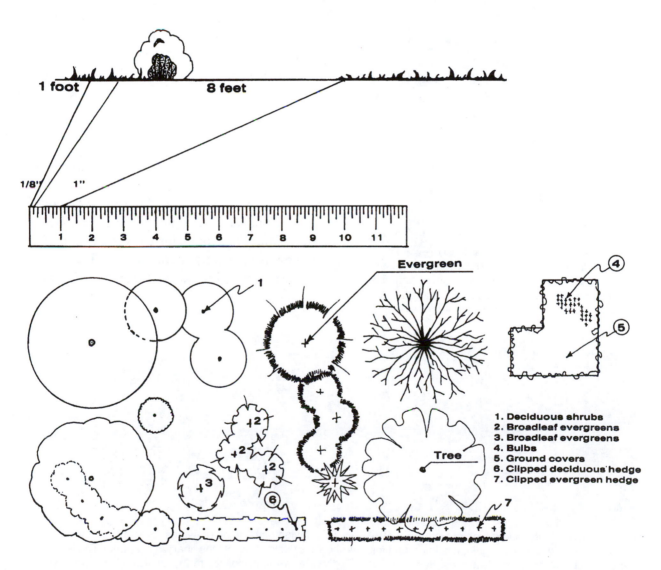

1. Deciduous shrubs
2. Broadleaf evergreens
3. Broadleaf evergreens
4. Bulbs
5. Ground covers
6. Clipped deciduous hedge
7. Clipped evergreen hedge

Figure 1. Every designer has a different style of drawing, which the contractor must be able to see and execute on the ground so the designer's intentions are maintained.

After a design has been finalized, it is inked. Color can be applied to help a client or contractor visualize a finished landscape.

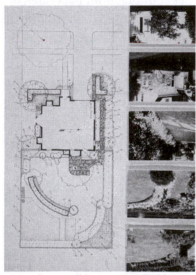

This design of a small house has five important areas, and the pictures at the side show how the designer wanted them to appear. It is important for a contractor to be able to achieve such designs.

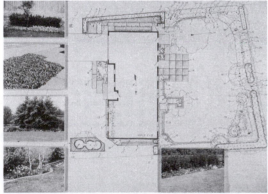

A larger plan with the same type of pictures. It also includes many structures. Again, it is important for the contractor to execute them correctly.

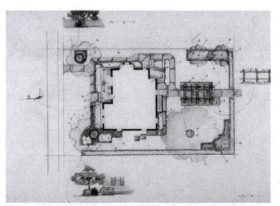

This design uses small drawings to help illustrate how the designer wants the final job to appear. That gives a vertical look to many of the important plantings and establishes scale of plants and structures compared to the home or business.

same time a good size to work with most landscape symbols. Plants and other objects are large enough to draw easily, and placement can be done exactly.

The installation should be done correctly, and the final landscape should be as the designer planned. This is extremely important to a contractor constructing a plan for another designer. Spend time with the designer and understand the desired look. Such effort can mean more work in the future if most of the designer's ideas materialize on the site. Tactfully point out construction faults or ideas for maintenance in order to help save installation and future upkeep costs.

Learn the symbols used in landscape planning—anything from a plain line indicating the space on the ground to an elaborate facsimile of the plant. Most designers develop their own plant symbols and other illustrative objects, making their drafting style as personal as their signature. When planning for home owners, it is a good idea to make a plan as descriptive as possible. Unfortunately, many designers fail to do so and do not communicate with their contractor or clients. Plans should be attractive, easy to read, and provide a feel for what plant material will look like when installed.

Staking out a landscape plan should be done before plant materials are purchased or brought to the site in order to avoid trips back to the shop for something that was forgotten. Staking also provides one more contact with the customer, ensuring that

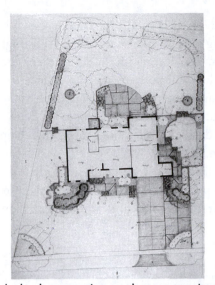

This design incorporates much more construction, and color has been used to highlight the areas. Execute the plan in a structurally sound manner and as close to the designer's wishes as possible.

the site and home owner are ready for the installation of the plan.

The plan should be done in the following order: install any and all hard materials such as edging, walls, or patios; stake out and prepare the planting beds; mulch; and, finally, plant and prune shrubs and trees where necessary. Water all plantings thoroughly before leaving the site. Lawn seeding or sodding is the last thing to be installed.

Figures 2–4 are three different styles of the same plan and should look the same when executed. The constant in all of the drawings are the dots or *x*'s marking the exact center of the new plant. The outline of each plant should be its mature spread. Often a designer will provide a perspective drawing of the

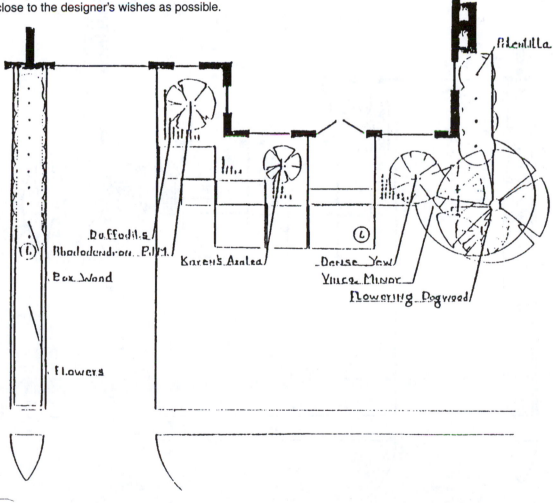

Figure 2. This drawing is done simply, with circles marking the mature sizes and a dot marking the center of the plant. It may take a great deal of discussion to arrive at a mutually satisfactory idea of how the plan should look.

landscape, portraying it at maturity. Such a drawing can be misleading and should be discussed thoroughly with the designer. The contractor's ability to engage in such a discussion will perhaps mean a chance to work with the designer on more projects. Clients should insist on participating in these discussions. By doing so, they will help decide on alterations rather than being surprised by them.

Staking out the plan can be just as important as drawing it. Make sure the measurements are taken from the drawing as carefully as possible and recheck them

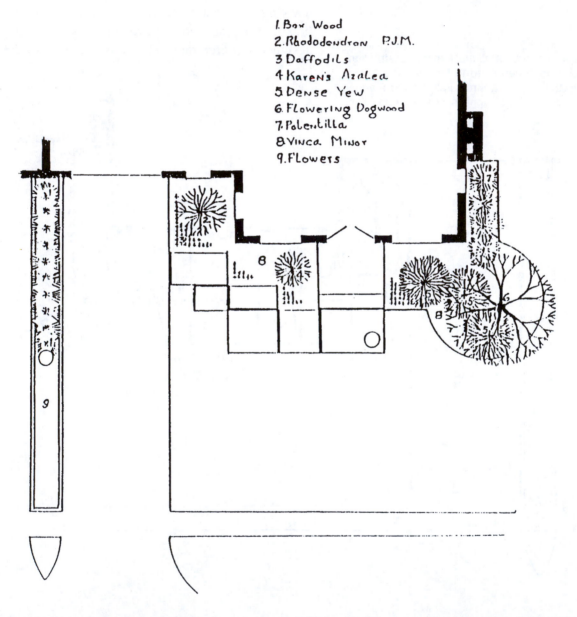

1. Box Wood
2. Rhododendron P.J.M.
3 Daffodils
4 Karen's Azalea
5 Dense Yew
6. Flowering Dogwood
7. Potentilla
8 Vinca Minor
9. Flowers

Figure 3. This drawing is more realistic than the first example; plants are marked using dots for deciduous plants and *x* marks for evergreens.

if there is any doubt of their accuracy. Then step back and look to see if the staking corresponds to your and the designer's mental images.

Many times a plan will specify a + with the letters *PP* (pivot point) following. That means that you swing an arc or radius of a curve or a circle (fig. 4). The *x* can be easily found on the ground and then the circle of curve can be marked off properly.

Many things happen on a job site from the time the plans are drawn until the job is completed. Underground utilities must be marked before digging starts

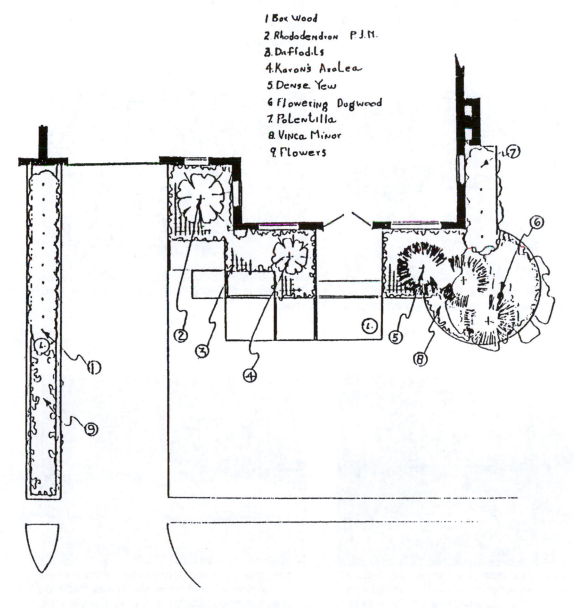

1 Box Wood
2. Rhododendron P.J.N.
3. Daffodils
4. Karon's Azolea
5. Dense Yew
6 Flowering Dogwood
7. Polentilla
8. Vinca Minor
9. Flowers

Figure 4. In this, the most realistic of the three examples, evergreens are not only marked with a + but the outline is also much darker and sharper than in the other two examples.

because these lines vary and seldom are laid as indicated. It may be necessary to obtain or make an as-built set of plans (as-built means that the original plan has been corrected and noted as to how it was actually built). These little changes cause more problems for the landscaper than for any other contractor or individual working on the site.

After the plan is completed, a checklist should be consulted to make sure that everything has been done and the plan will fit on the ground. Complete the take-off sheet and make sure every item on it is available to do the job a step that will save many trips to get things that were forgotten. Gathering material, equipment, and people after the job starts is expensive and time-consuming.

To ensure that everything fits, stake out beds and planting locations before beginning bed preparation and starting to plant.

This yew is suffering from too much water and shade.

Downspout water must be removed from beds. If it is not, plants will suffer and often die. The first symptoms are dwarfing, especially among evergreens. Foliage will brown and, in the case of deciduous plants, show fall color in midsummer.

These yews are dying because they were planted in compacted soil and no provision was made for drainage. Although the yews are on a slope, their individual planting pits have become watertight bowels.

Landscape Planting Bed Preparation

Planting bed preparation is the most important procedure in establishing a landscape planting (fig. 5). Good bed preparation can also prevent such later problems as poor internal drainage (percolation); without such drainage, a plant can drown on a hillside. It is very important not only to have a 2%+ surface drainage, but also to restructure the soil so that it will be open and aerated with good percolation of water down through the soil. Such drainage is often overlooked.

In order to achieve this aeration in most compacted soil around new construction, the soil must be worked up and a good amount of well-composted organic material added. Hardwood bark, pine bark, manure, and peat moss are all good but can raise soil pH. If the soil on the site is near or above 7.0, it should

Bed Preparation

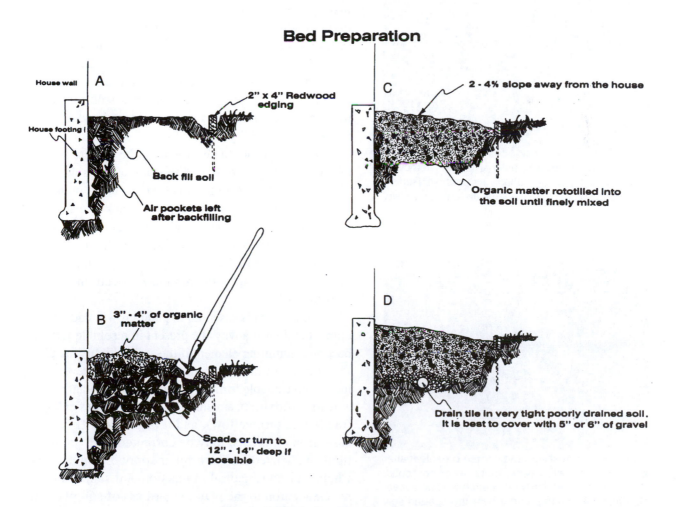

Figure 5. Steps to a good landscape bed.

In planting areas, make sure to strip away sod and rid the area of all rhizomes and weed seeds. Spray the bed area with Round-up to eliminate grass tops, roots, and rhizomes.

After all the sod and other material has been removed, spade or till the bed as deeply as possible. Rough-spaded soil is best if not too large an area is involved.

After spading or tilling, add coarse organic matter such as composted bark, manure, or corncobs. Here, manure and hardwood bark have been used. Use about 4″ and spread it over the spaded soil, incorporating it as deeply as the bed was spaded.

have some sulfur added to offset this rise; flowers of sulfur is the best material to use to lower soil pH (table A-1). Be sure to get rid of as many of the rhizomes and weed seeds in planting areas as possible.

After all the sod and other material is removed, spade or till the bed as deeply as possible. Rough-spaded soil is best if the area involved is not too large. When the spading or tilling is done, add coarse organic matter such as composted bark, manure, or corncobs; the material illustrated is manure and hardwood bark. Then incorporate about 4″ in the top 10–12″ of soil. Till this material until it is blended and the soil is loose and fluffy. The edging needs to be set at sod level so that it will not create a dam and retain runoff water. Install the edging and smooth the bed. An increase in volume will occur, so mound the bed to improve draining and compensate for the shrinkage that will occur later.

Iron sulphate (ferrous sulphate) is not recommended for acidification during the initial preparation of an alkaline soil because it can cause a buildup of soluble salts. When present in large amounts, these salts can be toxic to rhododendrons and azaleas. If supplemental water is alkaline, the soil pH may rise. In this situation, iron sulphate in weak solution can be used in small amounts as an annual top dressing to maintain soil acidity.

Aluminum sulphate should not be used to acidify the soil in which rhododendrons and azaleas will be planted, because aluminum is toxic to these plants and will kill them. Leaves will develop black spots, droop, roll, and turn brown. Terminal shoots and buds turn dark brown and then black, dying from the tip of the stem to the ground. These symptoms, which are similar to those caused by *Phytophthora*, occur uniformly over the plant.

Iron, which is essential to plant growth and development and must always be present in a soluble form, becomes a limiting element if the soil is highly alkaline because it is insoluble at a high pH. The iron develops into an unavailable form in the soil, and the plant is unable to absorb it. As a result, the plant becomes chlorotic (the leaves turn yellow), and it often dies. This disease, iron chlorosis, may be corrected with applications of chelated iron as a foliar spray or soil additive. Chelated iron is neutral in reaction and supplies the necessary iron to the plant, regardless of soil pH. This compound must be used according to manufacturer's

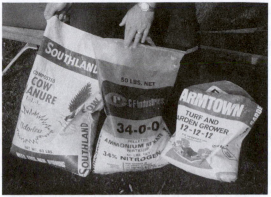

Apply fertilizer, especially nitrogen, to stop nitrogen drift caused by the breakdown of humus added as a soil adminitive.

After the soil is prepared, dig a trench for the edging. Now, not later. This is also the time to solve any drainage problems requiring tile.

Till the material until it is blended and the soil is loose and fluffy.

Drive in a ⅜" reinforcing rod at a 20-degree angle, every 3–4' and in opposite directions. A rod should be at each end of an edging board.

Rear-mounted tillers are good in open areas but not close to structures or fences. Front-mounted tillers are best used near walls and in small areas.

Install the edging and smooth the bed. There will be an increase in volume, so mound the bed to improve drainage and compensate for the shrinkage that will occur later.

Make sure the plant is replanted at the same depth it was grown. Cut strings only on shrubs, not on trees or larger shrubs. Since trees may need to be straightened later, their roots should be in a ball.

Stuff the string and burlap into the pit and finish backfilling by using the slurry method.

recommendations; excessive applications will cause foliage to burn.

When peat is used for organic material, make sure it is a good, coarse, acid peat and does not have a high pH. Add this organic material in a ratio of 3″ of organic matter to 10–12″ of soil that has been spaded to a depth of 10–12″ if possible (fig. 5B). Then add well-composted organic material. Before tilling, add about 5 pounds of ammonium nitrate per cubic yard of bark (or 2 pounds of ammonium nitrate if manure or peat is used) to offset the nitrogen draft caused by the breakdown of the incorporated organic material. Rototill the bed until it is evenly mixed and the soil is soft and has good overall tilth (fig. 5C-D).

After mixing, shape the bed so it is mounded high enough to compensate for settling because of the backfilling done during construction. Try to estimate this so that water, after the bed settles, will drain away from the structure and the bed will have a slope of not less than 2%.

In very flat areas where the soil is compacted and heavy with clay, a tile may be the only answer (fig. 5D). It can be placed easily and quickly and will improve any poorly drained site. On sites where soil is bad due to high clay content and/or construction waste, haul all the soil away to a depth of 16–18″ and replace it with good topsoil. A drain tile should be laid to ensure that all excess water will leave the site.

Raised Beds

All types of plants grow better in raised beds where soil can be more properly prepared and drainage is greatly improved. Due to soil type and conditions in some areas, the only efficient way to grow ornamentals and vegetables successfully is in raised beds.

Raised beds are an old method of growing, but still a good practice in compacted clay or in areas where the water table is high. They do not have to be very deep to be effective; 10–12″ is enough to grow most plants.

When beginning a raised bed in a low, poorly drained soil, dig the footing for the bed wall about 6″ deep and 16–18″ wide. If the trench is dug carefully, forms will not be needed. After the concrete is poured, work a ⅜″ reinforcing rod into the center of the pour and smooth the top with a smooth board or trowel. To make a good, snug fit, lay the first layer of stone while the concrete is still soft as soon after the pours as possible. The installation shown in figure 6 would

The trench being dug.

have been much better had it been backed up with weed barrier to stop soil from eroding through the free-laid stone wall. The rebar will hold the concrete together when it cracks, maintaining a good base for the bed wall.

Concrete being poured for the foundation and edging strip around the base of the wall and the turf.

The finished bed, including the edging or mower strip.

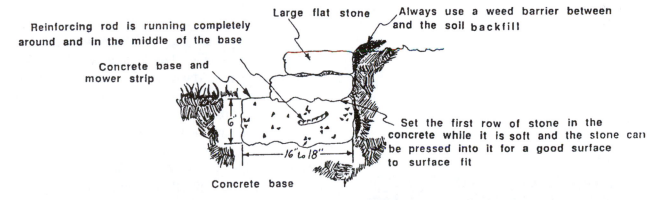

Reinforcing rod is running completely around and in the middle of the base

Concrete base and mower strip

Large flat stone

Always use a weed barrier between and the soil backfill

Set the first row of stone in the concrete while it is soft and the stone can be pressed into it for a good surface to surface fit

6"

16" to 18"

Concrete base

Figure 6. An end view of the concrete base for a raised bed.

Planting Shrubs

Planting shrubs is easy if a few simple steps are taken:

Digging the Pit. Dig a pit about ⅓ larger than the ball size of the plant to be put into the pit. Make sure that the hole is no deeper than required (fig. 7A). If too much soil is removed, replace it and firm the bottom of the pit so the plant will not settle or slump when watered in.

Shrub Planting

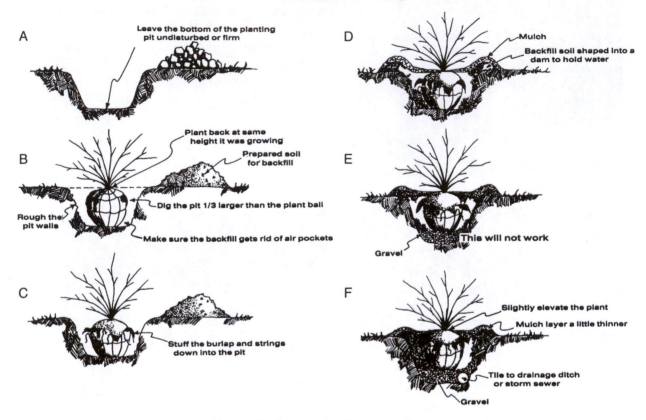

Figure 7. Proper planting procedures.

It is a good practice to cut strings on balled and burlapped plants because the string is sometimes made of plastic fibers that will girdle the plant.

Planting Depth. Set the plant into the hole and make sure the depth is right (fig. 7B). Always put the plant back at the same level or depth at which it was grown in the nursery. Make sure the walls of the pit are roughened in order to avoid an interface that will slow the establishment of—or in some cases kill—the plant. At this point, prepare the backfill soil by adding and thoroughly mixing organic matter and a small amount of starter fertilizer if needed. Some soils that are not compacted and are naturally nutrient-rich many not need to be conditioned before backfill.

Removing Strings and Burlap. Cut the strings off the neck of the burlapped ball. If possible, stuff strings and burlap down into the hole far enough to cover with soil in order to stop the girdling effect on the neck of the plant (fig. 7C). Burying the burlap stops the wick action so moisture can be held on the surface of the ball to help start rooting much faster. The rapid drying and soaking interrupts new root growth.

Backfilling. Backfill and make sure that air pockets are out. Firm the soil, but if it is wet do not compact it until all of the air or pour space is eliminated (fig. 7D). It is a common practice to backfill most of the soil as a slurry, simply adding soil and water as a thick soup. Fill the pit with slurry, then allow time for the water to soak out in order to eliminate air pockets and provide good contact between the plant ball and the soil. Complete the backfill with the prepared backfill soil. Always form a water-holding dam around each plant so the water will enter the planting pit and the plant ball and not run off.

Gravel in the Pit. It is commonly believed but not true that a layer of gravel at the bottom of a planting pit will provide drainage for the plant. The area filled with gravel will act as an air bubble, and perched water will be just on top of the rocks and intensify the water problem and eliminate space for potential rooting (fig. 7E).

Using Drain Tile. If a site is very wet it may be necessary to install a drain tile. If that is done, cover the tile with gravel to gather the free water and drain it into a ditch or a storm drain (fig. 7F). On such wet sites it may be necessary either to raise the planting up or to plant on a slight mound. Lessen the amount of mulch used around these plantings to keep the soil drier around the plant. Planting in this manner is not a substitute for drainage but will help grow some plants under conditions that are otherwise impossible.

Container-Grown Plants

No matter what a container is made of, it must be removed before the plant is put in the ground (fig. 8). Even papier-maché pots must be removed before the plant is put into the ground so roots are not circled or girdled (fig. 8). Cut the container away and either cut these circling roots or lay them out straight; in severe cases, do both (fig. 8D). If root straightening occurs just before planting, the process does little harm to the plant and a great deal of long-term good. Then proceed in the method discussed for balled and burlapped plants, a procedure that does the best job of breaking down the surrounding interface (fig. 9A-B) and gives the plant an opportunity to establish quickly and develop.

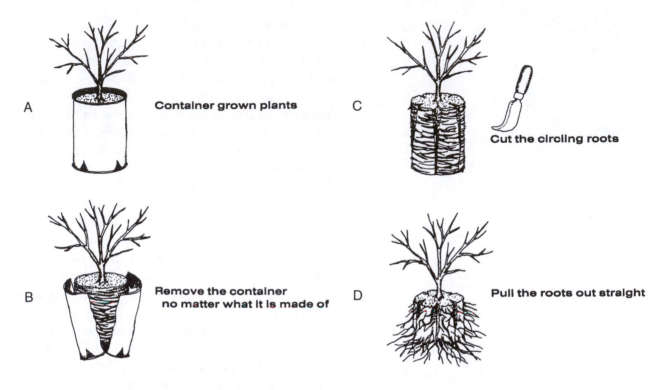

A   Container grown plants

B   Remove the container no matter what it is made of

C   Cut the circling roots

D   Pull the roots out straight

Figure 8. Remove any container and eliminate circling roots.

The papier-mâché container was left on this plant, which is dying from a lack of moisture. Even if water does get in, the roots will continue to grow in circles and establish slowly. What results is the death of a weak, unattractive plant.

Remove container plants from their containers and straighten or cut their roots to stop the circling growth.

Water-Absorbent Gel. This material is a super-absorbent crystal or powder that will take in enough water to 100 times or greater its weight. The material has the ability to repeat this process many times during a planting season. The first absorbent material introduced during the 1960s was organic and very expensive. Great improvements were made during the 1980s by cross-linking synthetic acrylamide, which gave rise

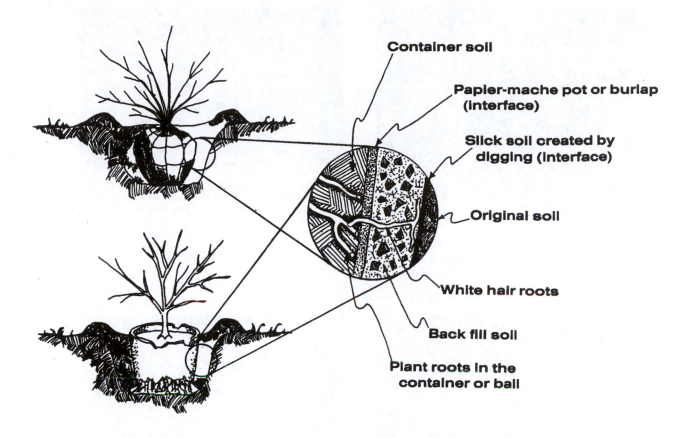

Figure 9. Roots must grow through the space between the soil in which the plant came and the soil on site. It is important that this process be speeded up; remove containers and break down the interface.

to new inexpensive superabsorbent materials (often called "super-slurper"). Mix the gel with water until it is a thick, sticky mass that resembles pudding to make an excellent dip when planting bare-root plants. Put the mixture in a large garbage can and dip the plant just before placing it into the soil. If plants are dipped off-site, too much of the gel will drop off before planting. The gel can also be mixed dry into the backfill soil and planted in the usual method. A powder can be mixed dry with grass seed before planting to yield excellent results.

Planting in a Slurry. Many people use this technique to ensure good results. The water and soil are added together, which results in a thick, muddy soup. The soil is carried into all air pockets to make good, instant contact with the ball and surrounding soil. It is a useful practice in the tight, uneven backfill found around new construction sites. Many designers and contractors recommend this technique for dry, sandy soils.

Straighten the roots, spread them out, and plant at once.

This tree was planted too shallow and is also crooked.

The results of not cutting and straightening. Even if this tree had lived it would never have been attractive. The mower has also inflicted severe damage.

Later, after the soil has settled, finish-plant and form a shallow basin to hold water.

Planting either too deep or too shallow retards growth and may kill the plants. This example was planted too deep.

Make sure the basin holds water before finish-planting and mulching.

Use a rake or shovel to form the walls of the basin.

The final step is to mulch and water-in well.

Landscape Mulches and When to Mulch

The many types of mulches are divided into those that are decorative and those that are functional. Both types have some of the same good mulching characteristics, but there are problems with many kinds of mulch (Table A-2).

Good, organic mulches such as hardwood bark and corncobs decay or break down in about a season and can rob plants of nitrogen, which must be replaced in the bed. Mulches such as stone can become a maintenance problem in later years. Shrubs cover the stone, and stone interferes with cultivation and lawn mowing.

It is advisable to carefully consider the plant or area to be mulched and then select a mulch that will provide the desired results.

1. Mulch should hold moisture throughout its mass and near the surface of the soil.
2. Mulch should moderate temperature and slow rapid temperature change from one extreme to another.
3. Mulch should also help control weeds. This is very important when establishing plants in a new landscape bed. Mulch is the single most important factor in establishing ground covers.
4. Some mulches should be attractive, especially when used as a permanent part of a landscape.
5. Mulches should often help control erosion while more permanent control, such as plants, takes over.
6. As they break down, many mulches release nutrients into the soil, a process that takes

Figure 10. Mulch the root area and provide a soil water basin.

a. Mulch should cover the soil around a plant but should not cover the crown or trunk (except of plants such as roses and rhododendrons).
b. Dam the soil to hold water.
c. Open around the base of the plant.

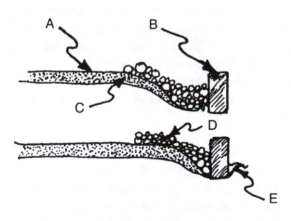

Figure 11. Proper installation of rock mulch over black plastic or weed barriers. The sand layer under weed barriers allows for moisture and air exchange.

a. Plastic or weed barrier.
b. 2 x 4″ edging.
c. Sand layer.
d. Decorative stone.
e. Plastic or weed barrier placed under edging before it is installed to help hold the barrier under the stone, no matter if it is woven or spunbond weed barrier or plastic film.

many months, depending on the mulch (table A-2). Nitrogen is the element that is most available after this decomposition occurs. If organic mulches are not composted before use they can cause a nitrogen shortage.

When to Mulch. The time to mulch varies with the group of plants to be mulched. For moisture conservation and weed control, most woody ornamentals should be mulched at the time they are planted. Annual mulches should be applied in the spring after the soil has warmed. Spring application is very beneficial to shrubs, such as azaleas and rhododendrons, that flower heavily, because a tremendous amount of water is necessary to maintain the bloom to completion. Spring mulching is critical for development of good wood for next year's flowers—indeed, for the development of next year's flower bud itself. Most plants benefit from a good mulch cover all year.

How to Mulch. It is a general rule to mulch the root area, but do not allow the main stem or trunk to become covered (fig. 10). That leads to rodent damage and plant disease. If the trunk needs protection, use plant wrap but do not bury the root area in mulch. Two exceptions to this rule, the rhododendron and the rose, must have their crowns or trunks protected in order to prevent winter damage. Depth of mulch depends on the type of mulch and the plants being mulched. Most of the stone or materials that do not break down should be no more than 4″ in planted areas and fill to 6″ in large, open areas (fig. 11). It is best to spread sand over planting beds before laying plastic. Plastic should cover as smooth an area as possible to prevent punctures. Always bury the plastic well in order to delay the time when it starts coming through to the surface. A good, solid bed edging can also help keep the plastic down. It is important to keep traffic away from these beds in cold weather. A plastic sheet will crack and break up, which begins the process of the material raising to the surface.

Light, fluffy materials are hard to keep in place. It may be necessary to mix materials like peat moss and compost with corncobs or hardwood bark. This improves both materials for use as a mulch.

Because many materials will mold and pack down, especially in damp or shady areas, it may be advisable to stir the surface with a rake. Corncobs and many composted materials and crop residues can become unsightly or have an unpleasant odor if not stirred and allowed to dry out on a regular schedule.

Hardwood bark has the unattractive habit of growing unsightly fungus. Keep the mulch fluffed and well aerated.

Extending the mulch ring as wide as possible is the best way to speed the growth of shade trees. This allows for a better area to fertilize and water. This also promotes good root growth.

Wood chips from a limb grinder are good for large areas and should be well composted. They are primarily wood, and termites like wood. This material is coarse; it would be much better to chop it finer and compost it for 3 to 6 months. Bark mulch does not attract or harbor termites.

Pine needles as mulch is very attractive when used near areas like patios or walks where it will be very visible. These clear mulch areas make good sites for bulbs and other spring flowers.

Bark mulch is excellent plant protection and can be visually important as well if it is replaced in part each year. Cypress is the best visually because it holds its color longer and does not break down as quickly as other bark mulches.

Pine needles are good in beds of acid-loving plants. The mulch from southern pines is sometimes coarse, and when using it in small beds it is better to grind it finer.

Start with clean, weed-free shrub beds when putting down mulch.

Rock over plastic mulch has been used extensively and creates many problems. It does not allow for moisture and air exchange and always breaks up and comes to the surface in a short time. The new weed barriers are much better in all aspects and much preferred over black plastic.

Mulch the root zone and don't pile too much around the crowns of plants. There are two exceptions: The crowns of roses need to be covered, and azaleas require mulching as shown here.

Weed barriers should not have organic mulch as on this bed because weed seeds germinate on top of the weed barrier itself. The material shown is woven; others, called "spunbond," are mats of fibers pressed together.

Hardwood bark mulch is likely the best to use on larger plants. Mulches vary in availability in various areas. The best mulch in the Midwest is hardwood bark; in the South and East, pine needles are good, especially if they are coarsely chopped. Compost from yard waste is also satisfactory if it is well composted and free of foreign matter such as plastic or aluminum cans.

There are two types of weed mats ("petro-mats," or all types of petrochemical sheets used in landscape work): woven and nonwoven. Both are widely used. Select a mat that allows water to pass through without much hesitation. Try several side by side and evaluate the material on its performance used the way you plant to use it and in your type of soil. Most are good as far as air and moisture exchange are concerned. Some types of weed barriers tend to clog, and air and moisture exchange breaks down. The material tends to rise through mulch, rock, or organic matter and must be tacked down firmly to slow that process. Grasses like quack grass and even Kentucky bluegrass will penetrate the fabric. Other weeds and grasses such as foxtail and pigweed will grow on top of the mat when organic mulches are used, which can be a serious problem in beds exposed to large wooded areas or farmland.

Pulling back the weed barrier would reveal nutsedge coming through. Many difficult weeds such as crabgrass, nutsedge, bluegrass, and quackgrass grow right through a barrier. Warm-season grasses like Bermuda and zoysia are particularly invasive because of their rhizomes and tough, drought-tolerant root systems.

Spunbond weed barriers increase water problems in wet-clay areas.

Plastic should be laid on a smooth surface to help prevent breaking up in cold weather. All of the materials become stiff and hard, and if they are laid on an uneven surface the mat will bend and break.

The material makes a good underliner before pouring concrete or stabilizing stream banks. It also does a good job of stabilizing soil under large rock or concrete blocks. Place a layer behind a retaining wall to stop erosion through the wall while allowing water to pass through.

When using stone, it is better if the material is smooth and has a natural look. This material spreads well and does not puncture or compact. In high pH soils, avoid using stone with high calcium content, like marble or crushed limestone, which will raise the pH. The finer the stone is crushed, the faster the pH rises.

Many woven materials are better than black plastic because they allow air and moisture to occur more normally (fig. 11). They have one problem, however: weeds will germinate on top of the material, and weeds like quackgrass will force their way through the mat and cause trouble (figs. 12–13). Weed barriers made like a thick felt will shed water if not in contact with soil. Water moves through the weed barrier by capillary action. Therefore, water will not be pulled through if the barrier is not in contact with fine material. Just below the barrier, the material tends to form an interface that holds water and can become a major problem.

Spray mulching

This large, truck-mounted sprayer applies a fiber mulch held together with latex.

The mixture on the ground. It does a good job in normal rainfall and is used primarily over areas where grass has been seeded.

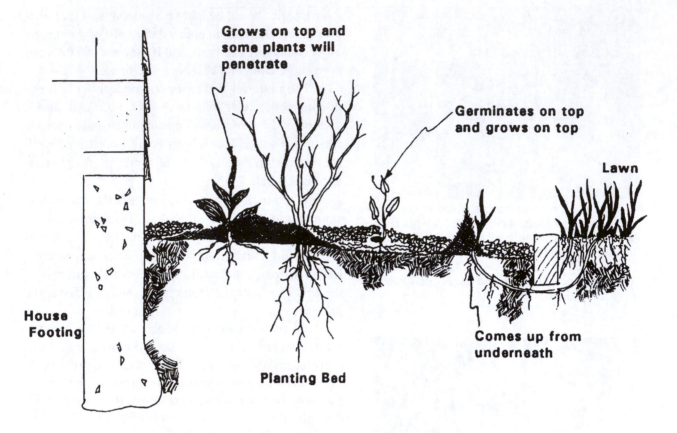

Figure 12. Weed barriers topped with organic mulch are a problem because of weeds.
  a. Some weeds will germinate on top and grow through.
  b. Some will come up and through the barrier by rhizomes.
  c. Other weeds will grown on top of the mulch.

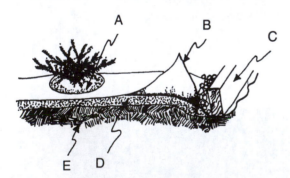

Figure 13. To improve a plant's chances of survival, leave a large opening in the plastic or mat for moisture and air exchange.
  a. Large opening around the plant.
  b. Plastic or week barrier.
  c. 2 × 4″ edging.
  d. A smooth sand layer on which to lay the plastic or woven mat to avoid winter damage.
  e. Prepare planting-bed soil.

The suitability and nutrient value of several mulches are given in table A-2, as well as major problems associated with each. Analysis of these materials is given in table A-3.

Planting in late spring or in areas where there are strong winter winds may indicate the need to use an antitranspirant to prevent moisture loss during the establishment period. In areas of severe winters, a material that contains both a wax or latex and a stomata-closing agent should be used. Apply as late as possible to avoid fall rains that will wash off much of the material or apply twice, once at planting and again after precipitation (i.e., snow). Many times this material is useful when digging plants late in the season or summer. Used in conjunction with pruning or leaf removal, it will help the plant get over the shock of being moved during an active growing state (table A-4).

Plant Covers

Spunbond plant covers are light enough to be supported by the plants, whose leaves are not affected as they would be under plastic (where they collect moisture and start to decay). Spunbond breathes and allows plants to dry.

Plant covers are similar to nonwoven (spunbond) weed barrier but much lighter and white in order to admit light. It is open enough to allow air to pass through but will not permit disication (the drying and burning of winter wind). It is lightweight enough to lay on top of the plants that it protects and will form a bright, warm area where plants can overwinter in good condition. First used over golf greens and over rows of vegetables, spunbond is used as winter protection for many types of ornamentals. The material is light enough to be laid directly on plants and transparent enough to allow enough light to maintain good growth. It does not collect moisture, and therefore the plant does not decay when the cover touches its leaves.

Spunbond plant covers are good for protection from frost.

Winter shade is an important consideration when working with broadleaf evergreens, especially new plantings.

Woven plant cover may provide more light and can also be used to prevent insect damage and bird- and rabbit-caused problems. An open net is available that will cover beds of ground cover or flowers and help protect them from wildlife. Be sure not to unintentionally pen rabbits inside fencing or netting.

Broadleaf evergreen ground covers benefit from winter shade. Here it is being provided with spruce boughs.

Landscape Bed Edging

Without edging, the lawn has quickly moved into the bed and destroyed the design. A lack of edging also invites mowers too close to plants and damages shrubs.

Hand-edging is recommended for large areas but will need to be done once or twice a month during the growing season. Soil and sod should be cut into a drop at the edge of the bed. That open space will stop grass from growing into the bed.

Chemical edgers such as Round-up will do a nice job of controlling this edge. It is also good to kill grass areas when more bed space is desired, as shown here.

Permanent bed edging must meet certain standards:

1. It must be strong enough to stay in place when walked on or driven over with a riding lawn mower.
2. It should compliment the rest of the landscape. For example, if brick or stone is used as an edging, it should be designed to complement and blend with the rest of the landscape and be waterproof.
3. It should be long-lasting.
4. It should be properly installed. Edging has two purposes—to separate shrub beds from lawn areas and to establish the design as originally drawn on the plan.

Bluegrass, the principal lawn grass in the Midwest, can be easily contained by an edging 4″ deep and 8″ wide. The exception to this would be metal edging. Open space will also control bluegrass by means of cutting and edging with a power edger or hand tool so the soil and grass can be removed to form a small cliff. Fill this space with something solid, such as wood, brick, or steel.

Chemicals can be of great assistance for the person maintaining weed control in a large landscape area. Never use chemicals for any purpose without a check study done in a small area out of direct view. That will provide a good gauge of how the chemical works on your soil type without damaging a large area. Chemicals react differently in various soil and moisture conditions and with exposure to wind and sun. The following list of chemicals can be used if labels are read carefully and small trials are used to fine-tune the application rate.

Round-up is a postemergence herbicide than when applied to green foliage translocates to the root system and kills the plant in a very short time. The area can be worked the next day and the root system will continue to die. Round-up is useful in spot killing and edging. Clean rings around the base of trees can be easily maintained to keep the lawn mower away. Sometimes Surflan is mixed with Round-up to lengthen the effective life of any one treatment. If the area to be treated will drain rapidly, Surflan could cause dead areas where runoff travels or settles.

All landscape beds should be edged with some kind of material that is structurally sound so it will be permanent, attractive, or unseen. That will maintain the design on the ground and separate the shrubs from the lawn area.

Surflan is a preemergence material used for edging and weed control in gravel beds, and flower beds. Surflan is used for more types of horticulture weeding than any other product. One feature that could cause a problem is that it is bright orange, but the color soon washes away. That may be a help in that you can see what has and has not been sprayed.

Dacthal is a preemergence used for annual grass in flower beds and as a crabgrass control in turf. This material is short-lived and works best if used in conjunction with good organic mulch.

Poast is a foliage spray for control of grass in woody ground cover. Application should be made when ground cover has hardened off after spring growth. Spray as soon as possible to catch grass while it is young. This is one chemical that it would pay to do a little trial experimenting with before too much area is covered.

There are many other chemicals available, but if chemicals are to be a part of your maintenance program, contact the local Cooperative Extension Service for their pest control handbook. Nearly all states have this service and some have booklets available on specific areas such as horticulture.

Edging Materials

Some of the best edging materials are steel (fig. 14), wood (fig. 15), brick (fig. 16), plastic (fig. 17), aluminum, and concrete.

Many contractors use plastic edging extensively, but it is less desirable than the edgings listed previously. If plastic is used, it will be necessary to strengthen the material by placing a ⅜" reinforcing rod down the hole on top of the edging and reinforcing the joints.

Although plastic edging is less expensive and easier to install than other edgings, its durability is poor and its appearance is artificial. It also has a much shorter life span than wood, brick, steel, or stone. In addition, plastic is very difficult to install in a straight line and almost impossible to keep in the ground. Of all materials used as edging, plastic is the hardest to install for a lasting, stable material.

If the flat plastic types of edging are used, nail (using galvanized nails) a redwood 1 × 1″ strip along the bottom of each strip where possible, even in curved areas, using 1 × 2 × 3″ blocks to help stabilize the plastic.

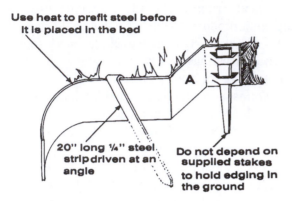

Use heat to prefit steel before it is placed in the bed

20" long ¼" steel strip driven at an angle

Do not depend on supplied stakes to hold edging in the ground

A

Figure 14. Install steel edging with slanted stakes after it has been fitted to the bed.
  a. 3–5″ or near that size.
  b. Prepare your own stakes 20–24″ long.

A D-handle shovel is ideal for bending steel edging.

Steel is one of the best edgings available, but too many jobs turn out like this because a few simple rules were not followed. The steel must be fitted to the bed before it is placed.

The steel edging around this mature bed has been in place for more than ten years and never been a problem.

To install steel edging, you will need a cutting torch and a hand grinder to groove the steel and make good, sharp corners.

The way steel edging should look. Nothing can be seen but a clean bed line.

Wood

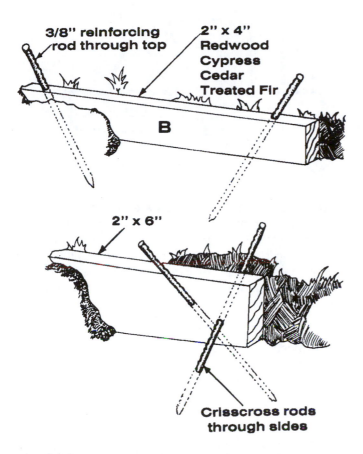

3/8" reinforcing rod through top

2" x 4" Redwood Cypress Cedar Treated Fir

B

2" x 6"

Crisscross rods through sides

Figure 15. Stake 2 × 4″ wood through the top and 2 × 6″ through the sides.
- a. redwood
- b. treated yellow pine or fir
- c. cypress

Wood edging is good if installed correctly. Dig it in at the correct height and drill ½″ holes at 30-degree angles.

Drive a ⅜″ reinforcing rod through the holes every 4′ or at the end of each piece of edging. Alternate the direction of the rods.

When installing wood edging, one time-saver is to use a bundle of smaller hardwood stakes to stabilize corners or any change of direction until permanent stakes can be drilled and driven. That is even advisable if wooden (treated fir or redwood) stakes are used. The hardwood stakes can be used several times and even as final stakes. Drive them straight down every 4′. This can be done as the wood freezes to the soil and will not pop up.

Wood can be curved if it is 1 × 4". Then, to make the width of the final edge wide enough to last, laminate another 1 × 4" piece and nail it together with galvanized 6 p. nails. It is best to soak the lumber for two or three days before bending.

The same installation three years later. Redwood, cypress, or treated fir is best used for edging.

Brick, Concrete Block or Stone

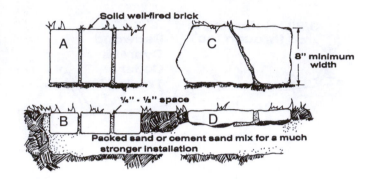

Figure 16. Install brick or stone edging on 2 inches of sand. To be an effective bed edging, 6–8″ is needed to separate the turf and bed edge. Concrete pavers make fine edging if laid in a smoothed level trench without sand. Tamp them into place and make sure they stay close together. For a permanent installation, use a mixture of 3 parts sand to 1 part cement.

Brick (A & B)

a. must be well-fired so they are waterproof
b. do not use house brick
c. concrete brick or interlocking paver

Stone (C & D)

a. at least 3″ thick or deep
b. at least 6″ wide to stop grass
c. sand or concrete base with reinforcing rod in concrete base.

Gravel or sand walks are attractive in some gardens or can be used for temporary walks. Use ½ × 6″ cypress if possible because it will blend well and last longer than any other wood.

An example of how not to use brick. It does not look sturdy and will move under the pressure of lawn mowers. Grass will quickly grow over and through this narrow space.

Brick can be satisfactory if properly installed, sound enough for outdoor use, and laid flat at 90 degrees to a bed as shown.

Edging, such as that made of these bricks, is an important part of a landscape design.

Plastic

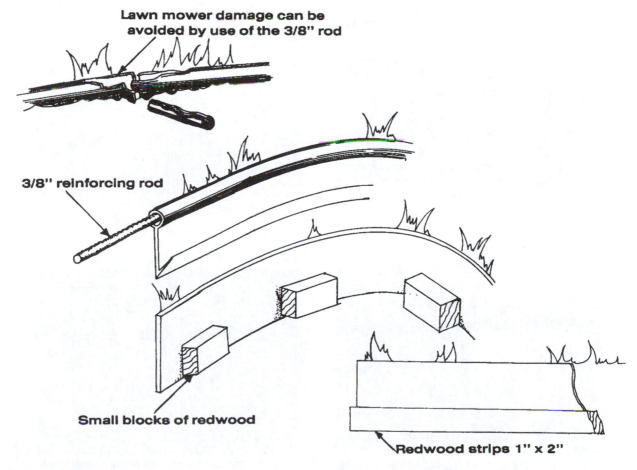

Lawn mower damage can be avoided by use of the 3/8" rod

3/8" reinforcing rod

Small blocks of redwood

Redwood strips 1" x 2"

Figure 17. Reinforce the rolled plastic with steel rods and nail a block to the bottom of the flat rolled-plastic edging.

Two problems often encountered during installation must be corrected before plastic edging can be classed as a fair-to-good edging. One problem involves the plastic's inability to stay in the ground during freezing and thawing. The other problem is its rigidity and inability to stay in a straight line.

Plastic edging with reinforcing rods down the hole in the spine to allow for either an even curve or a straight curve. Use about 10″ of the rods to fit into the next piece instead of the nipple provided. This makes the edging last longer when lawn mowers hit it.

This plastic edging is heavy-gauge and does not become brittle in cold weather but still seems out of place. It looks as though someone has forgotten to roll up a hose.

Aluminum Edging

Aluminum edging is made in two widths and two or more thicknesses.

This plastic edging is coming out of the ground at a joint and was destroyed by the lawnmower.

Bends like the one shown can easily be made with aluminum, which can be useful when doing interior landscapes.

Aluminum edging for brick is very good, especially for curves.

Many people think of this material when aluminum edging is mentioned. Soft, thin aluminum is completely unsatisfactory, and in many cases it can be dangerous. It should neither be sold nor placed in areas where power machinery is used. Fortunately, it is slowly losing in popularity.

Concrete Pavers as Edging

Concrete pavers are the best new edging material available. The units are larger and much heavier than the less durable, unstable clay brick, and the pavers come in many more different colors and shapes than any other type of edging.

Pavers provide an attractive divider that will remain for years with little or no maintenance between the grass and flower and shrub beds.

Pavers are used here to provide a clean, attractive edge to a perennial bed.

Some of the tools necessary to install paver or brick edging or floors are (left to right): a d-ring shovel, ½" plastic pipe, a stone chisel, a 6-pound hammer, a hacksaw, and a trowel.

A trenching spade and a flat-blade shovel.

Extruded Concrete Edging

This machine and technique has been used in other types of construction for a long time but is new to the landscape industry. The only problems entailed are the type of reinforcing used and the shape of the edging, which looks like a street curb. Varied shapes would make the extrusions more acceptable in the industry and by the public.

This edging would be better reversed when installed. That would yield a straight, vertical edge next to the turf to better use lawn-edging equipment. The strongest part of the edging would carry the mowers, and the bed knife of the mower would not cut into the concave part of the edging. As used here, it looks like a curb around a parking lot.

Crushed stone or sand base should be packed thoroughly. It can be done with a hand-tamper, but a power compactor is by far the best for laying floors or large areas.

Use a wetsaw to lay pavers in curves like this. Some edging pavers are now made to fit tightly into curves.

There will be many times when working with brick, stone, or concrete pavers that they will need to be cut. Brick and stone can be cut with a stone chisel. Always turn the beveled side of a chisel toward the waste. Harder materials like street pavers and concrete will need to be cut with a power saw that has a concrete cutting blade. Either of these procedures takes time and can be held to a minimum by careful planning and materials selection.

A close-up of a break joint in extruded concrete edging. This is done with a trowel as soon as the concrete is laid.

This new, extruded concrete edging is too overpowering and is hard on mowers. Turn the curb 180 degrees and put it back in the ground at sod level. With that change, it works well and is easy to maintain without damaging mowers and edgers.

Combination Edging

The use of brick and plastic edging in combination improves both materials. In this combination, the plastic should be placed in flat strips so it will fit close to the brick and not be visible.

When the plastic is placed in straight sections, it should have a redwood or treated fir 2 × 2″ strip nailed to the outside bottom of the plastic. If curved sections are used, place short blocks every foot or so around the curve (fig. 18).

Do not forget to edge posts or other objects that stand alone. A simple square of concrete around a post eliminates hand-edging.

Brick and Plastic Edging

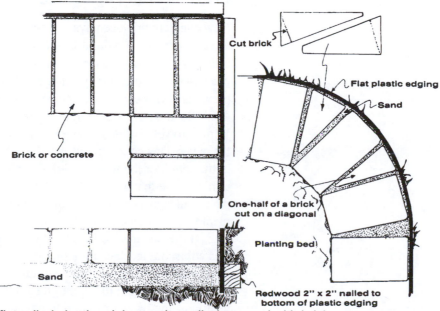

Cut brick

Flat plastic edging

Sand

Brick or concrete

One-half of a brick cut on a diagonal

Planting bed

Sand

Redwood 2″ x 2″ nailed to bottom of plastic edging

Figure 18. The flat-rolled plastic edging works well when used with brick or concrete pavers.

For a long-lasting edge, use a sand-cement mix in place of sand. Add 1 part cement to 2 parts sand and mix completely. Use very little water, just enough to keep the dust down. At this point lay the brick, sweep the same mixture into the cracks between the bricks, and allow the mixture to cure for 3 to 4 days. If this sand and cement mixture is used, fasten the plastic edging to the wood strip with forming nails. The first head tightens to hold the wood and plastic firmly together, and the other head protrudes to be set in the sand and cement mix. That makes the edging one unit.

This example of double edging, pavers and steel, makes a beautiful and durable bed-edge combination.

Entry and secondary walks provide excellent edging for grass and weed-free beds between the walks and the house. This is especially true when the walk is placed properly. This will be discussed in the walks section.

Concrete Brick Edging or Curb

New concrete brick or pavers are excellent for landscape use because they are durable and attractive. The brick is often used in patio construction, but it can be used any place that concrete or clay brick would have been used previously. It is useful to edge beds that are to be raised 4–5″. Set the pavers on end into a footing of concrete. With a trowel, form the concrete up around the bottom of the paver. This concrete will need a ⅜″ reinforcing rod in the center of the footing and about 2″ off of the bottom. Be sure that a ¼″ space is left between the concrete pavers, then sweep the sand and cement mix (1 part cement to 2 parts sand) into the spaces (fig. 19).

If the distance to be edged or curbed exceeds 20″ it is advisable to place an isolation joint or a curve in the curb to provide for more expansion in cold weather. The curve will give just enough to stop buckling or distortion of the brick or concrete pavers.

Dental Method of Laying Curb

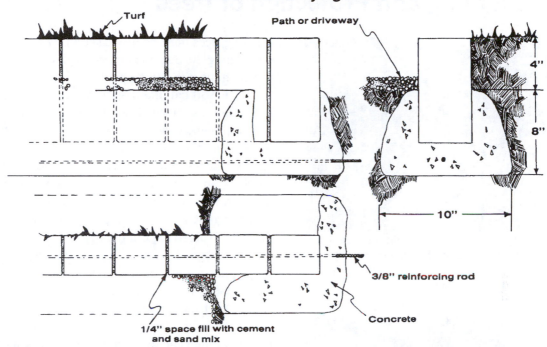

Turf

Path or driveway

4"

8"

10"

3/8" reinforcing rod

Concrete

1/4" space fill with cement
and sand mix

Figure 19. Brick or paver curbs or edging set in concrete make ideal curbs or raised edging.

Specially made bricks or concrete pavers set in concrete make an excellent curb for a drive or a raised bed.

The same curb after the walk surface is laid and the landscape is finished.

Paver curb completed before backfilling.

Ties placed at grade made an excellent curb and edging for a lawn.

The Planting and Protection of Trees

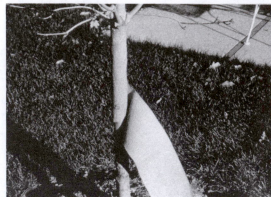

Wrap newly planted trees and tie the wrap. It is best to remove the wrap during the growing season because it could create an insect problem if left on during the summer.

A properly wrapped and tied tree. If the tree is planted in fall, wrap it after planting. It will also need wrapping if it is planted in spring but keep a check on it for insects.

The result of planting in papier-maché pots. It is important that any container is removed before planting and that roots be cut and straightened so they will not continue to circle.

Planting trees must be discussed in two sections: one concerning the tree, the other the planting pit or the soil in which the tree will be planted.

The soil ball the tree comes in should be solid, not soft or one-sided. The burlap wrap should be snug and well pinned and laced with heavy hemp twine. The lower trunk should be clear and not disturbed or damaged by cables, ropes, or other equipment while being moved. Sometimes trees are badly scored or damaged by cultivation long before they are dug. Reputable plant dealers would not sell such plants but would replace the tree if something did happen.

It is a good practice to plant then wrap. One wrapping method is easy and fast, the other takes a little more time to install but lasts longer. The first method (fig. 20) is to wrap the tree from the top down. Take the end of the wrap, drape it over the first limb, and bring the roll around and over the free end, locking the wrap in place. Continue to wrap until the soil line is reached. Tear off the wrap, leaving a foot extra to bury at the base. Spray the trunk with an insecticide if there is no treatment in the wrap.

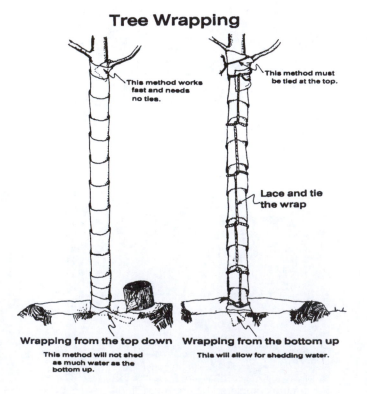

Figure 20. Two methods of tree wrapping.

Pruning Newly Planted Trees

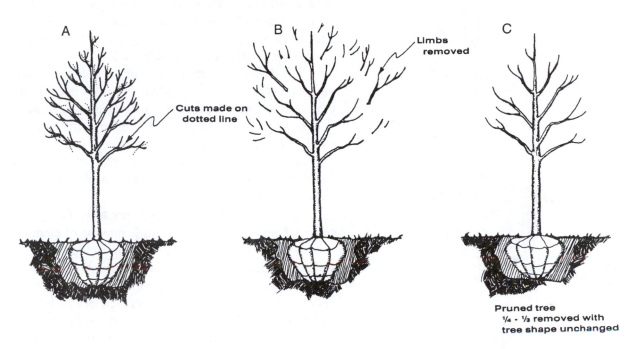

Figure 21. Prune new trees to maintain their natural shape and always retain their central leader.

Strings and wrap need to be taken off in spring and put back in late fall until a tree is growing well. This tree, which grew around strings that had been left on, will always have growth problems.

The dotted lines in figure 21A indicate the even removal of the limbs over the entire canopy, not disturbing the leaders and leaving smooth cuts and no stubs. Figure 21C demonstrates the pruned tree with the same basic shape and no stubs, for an even, shaved look.

The planting pit and planting site are the next considerations. If the pits are dug by hand, make them ⅓ larger than the tree ball. Dig the pit no deeper than the ball to be placed in the hole. Always plant the tree back at the same depth at which it grew in the nursery (fig. 21B). If the hole is to be dug with a tree spade, be sure to score or break up the sides of the hole to prevent the side from slicking. This severely hinders drainage and root penetration of this compacted layer. These layers of compacted soil are called interface. The plant must overcome the slick sides of the hole and the burlap as well as varying soils—that in which it grew, that in the backfill, and that in which it is planted.

Planting trees is basically the same as planting shrubs; when planting a tree, however, the strings must be left on the ball until there is no longer any danger of the tree shifting or settling out of the vertical. It is simple to correct a possible lean if the strings are still intact. If they have been removed, however, straightening may break up the ball, which could result

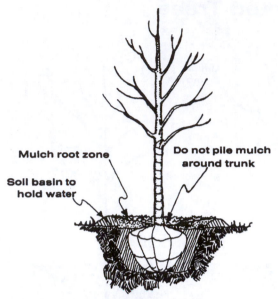

Figure 22. Properly planted, mulched, and wrapped.

Mulch root zone

Do not pile mulch around trunk

Soil basin to hold water

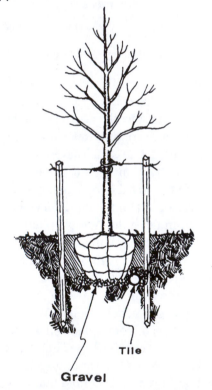

Tile

Gravel

Figure 23. A properly placed drain tile.

in losing the tree. Remember to return and cut the strings and tighten the cable. In species of trees such as maple and ash, this prevents increased borer damage. Such wrapping and spraying are all that needs to be done for the first year (fig. 22).

The method of wrapping from the bottom up has one advantage in that it will shed water. If either wrapping is to stay on over winter it will need to be laced with twine as shown. If possible, cut the string and remove the wrap in the spring. Rewrap and retie if this protection is needed for more than a year. Plant the tree and then wrap so everyone involved can see that it was planted under good conditions.

All new trees will need some pruning, if only to correct damage that occurred while moving or planting.

If a tree is to look right in a particular spot, sometimes pruning (such as raising the limbs above other plantings if the tree is planted in shrub mass) is necessary. When a tree is dug, moved onto a site, and planted, some of the canopy will need to be removed in order to lessen moisture loss from the top, which the tree cannot replace because of root loss. As much as ¼ to ⅓ of the canopy should be taken off in harder to transplant species. Never cut the leader and always preserve the natural shape of the tree (fig. 21A–C).

It is better to dig the holes with a bigger machine than they were dug with and then rough the sides and backfill with good soil. If the soil on the site is too tight, you may need to a consider a french drain, planting on a mound, or tiling (figs. 23–25). If tiling is necessary, run the tile at the bottom of the planting pit to one side. It would be good to cover the tile with a layer of creek gravel rather than crushed limestone. The tile should then be dumped into a sump or storm drain.

French Drain

The french drain works well if the site is on a hillside where the natural slope can be used. Cut a narrow trench through the wall of the pit and down the slope and fill it with creek gravel. The trench should be left open at its top for the first year or two after the tree is planted so the system will work better and corrections can be made more easily. Then allow sod to cover the top of the rock-filled trench. The sod's growth can be speeded by adding a few inches of good soil over the top of the gravel.

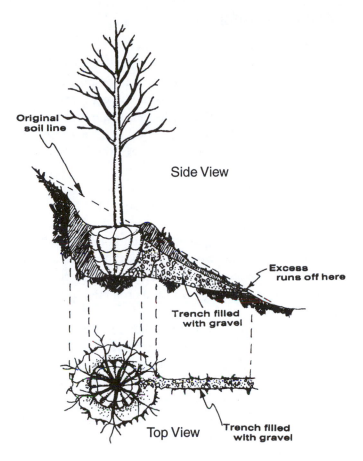

Original soil line

Side View

Excess runs off here

Trench filled with gravel

Top View

Trench filled with gravel

Figure 24. French drains are ideal to use on sloping sites where soil is compacted and will not drain internally.

This planting pit is in very poor soil, therefore a french drain was put in place before planting.

The next year: The trees are well established and growing.

French drains can be useful on compacted soil. There will need to be a slight grade in order to allow drainage down and off the surface, as shown here, or into a sump.

The same pines, doing very well—in large part due to the french drains.

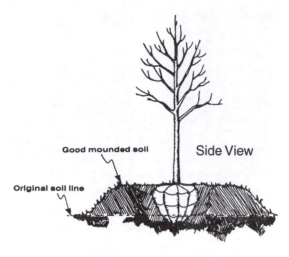

Good mounded soil

Side View

Original soil line

Figure 25. Mounds can be used to raise a plant above the water table.

A good way to move smaller trees is with a small machine. The hazard of doing so is that the machine operator will dig too large a tree. Dig only the right caliper trees for the size ball a machine can make.

This large, truck-mounted machine can move trees up to 6″ in diameter with little trouble.

Mound Planting

Mound planting will work for smaller trees on wet sites. Because this method is the most visible of the methods that correct drainage, it can be objectionable from a design standpoint. In some cases, however, it may be the only practical solution. If the mound is used, make sure it is made of good, porous topsoil. If possible, develop a mound as part of the landscape rather than as a little hill with a tree on it.

Staking new trees is important if they are large (3½–4″ caliper), planted in loose soil, or if the soil ball is soft. There are two factors to consider when determining if staking is needed: wind and pedestrian traffic. Traffic problems would be caused by factors such as lawn mowers, bicycles, and children; school grounds and city parks would need all the protection discussed, for example.

All wires used in staking that come in contact with the tree must be covered with a rubber hose. Make sure that these ties are loose enough to accommodate one year's growth and loosen them each year if necessary. Many commercial ties are satisfactory for holding a tree straight. Some are easy to adjust if they become loose or if it is time to remove them, and they can frequently be reused.

Soil in its undisturbed condition contains open space to be used for air and moisture exchange which is essential to plant growth. The absence of this space makes it extremely difficult to establish new plants, especially trees. Digging with a mechanical tree spade (fig. 26) can cause the loss of air space next to the tree spade surfaces. The soil particles and open air space next to the blade will be pressed until no air is left. As the blade is forced into the airless soil, it drags the soil and slicks it in the same way a potter would finish the surface of a pot to cause it to hold water. The more clay the soil contains, the worse the problem. Sandy soil, however, will not slick because sand particles are too coarse and contain too much air space. Sandy soil will not compress into a ball because of its coarseness and large air space; sand particles are already as close as possible. That is why sand is used under walks and concrete floors to provide a base that will drain quickly; the volume stays the same under wet or dry conditions.

Spades come in many sizes and vary slightly in the way they operate. Some machines have four blades and some dig with teeth like a chain saw. The sawtooth machine is large and works like an ice cream

A tree planting pit dug with a mechanical tree spade. The process slicks the sides and creates an interface that will hold water and interfere with root growth. Always rough the sides and make the pit ⅓ larger than the ball to be placed into it.

The chunk of compacted soil taken from the pit. It is impossible to encourage good root growth in this situation without a lot of work.

dipper. Diggers have been a boon to nursery owners and landscape contractors. Although they do a fine job of digging large trees, the tendency is to dig plants, especially trees, that are too large. It is easy to dig a tree with a large-caliper trunk and a ball that is too small. That produces a product with too few roots and far too much foliage and limbs.

Slicking the pit if it is dug with another tree spade or the same machine is a problem that must be corrected before planting. The sides must be roughened and widened to enable the tree to be positioned and backfilled properly. The ideal situation is to dig the planting pit with a larger diameter machine than the tree is to be dug with. When that procedure is followed, planting is easier and the percent livability will increase greatly. The walls of the pit will still need to be roughened to get rid of the interface.

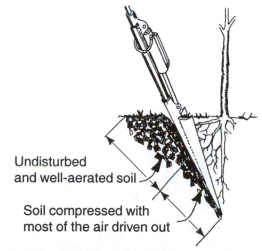

Undisturbed and well-aerated soil

Soil compressed with most of the air driven out

Figure 26. The side view of one blade of a mechanical digger, showing the location of soil compaction and how it comes about.

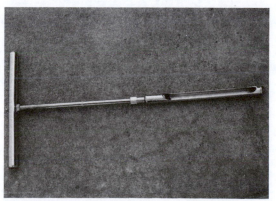

A soil probe has many uses other than pulling soil samples. It is the best way to see into the soil without disturbing plants growing on the site.

Tree Staking

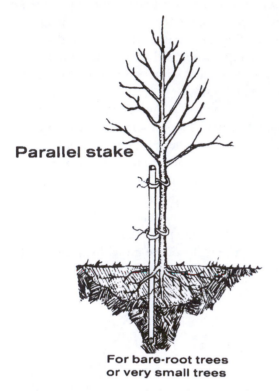

Parallel stake

For bare-root trees
or very small trees

Figure 27. One parallel stake is used for bare-root trees.

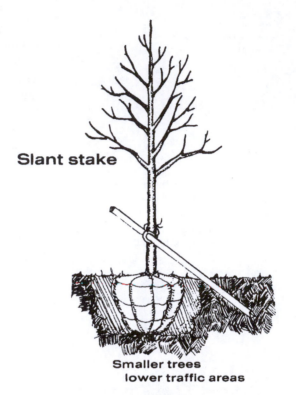

Slant stake

Smaller trees
lower traffic areas

Figure 28. The slanted 1-stake method.

Single stakes should be used for small bare-root trees. Make sure that they are tied securely in order to prevent them from rubbing together.

The slant stake used with balled and burlapped trees does little good for smaller trees and is not adequate for larger plants. Trees of this size and caliper, balled and burlapped, likely do not require staking.

Many times only one stake is used, which is an unsatisfactory procedure for large balled and burlapped material. One stake can be used on bare-root planting, however (fig. 27). The stake must be within 2 or 3 inches of the trunk and tied firmly in two or three locations. One slanted stake may be acceptable for small trees that do not need much help in order to stay vertical. The slanted 1-stake method should be used on

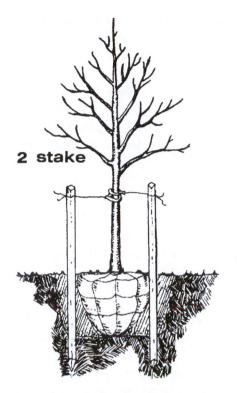

2 stake

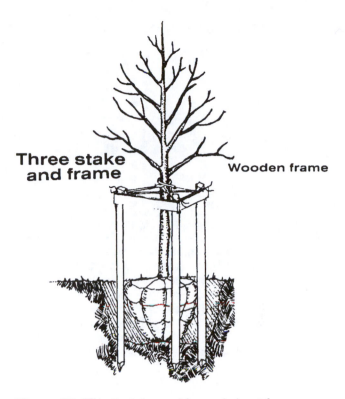

Three stake and frame   Wooden frame

Figure 29. The 2-stake method is the most used and likely the best in most cases.

Figure 30. The 3-stake and frame is best for high-traffic areas.

The 2-stake method shown here is the most widely used and quite adequate for small trees in most cases.

The 3-stake and frame method is highly recommended in public areas such as around schools, in parks, and on parkways.

small trees, and the parallel method on bare-root trees (fig. 28). The quick, pull-through plastic ties now available are satisfactory.

The 2-stake method is much more acceptable. Make the posts long enough to penetrate the undisturbed soil at the bottom so they will not collapse on the tree (fig. 29). The posts should have a good deal of tension put on them as the tree is tied to each. The best way to do this is to tie both wires to the posts at the same time. The tension should be the same so the tree

Wire Basket Trees

Trees balled like the one illustrated have caused discussion about whether the basket should be removed or retained. Some people think that the wires will eventually cause root-girdling, although the manufacturer says, and I agree, that the wire will rust away before girdling occurs and there should be no problem. Remove the string that attaches the baskets to the trunk as soon as possible, however.

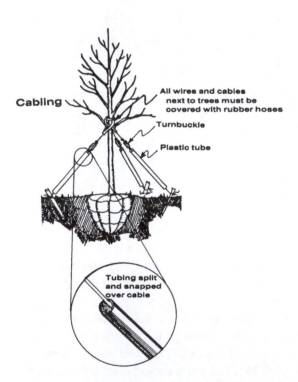

Figure 31. Cabled trees will need turnbuckles. Place them as high as possible. Cover cables with brightly colored plastic tubing.

is not pulled one way or the other during a growing season. If possible, place the rubber hose-covered wire above the first limb (the new tree ties are better if many trees need to be tied). That is not essential, but it helps stabilize the tie in one place.

The 3-stake method is the best method to use, but the extra expense of the third post and frame may not be warranted (fig. 30). The 3-stake and frame method will more than double the material and labor cost of planting the tree. For parkways, school grounds, and parks, however, this type of staking is necessary not only to stabilize a tree but also to ward off hazards such as mowers, bicycles, and snow removal equipment if the tree is close to walks or in a mall area.

Tree Cabling

The previous discussion concerns trees 4″ and under. Those with a caliper between 1½ and 4″ may not need staking. If it is necessary to do so, however, use the 2- or 3-stake method. Trees more than 4″ in caliper will probably benefit from some type of stabilizing. Staking trees that large is difficult and not very effective; in such cases, cabling may be the answer. The stakes used to anchor the cables to the ground are the weak link in the system, so make sure they are heavy enough and long enough to go into the ground 18–24″ for trees of 4–5″ caliper. For trees over that size, enlarge the stakes or use steel auger-type stakes, which can be reused. If wooden stakes are used, they should be made of a hardwood such as oak. The time given to selecting and preparing stakes is well spent.

It is essential that each cable have a turnbuckle so the cables can be tightened as needed. Loose cables are worse than no cables at all (fig. 31). Turnbuckles should be checked once a week for the first month or two they are in place.

If stakes or cables are being used in disturbed soil, the stakes will need to be longer and larger in diameter. It is far better to oversize a stake than undersize it. In these situations auger or duckbill anchors are preferable.

Cabling trees takes area on the ground, and therefore cables become a hazard for foot traffic and lawn equipment. If a tree is in a lawn area, extend the mulch area beyond the stakes. If there is likely to be foot traffic, split a white or brightly colored plastic tube and snap it over the cable to make the cable easily visible.

A cabled tree must have turnbuckles on each cable that can be tightened as they work loose. Wooden stakes can be used but are usually of little value. Auger or duckbill anchors are best. Install them on the same angle as the cable to provide a straight pull with no give. Mark the cables with bright objects.

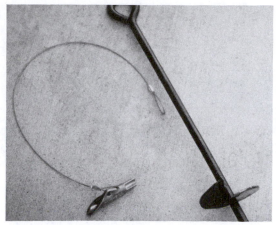

A duckbill anchor is very effective. It must be driven in at the same angle that the cable comes down from the tree, just as you would for an auger. It is driven into the soil with a special driver that makes installation easy. An auger provides the best way to stake trees when stability and strength are needed. Keep the auger in line with the cable to give a straight pull and eliminate spring in the auger rod.

When cabling trees, make sure that wires or cables in contact with the trunk are covered with rubber hoses or some kind of cushion that will not break up in cold weather. This is extremely necessary in avoiding trunk damaging.

Most wooden stakes are unsatisfactory. They are usually too small and driven into disturbed soil. They most often work loose in just a few days.

Guy wires are not enough to hold large trees rigid, and therefore a solid brace of either wooden poles or steel pipe must be used. If possible the feet of these braces must be set in and on solid ground. Braces can either be nailed or laced and tied at the top, which may be the only way to stabilize tall trees, especially those with a spreading head.

The turnbuckle is a tightening device used to take the slack out of a cable after the cable has been tied off. Place a screwdriver in the space in the middle of the turnbuckle and twist it clockwise. Check the cables weekly to ensure that they are tight; they are useless when there is slack in them.

To guy wire a tree, it is necessary to keep the cable tight and well insulated with a cushion of rubber hose or one made of manufactured material. Fast-growing trees such as this willow can fill the space left by the cable around the trunk. If the cable is left on, it could damage or kill the tree.

Tree Base and Trunk Care

One of the best tree protection devices is an area free of sod around the trunk of the new tree. This area should be edged to maintain a grass-free situation (fig. 32) that becomes an attractive containment for mulch in winter, bulbs in spring, and annual flowers in summer. In many cases a permanent ground cover, such as daylilies or English ivy, is attractive and is a one-time planting. Trees grown under this protection grow much faster and have fewer problems than trees with grass right up to their trunks. The protection can be removed after the tree starts to form bark plates (the corky, rough bark of a mature tree).

When trees are planted near busy sidewalks and malls, the soil surface left between the sidewalk and the tree must be protected. This space is necessary for water and air exchange. Tree plantings in urban areas often need to be screened with a galvanized wire mesh to keep rats and ground squirrels from completely undermining them. The screen may need to cover the entire soil area or just the hole around the trunk, depending on the size of holes in the grate. This grate might also need to be built for expansion; the rings can be cut out as the tree matures (fig. 33).

A good basin should always be placed around a tree. Doing so will help guarantee that the tree receives enough water. In wet areas, it may be advisable to remove the basin during the winter.

Fill the area with mulch, producing an attractive place for water, fertilizer, or flowers.

Young trees or shrubs need protection from sod competition and lawn mower damage. One good way to provide such protection is by wood edging filled with mulch or plants.

This tree is protected by a simple planting of a flowering ground cover.

Stake with wood or reinforcing rods as discussed earlier.

Ground cover planted early in a tree's life will ensure against mower damage and provide excellent growing conditions.

Tree Protection Devices

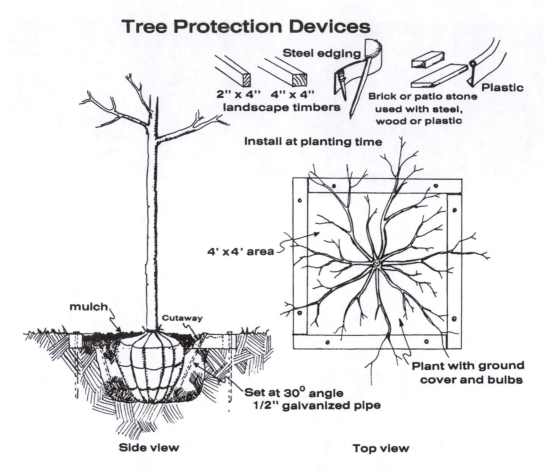

Steel edging

2" x 4" 4" x 4"
landscape timbers

Brick or patio stone
used with steel,
wood or plastic

Plastic

Install at planting time

4' x 4' area

Plant with ground
cover and bulbs

mulch

Cutaway

Set at 30° angle
1/2" galvanized pipe

Side view

Top view

Figure 32. Always use a tree protection device to keep grass away from the trunk. This area will also provide moisture and keep lawn mowers away.

In areas where snow removal equipment is used, tree trunks will need to be protected with something permanent, such as iron grillwork. The grill must either have the ability to be expanded as the tree grows or it should be installed large enough to accommodate a mature tree.

Hosta has been used as a ground cover around this large oak. Plant small plants around established trees so a tree's roots are not damaged. Plant a small area at first and increase it every year.

Trees in urban areas need as much protection as possible. Protection devices need to be maintained annually—in some cases more often. The small mesh hardware cloth around the tree is to prevent rats from living under the walks.

Sometimes trees can be protected, snow can be removed safely, and people can benefit because of a seat and a flower bed.

In areas where snow removal equipment is used, protect the trunk as well.

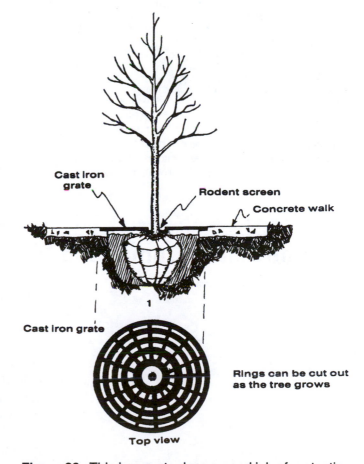

Cast iron grate

Rodent screen

Concrete walk

Cast iron grate

Rings can be cut out as the tree grows

Top view

Figure 33. This iron grate does a good job of protecting the planting area, but the trunk hole must be enlarged as the tree grows.

Correcting Sunscald on Young Trees

Young trees that are not wrapped and cared for properly are at high risk for sun scald damage. Be sure to remove all of the tree's dead or discolored bark. Cut it back until all of its edges are white or light yellow and are moist rather than hard, dry, and brown. Wound paint will not be needed for small wounds that are no more than 2″, but wider wounds could benefit from being painted. If wound paint is used, wait a few days before wrapping so that the wrap will not stick to the wound area, which would slow the healing process.

Young, smooth-barked trees will sunscald easily in open areas or in locations where the trees are under stress. Injury as severe as this can be corrected if the sunscald damage is repaired as soon as it is seen. Wrap the trunk in winter until healing is complete.

Construction Damage to Trees

Diagnosing Construction Damage

Symptoms of construction damage to trees appear from several months to several years after the damage occurs. This delay in the appearance of symptoms usually shifts the blame for construction damage to other causes after it is too late to treat the trees effectively.

The first symptoms are usually just a light wilting and the shedding of some leaves at the time of construction. Then in later years leaf-dwarfing, the dying of twigs, and, in the case of conifers, excessive dropping of needles occurs. Trees damaged by construction act abnormally in many other ways, most noticeably by dropping leaves in early fall compared

Tree roots should always be protected from construction. Here the trunks were protected but not the root area. These trees will likely die.

with trees of the same species in other locations. Early fall coloring usually accompanies early dropping of leaves. In cases of severe construction damage, off-season blooming occurs, which usually means the tree is about to die.

In addition to noticeable physiological change in trees, construction damage produces other symptoms. If the tree has been only slightly damaged, growth is slowed and resistance to insects and diseases is weakened. Borers, scale, and aphids, which can do great harm, move in quickly after construction. These insects must be controlled quickly or they will set the tree back or finish killing it.

Many diseases are soil-borne and quite destructive, especially in compacted or filled soil where the water drainage pattern has been changed. Verticillium is the most prevalent and destructive. It can kill individual limbs or suddenly kill the entire tree. Canker and root rot are other diseases that occur after construction damage.

Diagnosing compaction or smothering damage can be difficult because it takes quite a while for symptoms to appear, often several years. Trees sometimes die five to seven years after the original damage. The amount of damage, the species of tree involved, and the soil type will determine how long it will take for symptoms to appear.

Some species, the cottonwood, for example, have deep roots that give them the ability to survive for long periods in compacted soils that do not have enough air to support other species.

Control of Damage

Controlling Traffic. A basic means of reducing construction damage to trees is to reduce traffic as much as possible around the construction site. Talk this over with your contractor before construction begins. Establish definite traffic patterns and fence them off if necessary. Locate stockpile areas for soil and building materials well away from the drip line of trees you want to save.

Taking Care of Tree Roots. When you install temporary or permanent driveways or traffic lanes, cut nearby tree roots cleanly. Cleanly cut roots will heal well, and new roots will develop. Trenchers and backhoe equipment are most commonly used for such cutting (fig. 34).

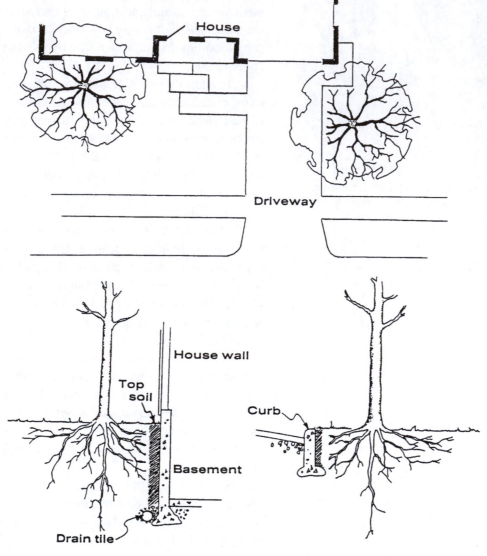

Figure 34. Various situations in which trenchers or backhoe equipment should be used to cut tree roots. Fill with good topsoil.

Bridging. Sometimes it is necessary for traffic to pass near trees. In this case use bridging as illustrated (fig. 35). Trees that have lost some roots and are in compacted soil usually need water.

After pruning a tree's roots, also remove a comparable portion of the top part of the trunk. Remove selected branches to the main trunk or to the crotch. Cut branches from throughout the tree to maintain symmetry (fig. 36).

Cut-and-fill damage can injure trees just as much as compaction. The symptoms of the two problems are almost identical, only in most cases tree injury and death occur more rapidly from cut-and-fill damage. Fill that covers the root system of a tree will smother it by

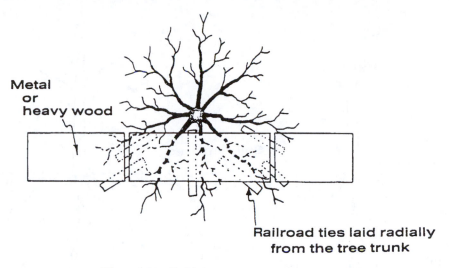

Metal
or
heavy wood

Railroad ties laid radially
from the tree trunk

Figure 35. Bridging to protect tree roots.

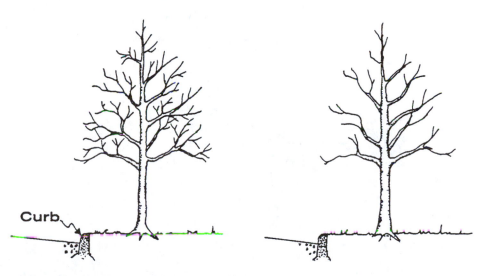

Curb

Figure 36. A tree before and after thinning or pruning. If part of a root system is removed, reduce the amount of fertilizer proportionately.

This well-constructed tree well is in an area where the grade was raised more than 2'. The tree survived and has grown well for several years; without this structure, however, the tree would have died.

cutting off its air supply and, sometimes, the moisture the tree must have to survive. Changing the grade by removing soil can kill trees as quickly as covering (fig. 37A-B). Leveling a steep grade also creates a problem, but the same procedures must be followed as shown in figure 37C-D.

To place fill soil over root systems, follow the procedure illustrated. Use the complete system for satisfactory results because installing any one part of it will do little good. Use 4″ or 6″ standard agricultural field drain tile. Lay it in the pattern illustrated. Cover the tile with 6–8″ of coarse, ½–3″ stone. Use creek gravel, not crushed limestone, which is commonly used for road work. Crushed limestone fill can harm the tree by raising the soil pH. The fill soil should be

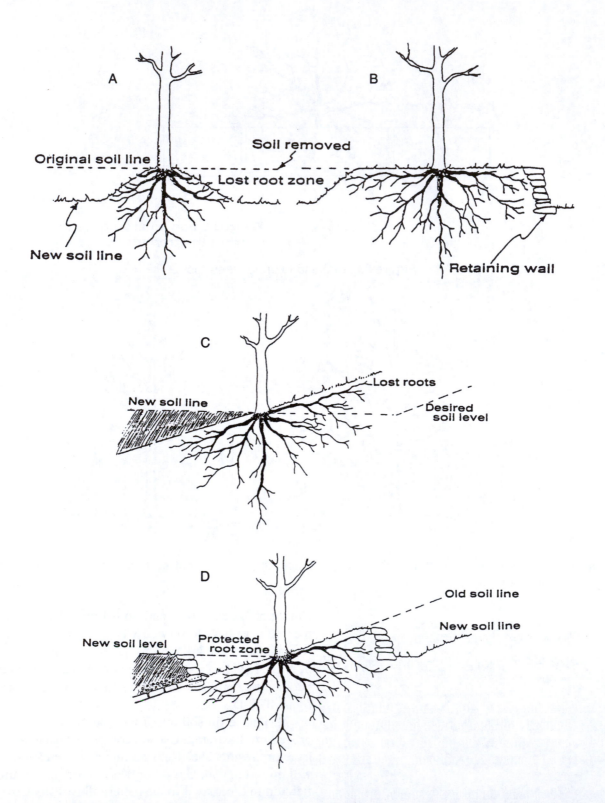

Figure 37. Drawing B shows the wrong way to lower soil level around a tree in a flat area. The right way to protect a tree from cut-and-fill damage is shown in Drawings C-D. The method in Drawing C will harm the tree.

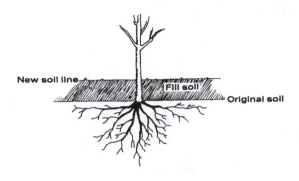

Figure 38. Completely covering the area above its roots will kill a tree.

as porous as possible or amended with sand or organic materials such a corncobs. Sandy soil permits more natural drainage of air and water than clay, which packs more easily. Two or three inches of sandy soil can be filled over a root system without harming the tree, while 2–3″ of clay soil over a root system will kill the tree (figs. 38–40).

Controlling Insects and Diseases. For insect control recommendations, contact a state land grant university college of agriculture for the most recent pesticide information.

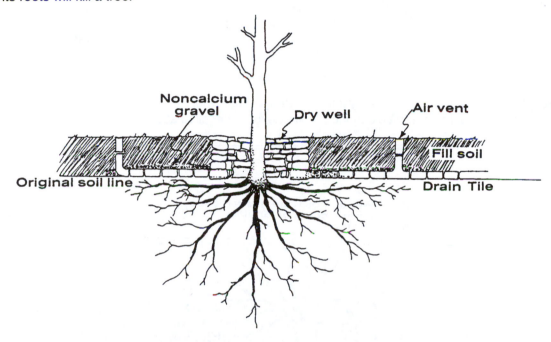

Figure 39. A side view of the proper tiling system to install when using fill dirt to raise the ground level around a tree. The dry well can be filled with stone or soil if the air vent is not hindered. If soil is used up to the tree, a vent tile must be added and the trunk must be sound.

For best results, fertilize trees a few inches below the surface. Drill a hole with an auger to a depth of 18–20″, add about a one quarter pound of a blended fertilizer, then cover or backfill with about 5–6″ of soil.

Fertilizing Trees

Use a good blended fertilizer such as 20-10-5 or 10-6-4. Fertilize in November or early spring to stimulate new root growth and help the tree resist diseases and insects.

The best method of fertilization is to drill holes with a 2″ soil auger, 18″ deep and 3′ from each other. With small trees 8″ in diameter and under, start the holes 2′ away from the trunk. With trees more than 8″ in diameter, start the holes at a distance from the trunk equal to 4′ plus 1′ for each inch of diameter beyond 8″. Holes for a 12″ tree would start at 8′; for a 15″ tree at 11′ (fig. 41).

For trees under 8″ in diameter, when using a 10-6-4 fertilizer, apply 5 pounds of fertilizer per inch

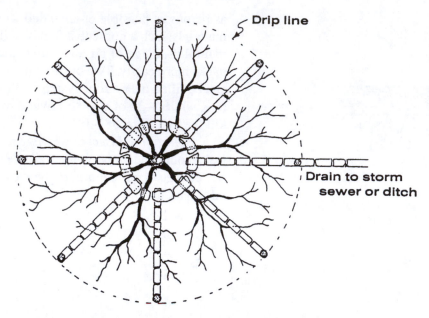

Figure 40. Top view of the drainage system of a tree located where the ground level is being raised by the addition of fill dirt. Vent tiles can be connected with tile for better circulation.

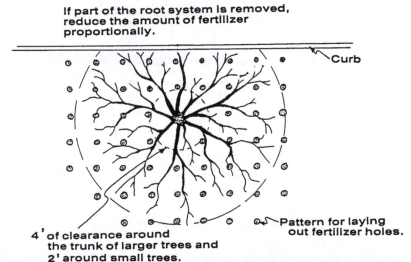

Figure 41. If part of the root system is removed, reduce the amount of fertilizer proportionately,
- 4′ of clearance on large trees and 2′ on small trees.
- Pattern for laying out fertilizer holes.

of trunk diameter (measured 3 or 4′ above ground). Distribute fertilizer evenly in the holes. When using a 20-10-5 fertilizer, apply 2½ pounds per inch of trunk diameter. Double these rates for trees more than 8″ in diameter. Thus, when fertilizing a tree 6″ in diameter with a 10-6-4 fertilizer, you would apply a total of 30 pounds in the holes you had drilled beneath the tree (6″ diameter × 5 pounds of fertilizer = 30 pounds total

Place the holes approximately 3' apart. Measuring cups are useful for apportioning fertilizer.

applied). Apply fertilizer after July 15 and then wait until a hard freeze. Avoid fertilizing in late spring and begin again in early fall. Water the fertilizer in if at all possible. Soak the area thoroughly.

The simplest, safest way to fertilize a tree is to drill holes every 4' starting 4' from the trunk, 6' or more for large trees. The holes should be 18" deep and 1 to 1½" wide. Put one cup of 12-12-12 fertilizer into each hole. When done over the entire area under the drip line, the tree will receive enough fertilizer and nutrients, but the roots will not be burned. If this is done properly and holes are sealed with sand or soil, grass will not be affected by burning or by a dark-green pattern of dots. That also takes into account areas under the tree that may be covered by drives and walks.

Another common way to fertilize is with a needle. Always use gravity flow or very low pressure and place the needle in several locations around the tree or shrub.

Lawn spreaders are the least effective way to apply fertilizer. The grass will use most of the fertility before the tree receives any benefit. Lawn grasses are formidable competitors for moisture and fertility.

Patio Design

The patio, lawn space, and enclosure combine in a functional and attractive way to make an outdoor living area. This combination varies in importance, depending upon where you live. For example, in California or Arizona the patio would likely be a large, hard surface that includes most of the lawn and would be enclosed with a fence or shrub screen. In the Midwest, however, the patio surface need not occupy as much space, and the lawn and enclosure plants become much more important.

It is important to see the outdoor living space as another room. Developing it requires careful planning to make it attractive and to provide as much privacy as possible. Outdoor living areas will not be used if they are open to the public or if they provide inadequate protection from wind and sun.

Patios need not be very large as long as the outdoor living space is designed to work as a unit to provide space and access to that space.

The rest of the outdoor living space is enclosed, making the area private. Access into the lawn gives all of the space needed.

This outdoor room should have a floor, walls, furniture, and a ceiling. The floor is the patio and lawn; the walls are hedges, screens, and mass plantings, including flowering trees and other plants that provide a framing for the windows so those inside have a pleasant view. Furniture can either be built into the enclosure or be commercial patio furniture. The "room's" ceiling is provided by well-placed shade trees, a shade structure such as timber covered with canvas, or an arbor covered with a well-maintained vine.

Make the access from the house onto the patio surface as convenient as possible. It should be as easy as going from one room to another in order to transport food and other items conveniently, otherwise no effort will be made to do so.

Grade the soil so the patio surface is even with or just below the floor of the house. If that is not possible, construct a large landing with steps down to the floor or consider a deck. The hard surface area of the patio must work with the lawn as one large floor. The patio's hard surface should be large enough to accommodate all family members who use the patio on a regular basis. The area should be adequate for family meals or entertaining. The lawn area allows for expansion to accommodate larger groups.

Construct the patio from either the same material as the house or from materials that complement it. Concrete can be a satisfactory surface if finished attractively. Dyes, exposed aggregate, and imprinting are three possibilities. Use redwood or troweled break joints for attractive, durable finishes.

In areas such as the Midwest, where patios are often enjoyed more from indoors than from outdoors because of weather and insects, the patio enclosure or surroundings become important in the planning. It is necessary to select flowering trees and screening with care so they can add beauty all year. Patio furniture should be durable and comfortable and add to the area's overall appearance. Plantings and furniture should not inhibit the flow of traffic or movement.

5 rules or steps to a better patio:

1. Make access onto the patio as easy as possible.
2. Access into the lawn should be easy and inviting.
3. The hard surface should be just large enough for use by the immediate family.
4. Make the patio of like or complementary materials to continue the style of the house.
5. The patio should be as attractive to view from the inside of the house as from the outside.

This desert home has a patio surface that uses all of the back yard, which is ideal in such a climate. In cold climates, however, a different approach is necessary.

Unfortunately, many people are left with such a situation. Consider how the 5 rules for planning patios could have improved this outdoor living space.

Patio Construction

When building or designing a patio, it is important to keep an open, easy traffic flow to the rest of the outdoor living area. This patio is enclosed and does not provide a feeling of spaciousness or a welcome to the outdoors.

The same design and setting without the enclosure wall. The hard surface and the lawn areas give this patio unlimited space.

Concrete is the most commonly used material in patio construction because the surface can be imprinted with a pattern to resemble brick, tile, or flagstone. Exposed aggregate is sometimes used, and many good dyes are available. For example, one of the finishes that works well is travertine with a light tan dye.

If a step is needed to reach the patio, it should be constructed by figuring the height (or riser) and width (or tread). It is important to make steps long enough to be in scale with the house and patio. A rule to follow in designing a step is $2 \times$ riser + tread = 24 (for example, a 4″ riser and a 16″ tread).

It is a good idea to incorporate redwood (1 × 4″ or 2 × 4″) into the design when working with concrete (see "Using Wood in Concrete") in order to stop the random cracking of the surface.

Free-laid brick made of clay or concrete makes an excellent floor if constructed properly (fig. 42). Make sure the brick is impervious to water. One way to test whether the brick can be used for a patio is to weigh a brick when it is dry, then soak it in water overnight and weigh it again. If the brick gains 5% or more of its weight, it will probably crumble or break in climates where there is a lot of freezing and thawing.

Brick should be laid on a well-packed and drained bed of sand. If the area is level and wet it should be tiled to ensure quick drainage of excess moisture. Do not use black plastic sheeting under the brick because it contributes to excess moisture that causes the brick to deteriorate much faster. Use torpedo sand under the brick, not crushed limestone that will raise the pH in the surrounding soil and stunt or kill plants. Limestone used this way is harmful to rhododendrons and hollies;

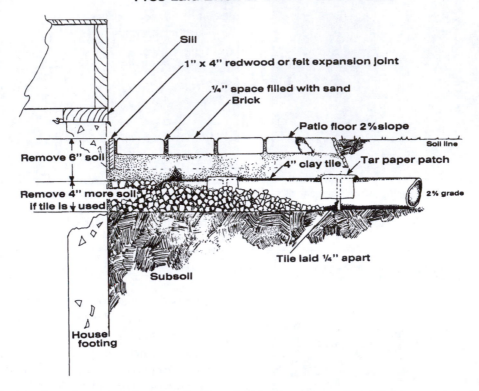

Figure 42. A side view of construction detail of free-laid brick or stone floor. Always provide drainage and a solid base upon which to lay the paving material.

This free-laid brick floor has a wide, low step onto patio from the home's porch. Free-laid floors like this must be enclosed in a curb or edging that will stop the brick from spreading.

the pH in these areas will be as high as 8.5. The best material to use as a base under walks, drives, and patios is crushed granite. It packs well and will not shift or roll like sand.

To construct a free-laid brick or stone patio, excavate and slope the base about 2% away from the house. Install treated fir or redwood 6 × 6″ landscape timber as a permanent edging; this stops the shifting. When this subbase is ready to be filled with gravel and sand, determine if tile is needed (lay it at this point, as shown in figure 42). Pack the base by tamping and flooding it with water. If tile is needed, make sure the sand is flooded into the rock base that covers the tile. It may be necessary to flood more than once.

There are many manufacturers designing and making hundreds of new shapes of pavers. For a specific shape or color, it may be necessary to shop a variety of sources.

It is important to have the edging material level when the floor or walk has had time to settle to a final grade. To achieve that, screat the sand off about ½″ less than the depth of the brick—more shallow than the brick or stone. Tamp until the surfacing material becomes level with the edging. Lay the brick with about ¼″

This front entrance has good scale for its steps.

space all around in order to provide expansion space, especially for large floors.

Treated Douglas Fir or redwood is best used for edging because of its straightness and resistance to rot. Stake with ⅜″ enforcing rods or ½″ galvanized pipe driven in at a 30-degree angle to prevent heaving out in winter. Timbers and pavers make an excellent combination in appearance and strength. Pavers must have a strong edging, and large timbers provide it naturally.

Set pavers or brick firmly into the sand bed by using a tamper. Place a large board—for example, one 2 × 12 × 18″—on the brick and tamp firmly. Here a sledgehammer is being used on a 4 × 4″ post to set the brick.

A packer is useful in small spaces and can prevent walks or floors from developing low spots and unevenness. It is also a good idea to lay weed barrier over a smoothed area. Then screat a 2″ layer of sand, granite chips, or fine limestone over the top of the weed barrier.

Using wood in concrete adds interest and, if done properly, will not affect the life or usability of the surface. Areas of concrete must be tied together and wood anchored into the concrete.

This patio was given an exposed aggregate finish.

This anchoring is easily done by using steel galvanized gutter spikes. Drive them in every 2' and/or at the end of each section.

This type of construction allows for surface expansion without leaving a cold joint (a rough connection between the old concrete and the new).

When using wood in concrete, edge all areas that touch the concrete so there is a smooth surface and a good transition from one material to the other. When that is not done, there will be an unsightly rough edge.

Set the wood with the galvanized gutter spikes as was done in the original surface.

Always cover and cure concrete for 48–72 hours before removing the forms or using the surface and be careful not to damage the concrete's edges when removing forms.

Ornaments made to match the rest of the patio complete the look of this outdoor living space.

Cross Section of Exposed Aggregate

This new pour is visibly lighter, but that will change quickly.

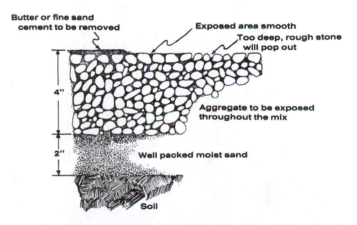

Butter or fine sand cement to be removed

Exposed area smooth

Too deep, rough stone will pop out

4"

Aggregate to be exposed throughout the mix

2"

Well packed moist sand

Soil

Figure 43. Use free-flowing water when exposing aggregate—never spray on the water. Wash off just enough to show the top of the stone and never wash until the stones are raised.

There is no visible difference one year later. Good, structurally sound furniture is always advisable, whether built on-site or manufactured.

This floor has been exposed correctly with low water pressure and a high volume of water. That allows an easy flow to carry off the "butter" or sand and cement mixture without damaging the concrete or losing the exposed stones (fig. 43).

The high-pressure nozzle that exposed this floor cut into the concrete too deeply and left streaks of pitted and overwashed surface.

Interlocking pavers are held together here with treated California cedar edging; the steps are made of 2 × 4 × 6"s.

The kind, size, and shape of paver to use is governed by the landscape style or the architectural style of the home.

Another popular style of concrete paver with a substantial edging.

The wood timbers used here do an excellent job of holding the pavers together and also provide a nice visual element. The best timber to use for this type of construction is redwood, treated fir, or treated yellow pine.

Seating can help emphasize the design of the patio and also be functional. These seats are not only functional but also provide a well-protected area for plantings.

Good, cushioned furniture is comfortable and attractive, but cushions retain moisture after a rain. They also tend to fade, and sun stains and discolors them. They are best used in a gazebo or garden house. These cushions can be used on custom-made furniture, which should be 6" lower and 8–10" wider. They will also stain if a ferrous metal object is left on them for a day or two.

Some furniture is expensive and must be used on a fine, hard surface. This furniture would be completely out of place on a smooth-finished concrete patio floor.

Custom-made furniture that matches and ties in with the rest of a patio's materials is always good design. Furniture built on-site provides an individual, custom look.

Good wooden furniture is always attractive but will take more care than other furniture.

This patio was built using flat, washed beach stones for an interesting, one-of-a-kind look. This type of hard surface takes much labor to fit and level enough to walk upon. The final product is an attractive, natural patio floor.

This patio was made from beach stone selected for its one smooth, flat surface and laid in sand. Bentgrass was sodded in the spaces between the stones to produce an interesting, one-of-a-kind patio that is level enough to walk upon and the product of much work.

The Tilesetters' Method of Laying Brick or Stone

The pattern of a walk must be selected and laid out to determine how wide the proposed walk will be. There will be no time to cut and fit each brick once construction is underway.

Once the setup is completed, all speed must be taken. The more rapidly brick is laid, the better concrete will stick to it.

The tilesetters' method is done much the same as the sand except a mixture of sand and cement is used (3 parts sand to 1 part cement). This mixture is almost dry, with just enough water to stop the dust. Use 3″ of mixture under the brick and sweep it into the crack around the brick. If the area is to carry heavy traffic, install a 3–4″ layer of rough concrete instead of sand under the brick. After the brick is laid it should be allowed to cure for about 48 hours. Then the floor can be acid washed (1 part muriatic acid to 10 parts water). Next wash the surface thoroughly with clean water so it will be free of acid or loose sand. The last step is to seal the surface with a silicon material to make it waterproof.

Never lay out more of the mix than can be prepared and finished in 30 minutes. Then set up and begin again. The first step to set bricks, pavers, or flagstones in the tilesetters' method is to place the forms correctly and to the exact grade. The forms will become the final grade of the surface. Cut the screat board to about ½″ thinner than the thickness of the brick, paver, or stone. The sand and cement mix should be 1 part cement and 2 parts sand. Mix with just enough water to settle the dust and for the mixture to become sticky enough to form a ball when squeezed. The mix should be about the consistency of damp sugar. Place the mix into the forms and screat it off to the prescribed depth. Now lay the floor and sprinkle raw cement over the surface of the mix to provide better adhesion of the mix and stone. Always use dry brick or stone. If the pour space is filled with water the cement will be diluted. This will result in poor adhesion of the brick to the base mix of sand and cement.

Remember that the screat board was cut ½″ less than the depth of the brick, therefore the bricks are all stuck ½″ above the forms. At this time, sprinkle cement right out of the bag on the freshly screated sand-cement mix. That will cause a good bond. Now bring the bricks into grade by tamping them into the soft sand cement mix, which will settle between the bricks. Add more sand by sweeping over the surface and cleaning off the excess. Dry weather may necessitate a light misting of the surface before it is covered with plastic to hold moisture. In order to cure, not dry, the surface must be kept cool as any good concrete pad would be. Keep the surface covered and free of traffic for 48 hours at a minimum to allow for curing. In cold weather (below 40 degrees), 72 hours may be required to cure the surface completely so that it can safely carry a load.

This walk area took 4 people about a half hour to finish. Begin to fill the cracks at this point so that is done when the final brick is laid.

Start to tamp the bricks flush with the top of the forms.

Sometimes, especially around water, it may be desirable to have harder, more waterproof joints than are created by the tilesetters' method. This walk has been finished with a cement slurry rubbed in to the joints with sponges.

When the cover is removed, a white film will be on the brick or floor surface that will need acid-washing.

The walk surface after it has been cleaned.

Brick Walk and Floor Designs

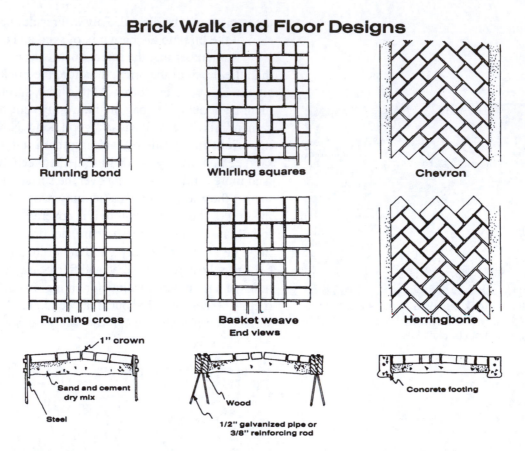

Running bond

Whirling squares

Chevron

Running cross

Basket weave
End views

Herringbone

1" crown

Sand and cement
dry mix

Steel

Wood

1/2" galvanized pipe or
3/8" reinforcing rod

Concrete footing

Figure 44. The design of a brick floor has a significant effect on the cost of laying it. All brick walks must have an edging.

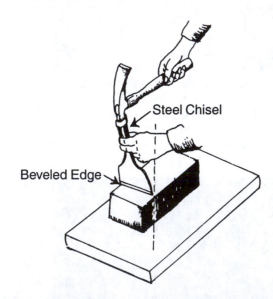

Steel Chisel

Beveled Edge

Figure 45. Brick, stone, and concrete pavers may need to be marked with a chisel or wet-saw before using a chisel. Always keep the beveled edge toward the waste, which may come off in pieces or all at once. Needed pieces generally stay intact.

Use a solution of muriatic acid mixed 1 part acid to 10 parts water. Badly stained surfaces may need to be washed with a 1 to 8 mix. Wash the surface completely and stop all reaction or it will eat into the mix between the bricks. To make sure that the reaction has stopped, wash the surface with a soda-water solution. Spray the surface with a silicone just as soon as the surface dries. The cleaner and drier the surface, the better the silicone will work to seal out water. Brick floors need to be treated at least every two years.

The cost of labor changes according to the pattern of brick used. Those that are more complicated require more cutting and fitting. The chevron design (fig. 44), for example, requires considerable time and makes for more waste. Hand cutting with a chisel is good for small jobs, but a saw will be needed to lay patios or driveways (fig. 45).

The subgrade and grout are prepared like the other tilesetters' method. The spaces between the bricks are filled with the same sand and cement mixture as the tilesetters' method, and a slurry of cement and water is spread over the surface to seal and smooth the mix. When the slurry begins to set up, sponge off the excess. Allow the surface to cure for about 48 hours and acid wash with a solution of 1 part muriatic acid to 10 parts water to clean and brighten the brick. Stop the reaction of the acid as soon as the brick is clean by spreading quicklime over the surface. Then sweep the lime water and what is left of the acid until all of the fizzing stops and wash the surface as clean as possible. The final step in this process is to apply a water seal as soon as the surface is clean and dry.

Wooden Decks

Installation of seats and deck rails is an important construction procedure if the deck is to look structurally sound and to last. All standards, legs, and rail posts must be installed through the floor and fastened to the joists or any floor supports. Surface attachments never look strong and will work loose. Surface attachments make the construction job look like the seating and railing were afterthoughts, not the impression that an expensive landscape structure should convey. Use ⅜ to ½ × 4″ long legscrews or bolts to secure these supports. Galvanized nails can be used to help stabilize the supports but should not be used in total.

Wood makes a nice patio floor. Redwood, treated yellow pine or fir, California cedar, and cypress are the best woods to use. Do not use sapwood (wood that has white streaks on its outer edges), especially if the wood is to come in contact with soil. Sapwood can be treated with Cupernol, but not with products like Penta, which can be harmful to plants and should be used only on posts. California cedar should be kept out of contact with soil because it does not last well as posts or bed edging.

Attaching a wood deck to a house can lead to severe structural problems if it is not done correctly. Deck joists must be attached to the house's framing rather than its siding (fig. 46). Remove the siding and install a copper or galvanized flashing to prevent moisture from damaging the house frame (fig. 47). Galvanized hangers are made in all shapes and sizes to fit each particular job. They make an easy, structurally sound connection between the deck and the house.

The joist has been notched to hold more weight and prevent slippage.

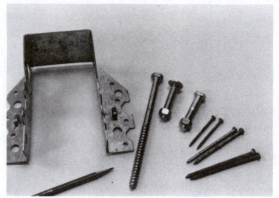

(Left to right) galvanized hangers, galvanized leg-screw, stovebolts, hexhead bolt, and nails.

The hanger makes an excellent connection to the house and is quick to use and inexpensive. These are good hinges for outdoor use because they are large and galvanized.

These posts can be set on top of concrete cores below frostline. If a hole is dug carefully, no form will be needed except at the surface for deck supports or posts. In this example, the holes have been dug with a posthole digger.

When seen from below, many good things are evident about this deck. The support posts are notched to receive the floor joist, adding great strength to the floor. The notch provides added strength in line with the joist to stop ricking. Deck railings are also fastened below the floor.

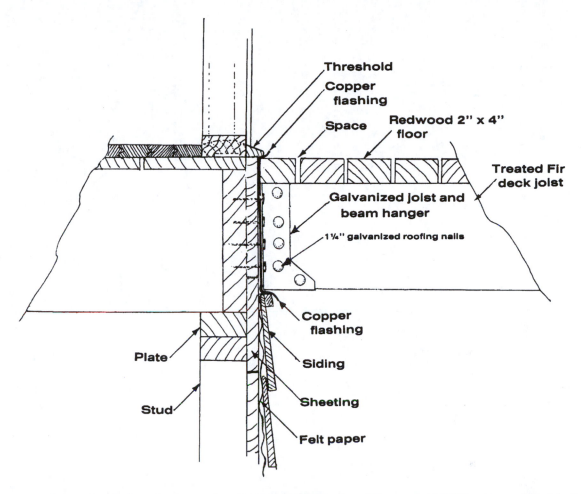

Threshold
Copper flashing
Space
Redwood 2" x 4" floor
Treated Fir deck joist
Galvanized joist and beam hanger
1¼" galvanized roofing nails
Copper flashing
Plate
Siding
Stud
Sheeting
Felt paper

Figure 46. Attach the deck to the house framing rather than to the siding material. If the house is brick, it may be best to let the deck be freestanding and not attach it. Leave about 1½" between the deck and the brick. This is the safest procedure to follow and keep the house brick intact.

Remove siding material when attaching a deck to a house and attach the support structure to the house's frame or sill. The only things between the structure's floor and the house should be copper flashing or termite shield and moisture barrier.

The deck structure and flashing are in place. The joists are mounted with the galvanized joist hangers. It is important to set the support posts below the frostline so the floor will not move and damage the house frame because of freezing, thawing, and settling.

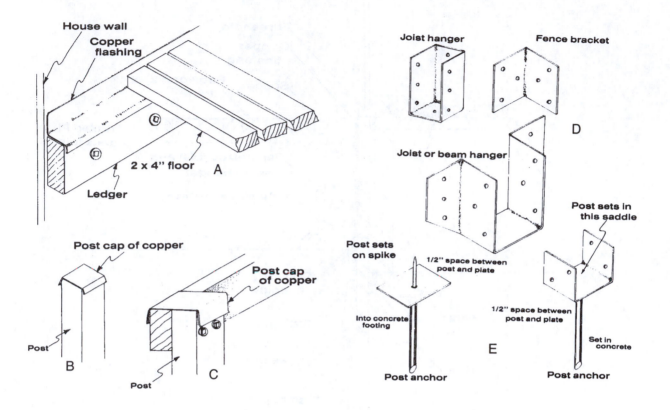

Figure 47. a. Place flashing over ledges to keep them dry.
b.-c. Cap posts before building over them.
d. Three different galvanized metal hangers.
e. Two kinds of post plates to secure posts and keep them off the footing and dry.

This deck is being built with aluminum flashing to protect the house from water and termites.

Ideally, any part of your structure that touches the soil should be redwood. Treated yellow pine or fir are the best woods for floor supports and joists because they will hold nails firmly. All metal parts such as nails, hangers, and bolts should be hot-dipped galvanized. It is also important to make sure that the deck is supported by posts set in concrete below frostline or on concrete pillars, also below the frostline.

The step truss in figure 48A is a standard measurement for house steps; the truss is cut from a 2 × 10″ board. The steeper angle makes these steps stronger because much of the weight is transferred to the floor. Steps with a lower rise and a longer tread need to be built with 2 × 12″ boards.

The truss in figure 48B is cut to accept a covering and give a 5″ riser and 15″ tread needed for outdoor landscape work. It is also evident that the weight is carried straight down at the junction of the riser and tread, making it weak. Avoid this problem by constructing the easier to build step box or stack step instead of the conventional method (fig. 49).

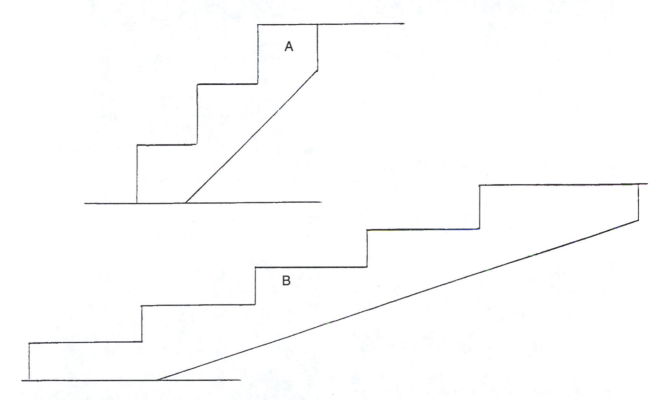

Figure 48. The standard step truss (A) is cut to support a standard house step. The truss in (B) is cut to meet the right scale for outdoors. Both trusses are built to reach the same height. Truss B is weak and will need to be braced in the middle to keep it from breaking.

Attach railings and seats through the deck floor and fasten them to a floor support or joist.

Steps are needed for this deck, which is raised a little higher off the ground. Make them as wide and as low as possible. The transition from the deck to ground is accomplished with low, deep steps.

Curved deck handrails require skill to build. They must be laminated from several thin pieces of wood, glued with marine glue, and screwed together with brass screws.

Here, 5 thin boards, ⅜″ thick and 3⅝″ wide, are nailed and glued together to form a handrail. The first board was nailed to the support post. The rest are then applied one at a time with marine glue and galvanized nails.

Curved seating requires all possible posts or supports, not only to make the seat sound but also maintain the curve in the wood. Such seats must be built in place and laminated one board at a time. Where possible, start the seat square and straight and then go into the curve.

Seats and handrails should always be attached to a deck's joists or floor supports, as illustrated. The railing is built in panels and attached to 4 × 4″ posts below the floor. All railings should close enough to each other so a baby's or small child's head cannot fit between them. It is important to check local ordinances before building a deck.

This rail and seat were built as one unit to add strength.

When working in small areas, it is important not to overpower the area with one item such as seats and railings, although railings are needed.

This low deck is built correctly with railing below the floor; low-growing shrubs screen the underside.

Decks built low to the ground must be closed to wild animals and vented to keep the area under the deck dry and mildew-free.

This pool-deck seat provides room for toys and equipment because it is constructed to have great strength and provide practical storage.

This low deck has many good features: It is easily accessible and attractive from the house or the lawn, although a deep step would be useful.

Correctly built deck steps are in scale with the outdoors. The risers are 4½" and the treads are 18", providing an easy climb to the top. Proven formulas for step construction are included in the portion of this volume on steps.

Screening this deck adds more private space if needed.

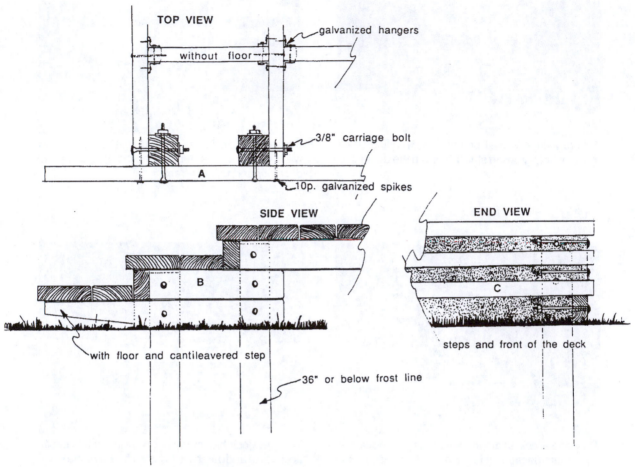

Figure 49. The box step method of building steps.

These steps are being made of 2 × 6" treated fir. It would be impossible to cut the long tread in a board as big as a 2 × 12". Even if the cut could be worked out, it would be too weak to hold up under much weight.

Strong steps can be built quickly using the stack method. Here, three risers are being built. Three boxes are built and stacked and then the tread and risers are applied (fig. 46).

Curved Decks

The beginning of a roundnose deck. It requires skill and patience to build facing for a curved deck floor. Here, the deck supports are in place, ready for the curved face or joist. The board must by curfed every ¾".

The joist and the curfed board, using scrap blocks to form the backing for the curved board.

The curf cuts can be seen here; waste blocks are nailed to the joist to support the curfed board. An even, sturdy face can be achieved for this deck. If more rigidity is required in the facer board, fit the shims behind the curfed board until the openings are filled.

Curved decks and other structures always create a problem for builders. The process is similar to that of curved handrails except that the wider, thicker boards will need to be cut across the grain several times ½–⅔" of the board's depth (curfing). Larger, wider boards should be curfed every ½" along the entire length of the board to be curved. It is also a good idea to soak the board at least overnight—longer if possible—because boards become more limber as they soak. Cut the curf after soaking.

Curfing is done by setting the Skillsaw to cut halfway through the board. Before the board is bent into shape, soak it overnight to soften the wood and help prevent breaking. The depth of cut will be determined by the radius of the curve and the type of wood; curves should not be less than an 8' radius. It is always best to use an even-grained wood like cypress or redwood.

If two curfed boards are to be jointed, cut several pieces of 2 × lumber to the same curve as the curved facing board. That will allow for nailing to a solid backing. For greater strength, use good marine glue on the curved backing. The nails and glue should give a smooth, professional-looking joint.

The joist and curfed facing board have been curved and are ready for the floor.

The completed deck is attractive and unusual.

Decks sometimes become docks. Put together, the two make an enjoyable addition to homes located near a water source. Setting the pilings for this structure usually calls for getting wet. Two flatbottom boats lashed together also make a solid platform from which to dive.

Before the curved board is applied, frame-in holes for the boxes to hold light fixtures. The nailer blocks will fit snugly against the box and prevent the curved board from splitting and peeling back or becoming straight.

The finished deck/dock includes a special place where younger people can board a small boat.

Landscape Surface Treatments and Preservatives

Aging Redwood Quickly

Common baking soda can give a redwood fence an aged look immediately. Mix 2 cups of baking soda with 1 gallon of water and brush or spray the solution on the wood, stirring the mixture often. As it dries the acids in the redwood combine with the soda to produce a dark, weathered appearance. Baking soda does not darken other woods as effectively as redwood and will weather out of redwood in a year or two, but by then a natural darkening of the wood will have taken place. The mixture can be used on rough or smooth boards; apply it evenly to avoid streaking.

Bleaching Oil

Bleaching oil is a refined and clarified Creosote oil containing a small amount of gray pigment and a chemical ingredient that actually bleaches the wood. When first applied, the bleaching oil colors wood a light gray. During the first few months' exposure, it gradually changes the color of raw wood to a beautiful, natural, even gray. If derived from nature, this effect requires 2 to 3 years of weathering, whereas it can be achieved with bleaching oil in 6 to 12 months.

Any exterior wood surface stained with bleaching oil is preserved effectively against decay. The oil contains mildew-resistant Creosote, which prevents blackening of the surface. Bleaching oil is an ideal finish for exterior wood surfaces of any type lumber.

Cupernol

Various preservatives containing copper naphthenate are satisfactory and are as safe to use in closed areas as wood preservatives, but this material does leach out of treated lumber and, over a period of time, protection against rot is lost. Many times the wood can be treated in place to prolong the protection.

Penta

Pentachlorophenol is an excellent wood preservative, however it should never be used on wooden surfaces indoors because the fumes are toxic to plant growth. It can be used on fence posts but not on large areas such as a board-on-board fence. The material will volatize to the extent that it will kill surrounding plants; such volatilization will continue for many years.

"Wolmanizing"

The treatment recommended for ground contact are Wolman CCA, chromated copper sulfate, and arsenic acid. They are injected into the wood in a water solution. Once the chemicals are in the wood, they react with wood sugars from insoluble compounds. Many formulations of salts are injected. In general, they have little effect on plants.

Creosote

Creosote is a good preservative, but treated wood should be used after it weathers to get rid of the excess creosote on the outside of the lumber. Creosote, a combination of aromatic hydrocarbons distilled from coal tar, is used primarily for posts and wood that comes in contact with the soil or is below-grade.

Wood Preservatives

Pentachlorophenol 5% in Stoddard Solvent and Pentachlorophenol 5% in #2 fuel oil will damage outdoor plants for 4 or more years. If these treatments are used, allow them to weather outdoors 3 years before use outdoors. The same treatment used indoors or in a greenhouse will be damaging for many years. It is not recommended for use in the landscape except on posts after they age.

Copper naphthenate 10% in Stoddard Solvent and copper naphthenate 10% in #2 fuel oil will give some light damage to plants indoors and a slight trace outdoors. Weathering one year before use usually eliminates all damage.

Products such as Erdalith, Tanalith, and Celcure gave only light traces of damage for 2 years.

Chromatid zinc chloride will give light to moderate damage for 2 to 3 years. It is best to age the lumber for 2 years before using it.

Borax is sometimes used but is not recommended because it has poor preservative qualities and will give severe damage to plants for the effective length of the preservative.

Creosote will give severe damage to plants for 3 to 4 years outdoors and can be much worse indoors. Creosote is not to be used where people and pets will come in contact with the treated wood; it is good for railroad ties and large landscape timbers used for posts and retaining walls.

Cupernol or copper naphthenate is best to use in general. It is excellent for wood used in concrete or decks.

If there is doubt about the effect of the wood treatment, put a tomato plant near the wood in question. You should have an indication soon, usually within 3 to 4 days.

A new wood preservative can be used in combination with CCA: chromatid copper arsenate. This material reacts with the sugar found in the wood cells. That makes a solid chemical bond. Paraffin is infused into the wood, making a stable, safe product to use for decks or any other project that will be exposed to the weather. The process makes lumber that is safe and clean to work with. If this wood is left untreated with stain or paint it will turn a soft, silver-gray in time. Stain and paint can be used, but the wood must be allowed to dry completely. Paraffin causes the wood to dry slowly, so wait and try the stain or paint on a piece of scrap. If that takes the stain or paint the wood is ready. That is the only difference between the paraffin-treated wood and any other type of treatment.

Etching Concrete before Staining

Etching works best on concrete floors that are extremely smooth. Clean the floor thoroughly with trisodium phosphate or a cleaning product whose main ingredient is trisodium phosphate. Use a stiff brush to remove all powder, grit, and oil.

Now test the floor by dropping a glass of water on one spot. If the water is absorbed within a minute or two, no etching is necessary. If not, you will have to etch it. Because etching material is an acid, follow directions carefully and use rubber gloves.

Etch with muriatic acid mixed 50-50 in water and be careful not to etch too deeply. When the process is done, flush the floor thoroughly with water. To halt the etching completely, sprinkle with hydrated lime and wash off slowly until all signs of fizzing or bubbling have stopped.

Concrete Dyes

Car-bo-jet is the best known of all concrete dyes, and it is a good one. The material, lamp black, has been used for years as a dye for mortar when laying brick. There are many colors of dyes, and they all should be mixed into the entire pour of concrete. Dyes are used extensively in prefabricated materials such as interlocking pavers and patio stone.

Exposed Aggregate

This procedure is done in two ways. The first and best method is done by mixing the aggregate that is to be exposed into the mix. For example, crushed limestone is usually mixed in as coarse aggregate is replaced with the attractive stone to be exposed. That makes a nice finish and is structurally sound.

The other method is to work the stone into the surface after the pour is made, as quickly as possible after the concrete is laid. If the stone is not worked in quickly, a cold-joint will be formed between the two layers of the exposed material and the original bottom concrete. The advantage of this type of exposed aggre-

The piles of stone, from top left, are: pea grade, B grade, A grade, and construction grade. The pile on the lower left is Merrimac river gravel.

gate is that it can be used to create patterns and save on the amount of expensive stone needed.

When exposing aggregate, do not wash too much off the surface. Remove only the "butter," or fine, smooth cement on top. Do not use high-pressure water, but flow the removed material off the surface carefully. Scrubbing the surface will remove too much of the material and leave a rough surface that will deteriorate rapidly. On large jobs, it may be necessary to apply a retarding chemical to slow curing of the surface so timing of the wash is not too critical. It is a good idea to practice on a small area and learn the procedure before starting a large area.

The most common stones used for mixing into the entire pour are Indiana creek gravel and Merrimac River gravel. Indiana creek gravel is a mottled stone that has many earth-tone colors in its mix. Merrimac gravel is an even, rusty-yellow brown and not quite as smooth as Indiana creek gravel. The stone is screened into pea gravel, grades A and B, and construction. The latter is straight from the quarry with no grading or cleaning.

Imprinting Concrete

Patterns such as brick or flagstones are made of steel in the desired shape. Some processes use a hard rubber mat to imprint the surface. The wet concrete is dyed to the desired color and the pattern is pressed in. It takes considerable practice to execute a product that looks like the original material.

Silicone Sealer

All outdoor floors and other surfaces would benefit from a treatment of waterproofing, which will give the surface a wet look and repel water. There are many brand names, and most are good. Before applying, make sure the surface is clean and dry and that the concrete is cured thoroughly. Silicone is a polymeric organic compound that keeps material flexible and waterproof. This material can be applied with a garden sprayer. The treated surface should be kept dry and clean until the sealer is completely dry. This material works well on brick and soft stone. The treatment should be repeated every 2 years, depending on how much traffic the surface receives.

One product seals and forms a protective shield. This surface can be redone every 2 or 3 years by reapplying, which redissolves the material and recoats the surface.

Arbor Construction

This arbor will last; the proportion of the pillars to the overhead structure is excellent.

Arbors are any type of overhead structure in a landscape. They need to be and look structurally sound. The smallest post for any structure of this type would be 4 × 4"; 4 × 6" is much better. If metal posts are used, the size is still important. Steel posts used for this purpose are usually square or rectangular and hollow. Set these posts on a frost-free, concrete footing that will raise them above the soil line in order to keep the base of the post dry and help slow rust (fig 47E).

Many times it is better to build a column out of 1 × 10" boards (fig. 50) to give a nice scale and plenty of strength. If this type of column is built, be sure to either cap the top or cover it with a copper or aluminum flashing to shed water and stop birds from nesting inside the post. Strength of construction is important if vines are to be used on the structure; vines have more weight than other plants of equal size because they support none of their own weight. If the arbor is in an open, windy location, the wind causes the foliage of the vine to act as a sail. The resulting constant movement

Box Post

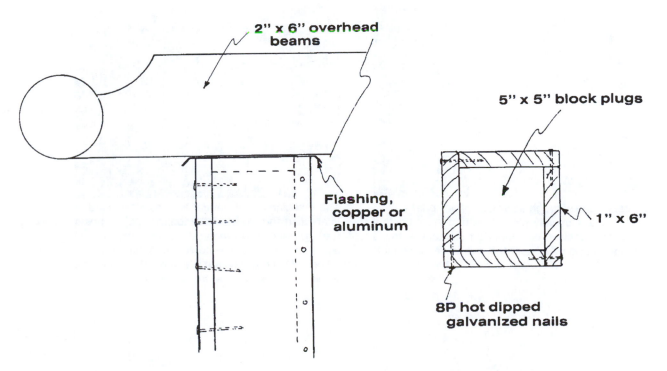

Figure 50. A box post gives the size, scale, and strength needed and is less expensive than other posts.

Posts for arbors should be set like screens but with more weight in the concrete footings to handle wind pressure and the extra load of plant material.

of the structure will gradually work the arbor's joints loose. It is a good practice to bolt the major joints of the arbor with strap metal or galvanized fasteners. Make sure the nails sold with each fastener or hanger are used (heavy galvanized roofing nails can also be used). Set the arbor posts in concrete and below the frostline (fig. 51).

The arbor shown is built of many small units. Its posts are made of welded bundles of reinforcing rods, and the entire structure is open and airy but does not appear to be flimsy or weak.

Posts made of rough-sawn California cedar 1 × 12″ lumber are usually placed around steel posts if much weight is to be supported. Remember that a rough-cut board is near the size under which it is stocked; a 1 × 12″ board is likely a 1 × 12″.

The combination of natural and painted wood is interesting and provides a Victorian look. The posts are large, and the overhead structure is also in good scale. The arbor top was copied from the eve decorations of the home on the site and will stabilize the weaker latticework used for screening.

The top decoration of the trellis.

Although well-built arbors are much stronger than necessary in order to support the vine, the bulk is required in order to be in scale with the rest of the garden and the outdoors.

Arbor Construction

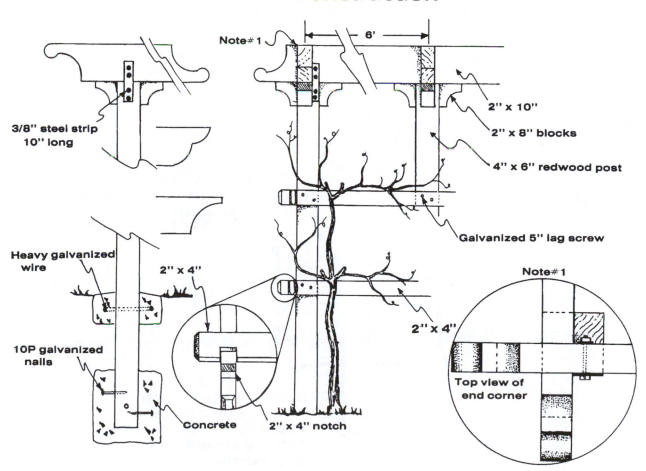

Figure 51. Arbors and other overhead structures are much like large screens. Set the posts in the same manner as discussed for fences. Figure 75 (p. 130) has more information on setting post.

Using Wood in Concrete

There are two reasons to use wood in concrete construction: as an expansion joint and as a design element. If construction is done properly, wood can be a functional and attractive design feature in walks, patios, and driveways. You should have good results if the following simple procedures are followed.

First, select wood that is decay-resistant or has been treated. Do not use any lumber that contains sapwood (light-colored streaks on the surface); even if treated, it is soft and does not wear well.

The next problem is fastening the wood into the concrete slab (fig. 52). Drive galvanized gutter spikes through the wood and then crimp the short end so it will hold securely in concrete. The nails should be placed 6″ from the ends of each board and about every 2′ or 3′ along the board. Try to drive the nails through one side and then the other. When pouring a patio, the outside form board should have these spikes

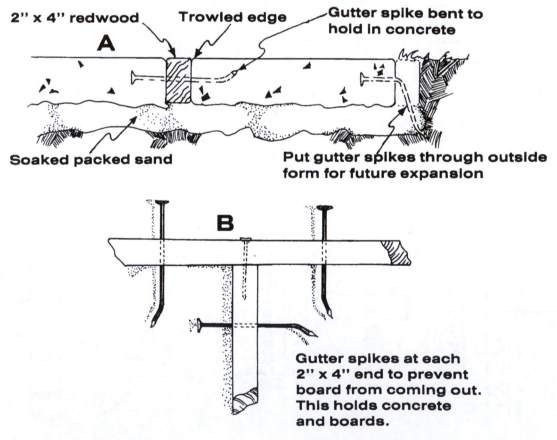

2″ x 4″ redwood **Trowled edge** **Gutter spike bent to hold in concrete**

A

Soaked packed sand

Put gutter spikes through outside form for future expansion

B

Gutter spikes at each 2″ x 4″ end to prevent board from coming out. This holds concrete and boards.

Figure 52. Anchor wood in concrete securely using a gutter spike or small reinforcing rod. This technique also holds the two pieces of concrete together as well as the wood in the container.

Gutter spikes were not used to hold the wood in this concrete, and a snow blade cut off the top, which would not have happened had the procedure shown in figure 52 been used.

Drive galvanized steel gutter spikes into treated wood headers to hold them in the concrete and hold the concrete squares together.

A keystone isolation joint should be used when putting together walls, walks, or driveways.

driven all the way through it. Then, if later expansion is to be done, both the old and the new pour will be tied together firmly. Make sure the concrete is completely cured before trying to remove the forms or the outside edge may break. It is a good procedure on outside forms to drill small holes just larger than the nails, then the form will slip off easily. The nail can be bent out of sight until it is needed.

It is also necessary to edge each board used in concrete, just as in finishing the edges of a sidewalk. If that is not done and the slab is troweled flat across the wood joint, it will leave an uneven, sharp edge. Edging makes the board look as if it belongs in its setting. The edging tool used can be modified to make a smaller, rounded edge than is usually found on sidewalks.

Frequently, sidewalks and patios are poured next to the house's foundation, which can cause a problem if not handled correctly. If the foundation is solid concrete, holes slightly larger than a ½–⅝″ reinforcing rod can be bored about 3″ deep. Place 6–8″ long reinforcing rods into these holes (fig. 53A) so they fit into the center of the walk or patio slab. If possible at the time the foundation wall is poured, form spurs that extend out so the patio can rest on this projection (fig. 53B). If the wall is made from block, knock a hole in the block just below the patio and allow the concrete to flow into the hole as a pour is made (fig. 53C). All these precautions are taken to prevent the walk or floor from settling and diverting water into the house's wall. The inward tilting is unattractive and will worsen each year because the backfill around the foundation settles for a period of years—a fact that must be considered when pouring concrete.

Although there are many fine finishes for concrete, exposed aggregate is one of the nicest for its appearance and the way in which it complements plant material. Exposing aggregate in concrete is the most abused and poorly executed of all finishes. When the washing is too hard and the stone is raised, the concrete breaks up in freezing weather. Use a small area such as a patio block to get the feel for how hard it is necessary to scrub and when to start. If the surface feels gritty as you drag your finger across the curing concrete, the surface should be about ready to be exposed. Always start exposing the concrete where the pour was started.

Concrete dyes are useful but be sure the color is mixed into the total batch and not put on the surface. Surface applications wear off in a short time, and it is difficult to get an even color throughout the entire surface. Mixing color into the batch eliminates these two problems. It is also less expensive to mix in the color before the pour.

Concrete wall

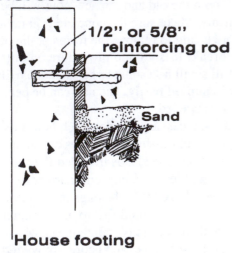

1/2" or 5/8"
reinforcing rod

Sand

House footing

Concrete wall

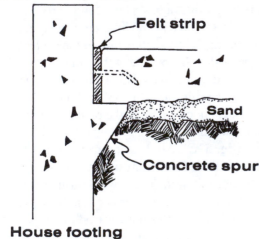

Felt strip

Sand

Concrete spur

House footing

Block wall

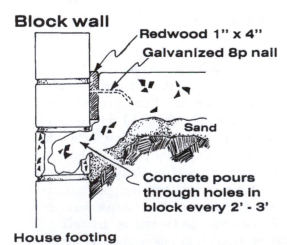

Redwood 1" x 4"

Galvanized 8p nail

Sand

Concrete pours
through holes in
block every 2' - 3'

House footing

Figure 53. Three ways to attach walks or patios next to a house to avoid settling.

To produce a travertine finish, pour and rough-trowel, apply a dash coat with a dash brush (this leaves small bumps and peaks), then softly smooth off the area. The dash coat is cement and fine sand mixed to a consistency of thick paint. A light yellow dye is used to further the look of travertine. Rock salt troweled into the surface leaves much the same effect. If that is done, be sure to spread the salt evenly.

Embedding or stamping a surface to resemble brick or flagstone is effective in large areas. A stamp or template is necessary in this process. It is a good idea to practice this technique in a small area before trying to apply it to a large area.

Reinforcing mesh will be needed in driveways, and in some cases reinforcing rods may be needed. Side-walks usually do not need to be reinforced, but if wood is used as an expansion joint or as a design feature, hot-dipped galvanized steel gutter spikes should be driven through the wood every 2' (fig. 52). That holds the two slabs together, prevents the wood from heaving in winter, and keeps them level across the entire joint.

This break joint was cut with a concrete saw after the concrete cured. Control or break joints are extremely important in preventing concrete from developing unattractive, random cracks.

This expansion joint is in wood fiber saturated with tar. The concrete on the left is dyed with Carbojet.

Concrete Walks and Driveways

This drive and hammerhead parking have proper dimensions. They are 18' wide, the radius of the hammerhead parking is 18', and the width of the parking is 18'. All of the break joints should be no more than 8–10' apart.

This circle drive is handy but puts a lot of concrete at the front door. The effect can be lessened by dying, exposing, or texturing the concrete. Planting a small hedge and a shade tree made the drive more attractive and will soften the area's appearance.

The entire drive. The small hedge and the shade tree help lessen the mass of concrete by screening it, and the tree casts a shadow. More glare will be eliminated when it matures.

Well-designed concrete walks, driveways, and patios can have a major impact on landscapes. Poor concrete and poor design can destroy the appearance of a home or business and be expensive because the concrete will likely need to be replaced. If the design is poor, the concrete may not function as intended.

Driveways with a turnaround (hammerhead) must have a turn radius of 18'. A two-car garage should have a drive 18' across to provide a 12" surface on each side making it easier to exit the car on the drive's surface. This also helps tie the drive to the front of the house. The distance across a turnaround is 18' (9' per car to be parked in the space).

Walks should be 3–4' wide, and expansion joints must be placed between a walk and a house or drive (fig. 54). The walk from the drive to the front door should be 9' on the center from the house wall (fig. 55). This spacing is the most useful for people leaving their car and walking to the door. The space left between the house and walk is then large enough in which to plant ground cover and flowers. All drives should have reinforcing mesh or reinforcing rods beneath them.

Break joints must be properly spaced in order to prevent random cracking. These joints are formed in two ways: with a trowel when the concrete is wet and by the use of a concrete saw when the cement has cured. The trowel method looks better for walks and patios. A saw can cut deeper and may be the superior tool to use in large areas such as driveways. Sidewalks should have break joints every 8', and large areas like driveways should have a break joint every 10' (figs. 55–56).

This asphalt drive inlaid with street cobbles serves three important functions: it marks the entrance to the home, it provides a clean, attractive place to leave the car and enter the building, and it creates an area that signals the driver to move on and not block the entry area.

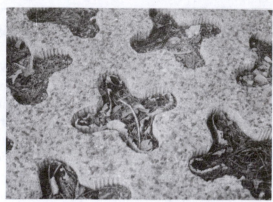

Any type of venting will help with air and moisture exchange; the forms come in many shapes. After forms have decomposed, fill the holes with sand so the surface will be easier to walk on. Leave the forms exposed to the sun at first to accelerate the breakdown.

For this drive, the problem is handled by marking the space for loading and unloading and entering the home.

This well-done driveway is beautifully finished. The curve ratio is correctly formed, and all of the correct expansion and break joints are in place.

Holes can be made in a vented floor by using a biodegradable plastic form that will disappear in time. The surface is difficult to walk on, but the tree will be saved. Plastic units are lighter and easier to install than concrete but will not take as much weight.

The white border makes this driveway too visible. The blacktop needs an edging or curb, but it would serve the landscape better to use a darker color that would be more inconspicuous. Curbs should not be more noticeable than houses.

Concrete Construction Joints

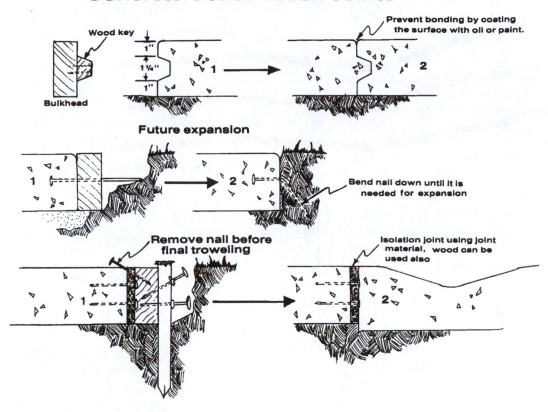

Figure 54. Isolation joints should be formed in at the edge of a pour if an addition is planned.

Walks and Driveways

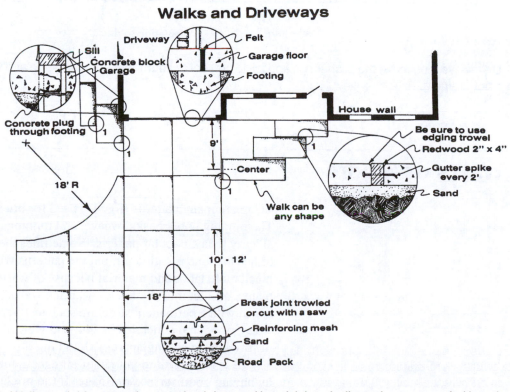

Figure 55. Walks and drives need expansion joints and break joints. Indicated are some vital location for each.

Driveway Construction

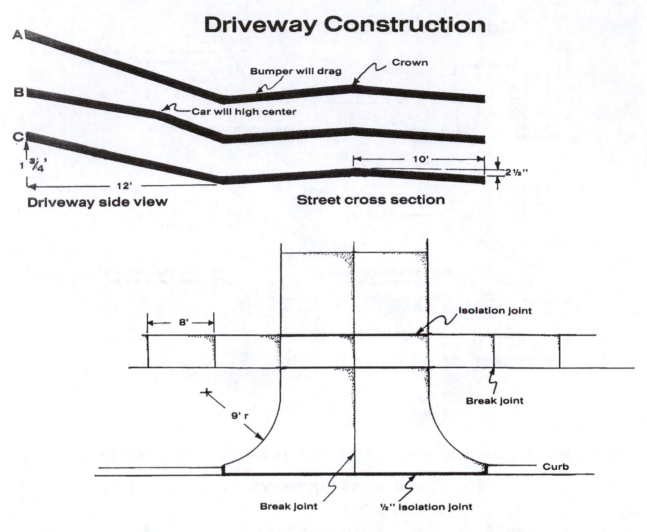

Figure 56. Driveways must have the proper rise and fall to prevent car bumpers from dragging and the road's surface from not draining.

Brick Walks or Floors

There are many patterns (fig. 44) used for brick walks. The running bond, basket weave, and running cross are all easy to lay, popular patterns. Sometimes the chevron or herringbone is called for, but the patterns will require much more labor and material because of waste and the many cuts that must be made. All brick walks must be edged with a permanent structure such as Ryerson steel, wood, or poured concrete (fig. 44, end views) to stop the brick from sliding apart or sloughing off.

It is important to get rid of all excess moisture by having good surface drainage. If the bricks are laid

This walk is edged with brick set in concrete and the walk is on sand.

Measure carefully or fit materials to avoid placing the small pieces next to the house wall.

Curbing or edging for this walk is made of treated 4 × 4" landscape timbers. The scale of the lumber is ideal because of its size and color. Six months of weathering will turn it a soft gray, and it will become part of a landscape that does not overpower the walk visually.

on sand, it must be able to drain rapidly in order to keep the brick sound and prevent standing water from causing soft spots in the walk. Surface drainage is greatly improved by planning a slight crown of 4″ for every 18′ of width. If the walk is 3′ wide, use a 1″ crown.

Any outdoor floor, primarily walks and patio surfaces, should be made of structurally sound materials. Driveways are often done with larger stone or concrete block.

If a walk has straight sides, as is the case with the running bond pattern, it can be edged with the same brick from which the walk was made. Set the brick on edge in concrete.

The tilesetters' method is the best and easiest way to lay brick. Mix 1 part cement with 2 parts fine sand just enough to stop the dust. It is important not to add too much water. Spread this mixture about 4″ over a sand base or 2–3″ over a rough concrete footing. Smooth and sprinkle this area with raw cement from the bag. Lay the dry brick or stone on the top of this, the paver, by using a wooden block and a hammer. Fill cracks with the same material and cure for 72 hours.

Flagstone

Stone cutting is easy if a few simple procedures are followed. Practice, of course, makes one more adept. Flagstone is marked by a power handsaw with an abrasive blade set about 4″ deep. Then set the stone on your toe or a block at the point of the cut. Take the stone chisel and set it in the groove left by the saw. The one beveled edge of the chisel must be facing away from the piece you want to keep. This procedure works well for flagstone and clay bricks. Concrete, granite, and other large boulders must be cut differently.

Flagstone walks should be built of stones large enough not to tip when stepped on. Larger stone is less expensive to lay, better looking, and easier to walk on than smaller stone.

Groove about ¼″ deep with a stone cutting blade.

Many designs of stones are available for informal walks. These can be used to great benefit in secondary areas.

Flagstone or brick can be best laid by using the tilesetters' method.

The beveled edge of a chisel should be facing away from the piece to be saved. See Fig. 45 page 68.

Place the stone and set it firmly with a piece of lumber and a rubber hammer.

Spread raw cement over the cement and sand mixture to make a good bond.

The same floor several years after completion.

Fitted and Filled Flagstone Walks

These walks are much harder to build than plain flagstone walks but are worth the extra trouble. It is also the type of walk required in the construction of a Japanese garden (fig. 57).

Fitted and filled flagstone walks are excellent. They must be set on a good base and then the stone set in concrete.

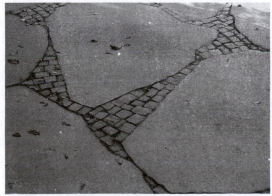

A fitted and filled sidewalk that has a more controlled appearance. It would also need to be set with the tilesetters' method, which would hold smaller stones in place.

Fitted and Fill Flagstone

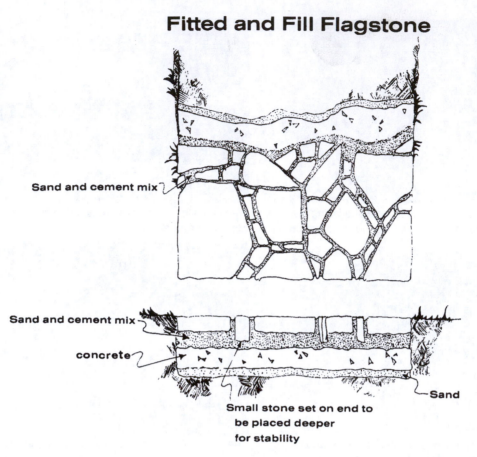

Figure 57. Stone walks in which small pieces have been used to fill between large stones must be laid with cement and sand (the tilesetters' method), which stops movement. The small pieces cannot turn over under foot or work up and out to trip people or be picked up by mowers.

These walks must be set on a concrete footing on top of a soil-leveling layer of sand. This concrete should be leveled with a garden rake and left rough. The surface of the concrete should be 4–5″ below grade. After this slab cures, lay a 1½″ layer of sand and cement mix over it as described in the tilesetters' method of bonding brick and stone. Spread the layer a foot or two at a time so there will be no need to walk on the mixture and compact it before the stone is laid. Lay the larger stone first and then fill in the space left with smaller stone fragments. Try to use the small pieces on their edge or place the longest dimension down so there is more surface to hold the stone in place. Then sweep the cracks full of the mixture and let it cure. Figure the depth of soil removed and material put back so the finished surface will be back to grade.

Flagstone walks can be cut out of the sod an inch or two deeper than the stone. Place just enough sand on the bottom of the cutout to make leveling easy. That small amount of sand will also firm the stone so it will not move. Use large, heavy stones approximately 18–20″ in width and 1½–3″ thick for this type of walk.

This concrete paver entrance is laid on sand and edged with steel edging.

Finishing touches make the difference between a good job and an excellent job. These pavers are attached to the old porch with marine glue.

The curbing material shown here is good on straight runs but a problem on curves. The stakes shown must still be driven in at an angle to help prevent heaving in the winter. Some strips of edging are notched for curves.

Concrete Pavers

Concrete interlocking pavers are one of he best walk materials but check when buying quantities of them to see whether the pavers have a foot or projection at their bases. This happens when the mold in which they are made is worn, allowing material to spread out under the bottom. Sometimes the material is mixed too wet and the paver slumps when it comes out of the mold, giving the walls of the paver a slight bulge. That makes the paver difficult to lay and the cracks between the pavers difficult to keep uniform.

Paver Walks

Concrete is excellent for walks and drives as well as for patios. The porch is veneered with the same pavers, and a ready-to-mix powdered glue is used to attach them to the porch.

The walk is edged with steel (which must be set as described in the section of this book on edging) set about 1″ below the top of the paver. Set it and then make your own stakes, 30″ long and ⅛″ thick, of mild steel strips. Drive them in at 30 degrees and bend them to grip the steel edging. Pavers used on the sides of the porch need to be set on a ledge, which can be poured concrete or—as in this case—a treated fir 2 × 4″ attached to the side with a nail gun. The same adhesive is used to attach the pavers to the concrete porch.

Concrete walks are the most durable, the easiest to build, and probably the least expensive if all factors—for example, the speed of installation and the skill required—are considered. The designer and

Edging as shown here is straight stock; curved or round edging stock is available to handle sunburst patterns.

This walk was built to match the entrance. It is useful and ties the overall appearance of the landscape together.

Sunburst patterns made of concrete pavers are available in kits, packaged and ready to lay. Take plenty of time when laying the first sunburst and make each ring complete before starting the next. Make sure the spacings are all equal. Use a string compass frequently to ensure the sunburst is indeed round and not lopsided.

Small walks with many changes in direction and curves are best edged with steel or heavy-gauge aluminum.

This large sunburst floor is attractive and not difficult to put together. Remember to work in circles and check every 2 or 3 courses to make sure the circle is still round.

Walks built in the chevron pattern are attractive but cost twice as much as a simple running bond, a factor that should be kept in mind when designing and bidding. Curves used as illustrated add even more to the cost.

A walk dyed tan and complemented by brown Merrimac River gravel provides a warm welcome to this home. Such uninterrupted space provides an excellent place to showcase objects such as a spruce tree in a large container.

Inlay walks with whole, weatherproof bricks or concrete pavers applied with cement and sand. If the base of the ledger area is smooth, a concrete glue can be used.

This large walk, to be used for foot traffic and small vehicles, features brick borders and expansion joints laid on their own concrete foundations. The entire walk is tied together with reinforcing mesh.

the builder should make the surface special by finishing it in an attractive and enduring way, sweeping, exposing, and using wood to form designs in the concrete, for example.

Side-dressed Sidewalks

Brick trim on a concrete sidewalk is attractive but can be disappointing if done incorrectly or with the wrong materials. The bricks used in figure 58 are house brick and will last for perhaps one winter before they start to break up. Make the masonry ledge a little longer than the brick or piece of brick to be used and then select a concrete paver or a well-fired patio brick to inset into the ledge. If brick is to be used, affix it with mortar. Concrete pavers are best applied with an adhesive.

A side view of the walk (fig. 59) shows the structural steps taken. Vertical pavers should be set exactly for height, and the concrete should be deep enough to cover the rebar where the bar goes under the vertical paver. The expansion joint at the base of the vertical paver is important to keep the paver from being broken in half. Make sure the top of the concrete part of the walk and the paver section are at the same height or are level (fig. 60).

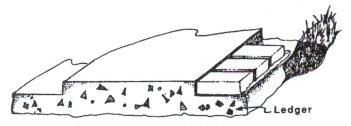

Figure 58. Inlaid sidewalk with a ledger plate formed. Pavers can be set in mortar or in a sand-and-cement mix used by tilesetters.

The completed walk. The concrete was dyed black or dark gray.

Home walks should be at least 3' wide, and 4 or 5' can add greatly to most entryways.

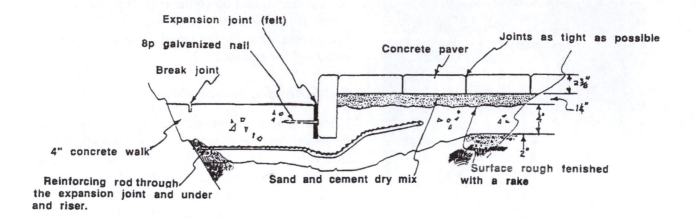

Figure 59. A side view of a walk in which brick is used as a step riser.

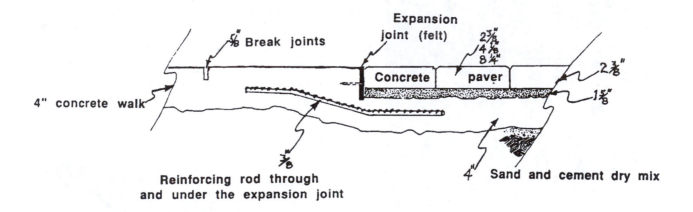

Figure 60. Concrete and paver walk construction.

It is often a good practice to design an access walk to the back of a house. Keep it in close and place a corner planting in front of it. Such placement will help hold the planting away from the home and also conceals the service walk.

The walk provides a splash pan for downspouts and useful service access to the rear of the home.

A concrete walk that has been given a new look with the addition of grooves cut to simulate flagstone.

This brick walk was built to take traffic from a garage and parking area to the front door, which is out of sight. The large brick area acts as a front porch to welcome visitors and point them to the front door. Begin walks about 9′ on center from garage doors.

Exposed aggregate provides an attractive change from plain concrete. Here, the walk to the house flairs out so there is more area to pick up traffic. That also provides a safe place to install a light post and protect it from the lawn mower. It will also eliminate hand-edging around the post.

Move the walk far enough away from the house to provide a planting area that will allow development of an attractive entry court.

Grass can make a usable, cost-effective walk in large areas. It also allows access into areas that need to be controlled. Because it can be easily changed or moved, such a walk works well in flower gardens.

The walk is broken by enlarging areas and changing directions. Small objects along the way, as here, help lessen distance.

Small paths of stepping stones can be attractive, and easier to walk on, if not laid in a straight row. Change directions by laying the stones 2′ wide and staggering them.

The walk is carried along the porch, to end in a small pool. That also makes a pleasant view from the house.

Here, a concrete step is formed into the walk, making a structurally sound walk and marking the location of each step.

Pavers are used in this project to change the level or to provide a change of texture and color in the walk.

The concrete is poured and cured, and the depression is ready for the pavers.

This construction is much the same as the raised step discussed previously.

In this walk, pavers will be set at the same level as the rest of the concrete. The form board is across the walk just behind the ready-mix delivery shoot, and a 2 × 4″ plus a shim nailed to the bottom of the 2 × 4″ provide the proper depth. This will provide room for the sand and cement mixture as well as pavers.

The completed walk, as shown in figure 58.

Fine detail work is possible with a concrete wetsaw.

An all-too-common mistake in walk and step construction is to make a walk too narrow. All main walks should be 3' wide or more. Here, too, the steps are too much like a ladder.

Wood and pavers work well together to form a walk in scale with its location. The steps are 5½" high, making them much easier to climb than those of the previous example.

All walks and steps should seem to fit the scale of their surroundings.

Free-laid Steps

These steps, excellent examples of scale for objects used outdoors, are built like those in figure 63.

Free-laid steps should have the same base of the same material. These have wood all the way down and back under the top step (fig. 61-C).

Free-laid steps must be built with the same footing under all steps in order to put each step on a solid foundation. The area to contain the steps should be excavated until the first step is grade height, and this depth should be carried back 3 or 4 steps. If more steps are required repeat the process until the top step is at grade at the top of the rise (fig. 61). The method would be the same for wood, stone, or block steps. If the steps are likely to hold water, tilt them forward slightly. The tilt should not be noticeable but should be enough to drain off most of the free moisture.

From a design standpoint the treads of the steps need to be 16–18″ deep and have 4–6″ risers. Do not vary these measurements. There are 2 formulas to use in figuring dimensions to keep outdoor steps comfortable to use and in scale with their surroundings. The English method (2 × riser + tread = 24) is the most common. If larger steps are required use the formula that holds that a riser should decrease ½″ for every 1″ increase in tread.

If step dimensions are to be changed, a landing should be placed between the different dimensions to allow pedestrians to readjust their strides before continuing up the steps.

If the incline is not too steep, a ramp may be the best structure to use. If so, do not exceed a 5% slope and give the surface a nonskid finish. Sometimes a break or shallow step may be needed to stay below the 5% grade. If that is done, use 7′ between the steps to allow for 2 comfortable strides before the next step up.

Plan outdoor steps to be large and inviting and use the rise-to-run formula.

This example uses the same pavers and wood, showing the value of a landing—especially when turning a corner or changing the height of steps. Doing so gives people time to adjust to the new height.

Free Laid Stone or Wood Steps

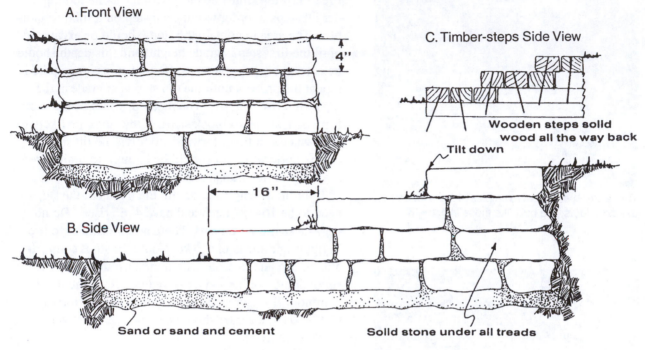

A. Front View

4"

C. Timber-steps Side View

Wooden steps solid
wood all the way back

Tilt down

16"

B. Side View

Sand or sand and cement

Solid stone under all treads

English method

2 x riser + tread = 24

For every 1 inch increase in tread,
the riser should decrease 1/2 inch.

Figure 61. Steps made of stone or wood should have a common footing so the entire step unit will move rather than individual steps.

Old concrete steps can be given a facelift by veneering them with flagstone.

These brick steps are much too steep and could be dangerous.

When grade is not too steep walks can raise gently to the bottom of a porch so there is one 6″ step onto the porch.

The same concrete units used to hold soil so that it will hold on a steep slope.

Large units laid to make a walk or drive and still have all-weather access. They are unattractive, however.

The best way to install a timber curb is to stake the timber with galvanized pipe or ½″ rebar. The timber shown, however, should not be used as a parking bumper. The car extends over the lawn area and will interfere with mowing. Install smaller bumpers that will stop a car before it reaches the curb, regardless of the curb's construction.

Acute Angles and Other Wasted Areas

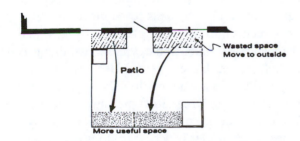

Figure 62. Place concrete on any patio surface where the area will be used. Surfaces near a structure will not be used, so move the structure into the open.

The first area to eliminate is the point at which the patio joins the house, a 3–4′ strip of concrete that is wasted because no one will sit or stand so close to a wall. The area should be put where it will be used (fig. 62), on the patio's perimeter. If the area near the house is planted with ground covers or flowers, the patio is much more pleasant, comfortable, and usable without using extra concrete or flooring material. Plantings in this area will also help cool the house and patio.

Acute angles or narrow points of concrete or planting beds are usually too small to plant anything in. These points of concrete will break off with weight or with freezing and thawing (fig. 63).

Another frequently unusable space is the thin strip of soil between the curve of the driveway and the

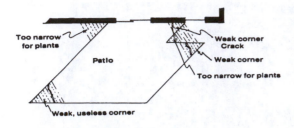

Figure 63. Sharp points of concrete are prone to causing damage or breaking off.

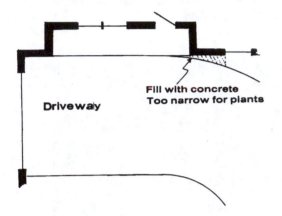

Figure 64. Small, acute angles in planting beds are not large enough to hold plantings and will become maintenance problems.

house's wall. Cut this wedge off far enough back and fill it with concrete. Then the area will at least be clean and maintenance-free.

Space between the front walk and house is often small, narrow, and wasted. Many times it is only a foot or two wide and does not give enough distance from the house for easy access to the home (fig. 64). Widen the area of soil between the walk and house so there is enough room to plant at least flowers and ground cover.

Acute angles should be avoided if possible. This area is too small for plants and, like other such problem areas, should be solid concrete.

Retaining Walls

A simple concrete wall constructed as illustrated in figure 67. Overflow water is carried off by weep holes, and a swale has been built to carry water along the top of the wall and dumped at its end. All solid walls must have a frost-free footing.

Retaining Wall Stress Points

Many forces apply pressure to retaining walls, and these pressures come from many directions. The pressure in the top 10–20″ of the wall is the most dramatic and destructive to the top of free-laid walls such as railroad ties or stone (fig. 65). This force moves the wall in small increments during freezing and thawing, which could happen many times in the winter. Two things can be done to lessen such pressure: (1) Use a freeze taper at the top inside of the wall to allow the frozen layer to slip up instead of applying direct pressure to the wall; and (2) provide surface concrete for reinforcing (fig. 65). In heavy clay soil it is necessary to use a "dead-man" every 4–6′ along the wall as well as to provide a weep hole. The dead-man can be replaced with a winged buttress, which can be placed in front of the wall for best results if it will not be in the way or be

Pressures on a Retaining Wall

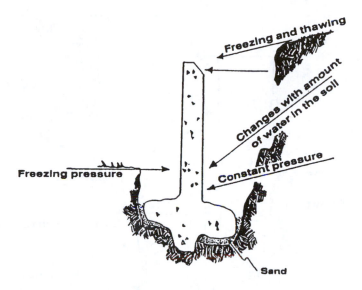

Figure 65. Many pressures affect the basic structure of a retaining wall and must be countered if a wall is to last.

Enough time was taken with this well-built wall to form in a design that adds interest. Again, attention to detail makes the difference between successful and unsuccessful landscape construction.

Small concrete retaining walls such as this one can be helped greatly by the addition of evergreens, especially when they are planted at the top and allowed to weep over.

unattractive. The buttress can, however, be built behind the wall with good results so it will be out of the way and not detract from the wall's appearance.

The heel built at the bottom of the wall is useful in stabilizing to prevent slippage and damage to the veneer. All solid concrete wall foundations should be below frost line. All veneer walls must have a waterproof cap or coping. The wall will break up if water is allowed to get between it and the veneer material.

Concrete-veneered Retaining Walls

The veneered wall can be built vertically on the soil-retained side of the wall. The solid concrete behind the veneer should be constructed as described in the discussion of solid concrete walls. Water should be collected, drained parallel with the wall, and dropped to the lower grade in a morning glory tube and concrete spillway. Another point that works with this layer is the pressure the same freezing and thawing applies to the base of the wall. This stops all movement at the base and causes the wall to break over. It is preferable to install weep holes every 4–6′ in solid concrete walls in order to help stop the added pressure of freezing water behind the wall at these points (fig. 66).

Because the pressure applied to the entire wall is caused by a combination of factors, the greatest variable is the soil type. The more clay the soil contains, the more water the soil will hold and the more weight

Concrete Retaining Wall

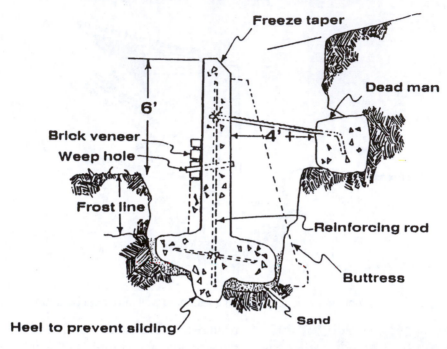

Figure 66. Any brick veneer wall must start with a good concrete wall. The basic structure is the same whether or not the wall is veneered.

Free - laid Stone

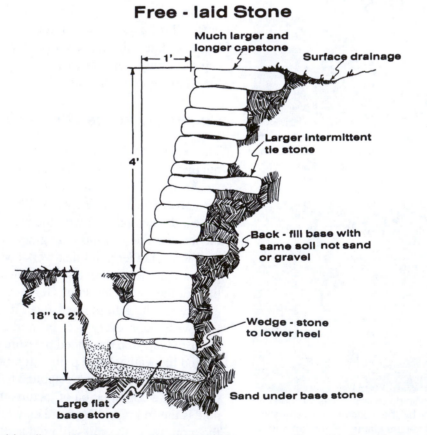

Figure 67. Free-laid walls made of stone or wood should be no more than 4' tall and have a 1:4 tiltback ratio.

will be applied to the wall. Sandy soil drains rapidly and will apply much less pressure to the wall.

Consider each of these pressures when designing and building a retaining wall. If the wall is to be higher than 4′, also consider having an engineer design it.

The final stress point on walls is heaving from below, so the foundation should always be set below the frost line. This is unnecessary in free-laid walls of stone or ties, which are flexible enough so the wall does not crack and fall apart.

This stone wall is backed with a woven weed barrier to prevent soil from eroding through the cracks. The woven material will take a lot of rough handling and still hold together and last indefinitely.

Unplanted free-laid walls can be built a little more upright. If they are properly done they will last a long time. This wall is more than 70 years old.

A trench is dug 18–20″ deep and filled ⅔ full with granite chips to form a base that is solid but easy to work and move around in.

Large cut and fitted stones such as these will also need a small tiltback. Their weight will help, but the weight of the soil will be greater. Use the tiltback ratio wherever possible.

This home was built on a hillside and set back into the slope. Large stones tie house to ground nicely and cover the large concrete foundation.

Free-laid Stone Retaining Walls

Stone retaining walls are the hardest walls to build and also the most expensive from a standpoint of material and labor. The stones must be wide and reasonably flat so they will lay and fit together easily. The stone's thickness needs to be great enough to prevent breaking while handling. The maximum height of a free-laid stone retaining wall should be near 4′ or as close to that as the material will allow. If more height is needed the wall should be terraced back and another begun.

If the soil is particularly erosive, special care should be taken. Use the same soil when backfilling behind the stone; do not use gravel or sand, which will cause erosion behind the wall material and then cause it to collapse into itself (fig. 67). If there is a lot of open space in the wall's face, back the wall with a woven weed barrier.

Stone walls built with a coarse gravel backfill that is too rounded and small and will never last very long, no matter how much backing or planting occurs. The wall will erode easily and eventually collapse into itself. Planting such walls is also difficult because of the gravel backing.

Free-laid planted walls need a little more tiltback to provide a place against which plant material can rest. This wall is too straight and the plants swing free and break off, making the wall unattractive. The plants will not do well, either.

Concrete parking bumpers can also make attractive strong retaining walls if cut and fitted and given the proper tiltback.

Large stones at the bases of walls built from boulders strengthen the walls. Small amounts of concrete should be used to level stones or prevent them from rolling out of position. On loose, open walls, use plants that will take these kinds of conditions and hold backfill soil in place.

A poorly constructed, planted wall will soon become a weedy rock pile.

The terrace should be planted with small, fibrous, rooted shrubs that will help stabilize the area (fig. 68). Roots will help hold the stone together. Both woven and spunbonded weed barriers work well, but woven barriers will stand more pulling and stretching without tearing. Always leave a lot of slack behind stone walls so the weed barrier can fill all the holes and fit in the uneven surfaces behind the wall. If a situation calls for a larger structure than described here, an engineered concrete wall is likely needed. That usually calls for specially constructed units or reinforced concrete walls.

Plants for retaining walls:
Sedum sp.—*Sedum sp.*
Dwarf daylilies—*Hemerocallis* 'Stella D'Ore'
Ivy—*Hedra helix*
Birdsfoot trefoil—*Lotus corniculatus*
Rock soapwort—*Saponaria ocymoides*
Catmint—*Nepeta* × *Faassenii*
Creeping phlox—*Phlox stolonifera*
Hosta—*Hosta sp.* (shade)
Ferns (shade)
European ginger—*Asarum europaeum canadense* (shade)
Sweet woodruff—*Galium oderatum*

The tiltback of a stone retaining wall is very important. There should be 1′ of tiltback per 4′ of rise. As the wall goes up, check frequently to assure that the tilt is being maintained evenly all the way up.

Planted retaining walls need much care and therefore should be of a size that is easy to reach. This excellent wall has good top and bottom access.

Planted, Free Laid Retaining Wall

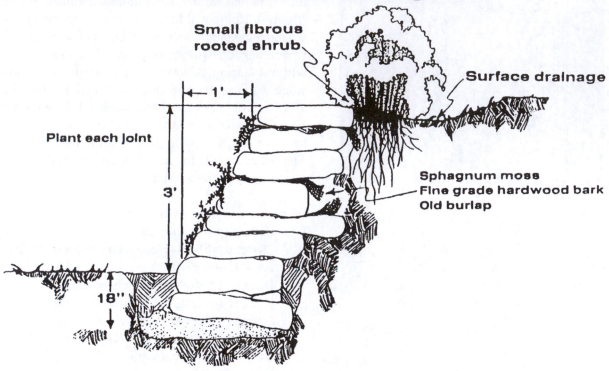

Small fibrous rooted shrub

Surface drainage

Plant each joint

1'

3'

Sphagnum moss
Fine grade hardwood bark
Old burlap

18"

Figure 68. A planted wall should be lower than 4' and have a 1–3' tiltback. That allows plants to make contact with the wall and become established. Wind will not be able to swing plants and slowly break them off.

Planted Free-laid Retaining Walls

It is also advantageous to use old burlap or sphagnum to stuff cracks in order to prevent erosion through these cracks until the soil settles, which usually takes a year or more.

If plantings are to be used between stones, shorten the height of the wall and increase the tiltback (fig. 68). Walls that are steeper than this will not support plants. If the wall is too steep, the soil behind stays too dry and the plants have difficulty clinging to the wall. The weight of the plant will then cause it to swing free and not attach to the wall. Many plants, such as sedum, will break loose. These two factors cause plants to gradually die. The height of the wall illustrated allows for easy maintenance because all parts of the wall can be reached. Planted walls can require increased upkeep time in order to prevent them from looking weedy.

Railroad-tie Retaining Walls

Railroad-tie retaining walls can be an attractive addition to a landscape if they are properly designed and built (fig 69). Change direction, add steps, and prevent

Railroad-tie walls can be unattractive if poorly built. They can be useful for a number of years if well designed and built, however.

Tie Wall or Landscape Timber Walls

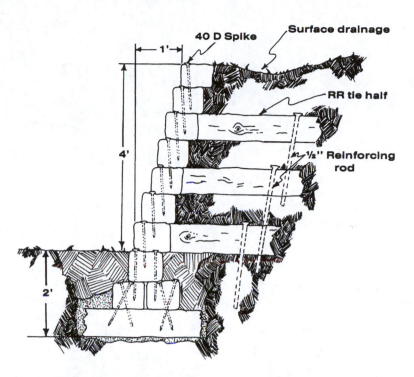

Figure 69. A tie or landscape timber wall needs the same tiltback as a stone wall. All timbers should be nailed together with 40-D spikes. Any retaining wall of 4' needs to be stabilized with a dead-man anchor.

This wall has the proper tiltback and dead-man ties and many other features to make it last.

overrun of surface water when designing a tie wall. The wall should have a tiltback of 1' per 4' of rise in order to take advantage of the weight of the ties themselves. The ties should be fastened together with 40-D spikes or bridge spikes. In order to drive such large nails, drill a pilot hole and then dip the nail in liquid soap. Do not use oil because it makes the nails stick. A 6-pound hammer is desirable for driving these nails.

The cutting and fitting of railroad ties can be a difficult and time-consuming process. The best tool to use for cutting is a reciprocating saw rather than a chain saw. A conventional chain saw will become clogged with Creosote and overheat and the chain can be ruined. A reciprocating saw does not clog or over-heat, and the blade will last much longer. New land-scape timber can be easily shaped with a chain saw be-cause it is most often treated with Cupernol or Penta (be careful with Penta in landscape timber because it will burn and kill plant material). Cupernol is the best and safest wood preservative. Creosote is also good, especially if the timber is well weathered. Wolmanized new timbers are satisfactory because they are cut to a dimension that is easy to nail and lay.

A reciprocating saw is a necessity when cutting old ties. The one shown is gas-operated but there are also electric saws that work well, although they usually require a generator on new building sites.

Ties are good in cases when a wall is large and will not be close to people. These walls can be planted to soften or hide the ties.

A gas-operated chain saw is useful on timbers not treated with Creosote. Railroad ties have another drawback: embedded stones, spikes, or other metal objects.

Many new ways are used to tie back retaining walls. Here, 6 × 6″ timbers are used to make a shallow curbing.

It is best to use a weed barrier mat behind the ties in easily eroded soil. This wall must be higher than 4′, so one 4′ wall was installed, then a terrace, and then another 4′ section. Another terrace and wall may be necessary.

The wall after the first two terraces were completed. There will be one more terrace and one more 4' wall.

A wall with no tiltback and built too tall without terracing. What results is an expensive wall about to collapse.

If a wood or tie wall is to be built higher, use the cribbing technique. Place the dead-men every other layer, forming a large box or crib. Doing so gives a wall 8' thick boxes to hold soil and makes the wall 8' thick.

A long-lasting wall built with the correct tiltback and with a terrace and change of direction.

One of the most important methods with which to stabilize the wall is to install "dead men." The number and location of these will depend upon the type of soil behind the wall and the amount of moisture the soil holds. These anchors are made of half-ties, or ties that have had ends that cannot be used in total. There is no need to use weep holes to provide drainage with a tie wall because there is enough drainage between the ties. In fact, if the ties are rough and knotty, a sharp axe will be needed to chop them smooth so they will fit close enough to stop burrowing by rodents. If there are cracks and openings between ties, it is desirable to use old burlap in these cracks to stop erosion until the soil settles and becomes firm enough to hold on its own. In highly erosive soils, line the back of the wall with petro-mat to allow the water to drain through the wall without any soil loss.

The boxes need to be filled slowly and compacted as the fill goes in.

Do not build a wall in a location where it does not fit. The solution here would be to put the ties on end.

Vertical Timber Retaining Walls

This type of wall is good in cases where the wall is less than 4′ high; it is often a welcome relief from the usual horizontal tie walls. A vertical wall is much harder to stabilize, however, and more labor will be required to install it. If the wall is to be straight (no curves, just sharp angles), the mower strip at the base can be made of the same material as the wall: wood or concrete. The horizontal timber at this point strengthens the wall and gives a trouble-free, labor-saving mower strip that does away with hand edging. The wood should be nailed to the wall with 40-D spikes and staked with reinforcing rods or a ½″ galvanized pipe. If the wall is curved or has many angles, concrete is the best and least expensive way to install the mower strip. When pouring this strip, make sure it is as least 6″ wide and 4″ deep. Always use a reinforcing rod or heavy galvanized wire to hold the strip together when it cracks.

U-bolts are used as anchors, frequently in tree cabling and bracing work.

A convex wall is difficult to control. The pressure pushes the timbers apart.

Vertical ties make the construction more interesting and are useful in building a concave curved wall that is forced together by the pressure.

Concrete posts make an interesting wall. The small, scalloped depression on one side acts as a tongue and groove to allow for good close fit.

Set the tie or timber as deep as it is high above ground in order to offset the pressure above and behind the wall. Always set the timbers slightly back into the soil that is to be retained and tamp large rocks and gravel on both sides of the wall using a large steel rod or a length of 1″ pipe (fig. 70). If there is room to work in the trench, use a power compactor.

Because vertical timbers are prone to separation, special effort is necessary to bind them together securely. A cable laced through holes in the timbers can be pulled together tightly and locked on each end with a U-bolt. Double the cable back and clamp it with a U-bolt to form a loop at the end, then place a crowbar 10-12″ through this loop, pry the cable tight, and lock it with another U-bolt. Then remove the U-bolt used to pull the cable tight. It is also a good practice to toenail the timbers with 40-D spikes before backfilling.

Vertical Landscape Timber Retaining Wall

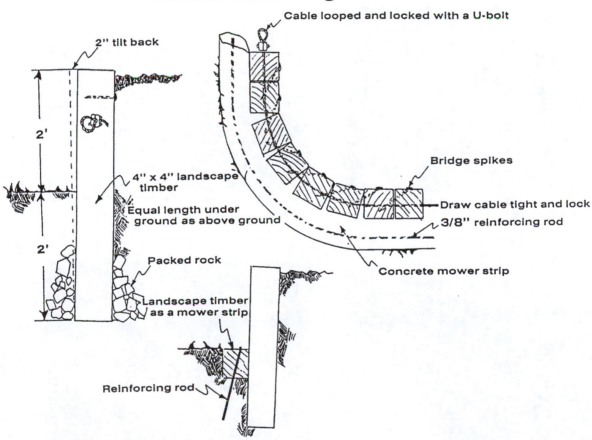

Figure 70. Vertical tie walls work well in curved situations. Allow at least 2′ to be buried underground—as deep as the wall is high above ground.

The most effective way to stop timbers from spreading is to use a U-bolt with a loop and another U-bolt as a knot to stop the cable from pulling through the post (fig. 70). Then use a steel post as a lever in the loop and pry the post against the vertical timber. To maintain the slack in the cable, place a U-bolt tightly against the post and tighten it as a lock to keep the cable from slipping back through.

Precast Retaining Walls

Retaining walls made in the precast method are excellent and can be laid quickly. This material is built to interlock at the correct tiltback and be equipped with a weep area. There are several types on the market, and most are good. Precast concrete retaining walls are fabricated in several patterns and colors. There are very large units that weigh more than 100 pounds as well as small units that can be easily picked up and laid. Select a size and weight that will do the job.

Here, the interlocking and dead-man features are exposed behind the wall.

A rounded front gives varied texture to this different wall unit built for more upright installation

These large, precast retaining wall blocks are excellent and lay beautifully. Interlocking and dead-man features are built into each block.

This block is laid and fastened together as the wall is built.

Plastic rod is used to pin the wall together; the unit is extremely flexible. Curved walls are easily built. This wall has no ability to have a tiltback, which will likely lead to its collapse.

Several types of lights to use with free-laid concrete unit walls. Lay and install the lights as the wall is built.

Concrete retaining wall materials comes in all sizes. This one is good for 2–3′ walls but do not forget the tiltback rule.

While laying wire, chip a groove in the concrete unit to allow the wire to move freely. Most are 12-volt systems, as is the one shown.

The ideal size wall for the unit. Be sure to back the wall with weed barrier.

Gabion Walls

Gabion walls, used for shoreline control and to make retaining walls, are about a square yard in size and constructed of large, galvanized steel wire. They can be filled with large rocks or similar material (fig. 71).

This gabion wall is being used to stabilize a pond wall.

The slope of the bank and of the gabion wall are at the same angle. The wall will last for several years, but it will be necessary to fill in with soil and plant the rock area. The wire will gradually rust away, and the rocks will slough into the water. From the beginning, work to establish water's edge plants that will help slow the process.

Individual baskets are laid parallel to the pond bank.

This nicely constructed and planted wall uses fist-sized crushed stone. The wall and the pond were constructed at the same time, and the stone goes from the bottom to the shrub line.

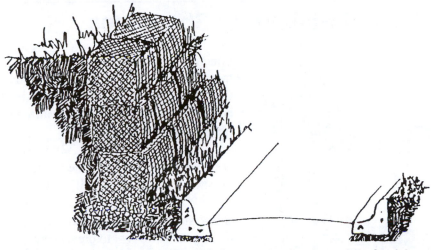

This kind of wall is built with large wire baskets filled with rocks and set in place by a crane. These are being used for a road embankment.

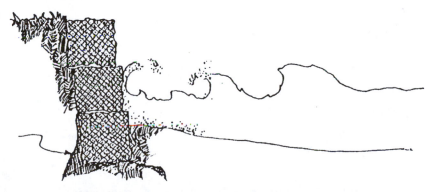

Always back walls like this with the weed barrier mat to stop the waves from pulling the soil and sand through the rock, causing the wall to collapse back into itself. Set these walls back just like any retaining wall: 4' rise and 1' tilt-back.

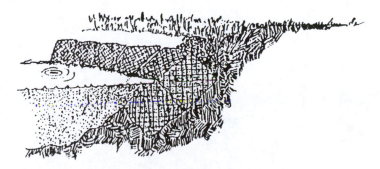

Shore protection for ponds is needed to stop wave action and animals like ducks and rodents. After the baskets are set into the bank, cover the top with gravel and feather it back into the bank as shown.

Figure 71. Gabion walls and some of their good uses.

Shore Walls and Stabilizing Shorelines

This pond bank has stone set in concrete, which produces an easy shore to maintain and protects banks from waterfowl or muskrat damage.

Pond and lake shores are difficult to stabilize and maintain. There are three major ways to handle shorelines. One is with plant material, another is with stone and concrete, and the third is with railroad ties or landscape timbers or posts.

The first method (fig. 72A), using plant material, is easy but can detract from the water feature during winter months when the shore will be left open to erosion.

Pile stone against the base of the wall on the water side to stabilize it and stop erosion. As the timbers are set, roll out the petro-mat to prevent erosion of soil between cracks. Wave action can be devastating, and the mat does a good job of controlling erosion (fig. 72C). It is also good to nail 2 × 10″ or 2 × 12″ treated lumber on the

Shore Walls

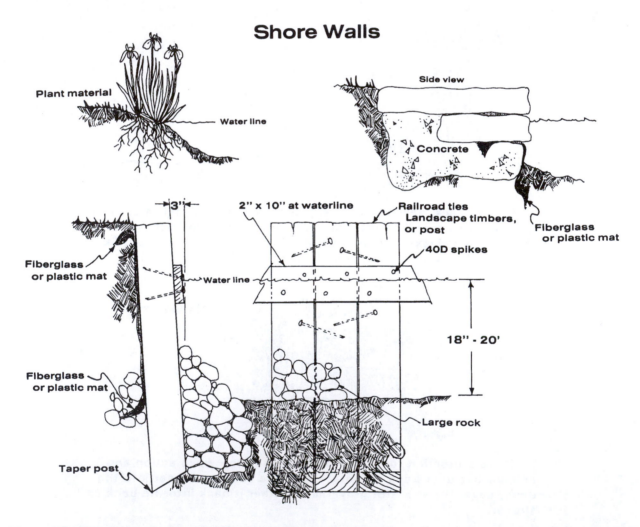

Figure 72. Shorelines can be stabilized by plantings or by a structure. If a structure is used, make sure that turf that meets it can be mowed without too much hand-edging.

The concrete footing is just below the water surface.

A shoreline made with dyed concrete that had been embedded with beach pebbles while still wet.

This wall, or any wall used to hold shorelines, must not only have all the factors necessary for a good retaining wall but also control wave action and the erosive effect of water (fig. 72C).

front of the wall, right in the middle of the water line. That is all that is necessary if the water line is stable, which is not always the case—thus the necessity for backing the wall with petro-mat. It is also important to cut the base of the post with the toe toward the shore side. Drive the timber into the base; this taper helps firm the wall back against the soil. Tamp or pack the stone on the lake side as hard as possible. Even under good conditions the stones will slump as water covers them and softens the soil.

In the second method (fig. 72B), the stone and concrete should be poured at least 6″ deep and 2′ wide (back into the shore). The concrete should be capped with stone or be disguised with dye or exposed aggregate. The water side of the pour should be covered with petro-mat and the top portion secured between the base stone and the concrete pour. The part of the mat that goes down and out into the pond should be buried to stop erosion and bank damage by rodents and waterfowl.

The last method (fig. 72C), using large timbers such as railroad ties, takes more labor to install but is attractive and ties in with docks or bridges. A shore wall made with landscape timber should be no more than 3′ tall. Make sure that the base is deep enough to offset the soil drainage to the ends of the wall.

When working with large areas of bank it is probably best to use a large sprayer to spread mulch and seed at the same time so the mulch will hold the seed in place until it germinates. Sprayers are often owned by large companies that will custom-apply the mixture of seed and mulch. Large, steep banks are probably easier and cheaper to control in this fashion, even if the initial outlay is substantial. The material works well, but after

This small concrete pool has no erosion problem, but it needs a shoreline emphasized by plants such as Joe-pye weed. Many other native plants can also be effective for naturalized shorelines.

This material is composed of very fine organic fibers and an adhesive. When combined with the prescribed amount of water the mix resembles a fibrous latex paint.

Stabilizing pond banks and still maintaining a natural look is difficult. Plants are the best choice; Siberian iris have been used in this example.

a sudden cloudburst some gullies will appear and need to be repaired.

The top stone should be broad and flat to make mowing the shore easier and to make it serviceable and natural-looking. Small stones are unstable and increase the labor necessary to keep the shore neat and clean.

Properly planted water features such as the one shown use native plants that are natural in appearance and require little maintenance. Reeds canary grass is one of the best plants for large ponds and streams because it is not invasive, will only grow in or near water, and provides a large amount of bird food in winter months. Yellowroot is the best plant to use in a flood plain where ground is inundated several times a year.

Plants that help stabilize the shoreline:
    Daylilies—*Hemerocallis sp.*
    Japanese iris—*I. japonica*
    Siberian iris—*I. siberica*
    Yellowroot—*Xanthorhiza simplicissima*
    selected ornamental grasses
    Joe-pye weed—*Eupatorium maculatum*

Seed to spray on over banks:
    Bluegrass—*Poa pratensis*
    Fescue sp.—*Festuca arundinacea*
    Annual and perennial ryegrass—
        Lolium multiflorum
    Timothy—*Phaleum pratense*
    Brome grass—*Bromus inermis*
    Reeds canary grass—*Phalaris arundinacea*
    Bermuda grass—*Cynodon dactylon*
    St. Augustine grass—*Stenotaphrum secundatum*
    Zoysiagrass—*Zoysia matrella*
    Legumes, white clover, birdsfoot trefoil, red
        clover, and others.

Solid Masonry Walls

Any solid wall needs to be on a frost-free footing (fig. 73). It is ideal to place reinforcing rods into the footing. Any wall exposed to weather will need a capstone; large cut stones or concrete capstones can be used. The caps should be ½″ wider on each side in order to allow water to drip without running down the face of the wall. If the brick or other materials of which the wall is made are to be used as the capstone as well, it will be necessary to

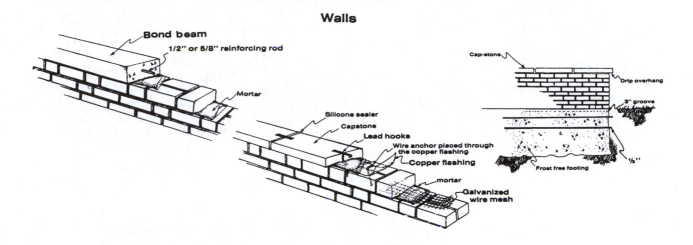

Figure 73. Block, brick, stone walls, or veneered walls must have a capstone to keep water out of the inside of the wall. Use a bond beam on high walls for added strength.

Damage on the lower face is apparent on this veneered wall with no capstone. Moisture is leaching through the inside, carrying lime and other chemicals. Soon the mortar will dissolve and the brick will fall off.

install copper or aluminum flashing below the last course. That will stop deep penetration of moisture into the wall. If this is done, only the top course will need to be relaid from time to time. A strip of galvanized wire mesh should be placed between courses of brick near the top to help compensate for the reinforcing rod in the poured concrete bond beam. If cut stone is used, fasten them with metal hooks made of lead, brass, or copper.

Surface joints on a capstone should be filled with a silicone sealer, which is much more functional than mortar because it will stay soft to allow for freezing and thawing and is water-repellent.

Serpentine Walls

Serpentine walls can be attractive and interesting if built properly. The basic structure differs very little from a solid wall. Footings must be below frost line and the wall. A capstone will be needed to shed the rain that comes off the wall. It should have a poured concrete cap and a reinforcing rod down the center of the concrete. If a prepared stone is used, place a galvanized wire mesh between the last course of brick or stone and put the capstone on top of that.

Some minimum dimensions need to be observed if a satisfactory serpentine wall is to be built. In addition to the frost-free footing, the minimum distance for the radius is 5'. The shortest distance advised from the center of one outside curve to the center of the next curve is 20' (fig. 74).

Serpentine Wall

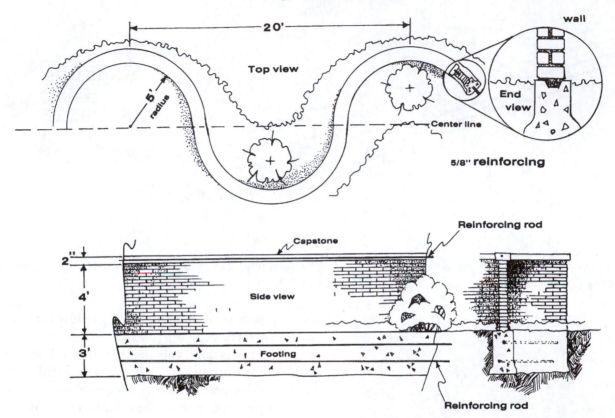

Figure 74. Serpentine walls should not be built smaller than the dimensions given. It is also important to have a frost-free footing and reinforced bond beam. The 3″ groove in the wall footing is important to the stability of the wall (end view). This is done by placing an oiled 1 × 3″ board in the top of the cement as the top of the footing is finished to grade.

The final recommended structural feature is the groove left in the concrete footing to add stability and help bond the wall to the footing.

Slave Walls

Slave walls in the South are probably the best example of this type of free-laid wall construction in the United States. The walls are made of large, flat stones 2–4″ thick and carefully laid. Small stone shims were used to level each layer before the next layer was begun.

Stone Walls

Large, rectangular rocks are excellent for building freestanding walls.

Precast Concrete Walls

Concrete panels cast in 10′ × 8′ × 1½″ planks are excellent fence material and fine sound barriers.

A good fence to use in areas close to car and truck traffic and also to plant along. It provides wind protection and some support for tender plants. The wall is better than plants at cutting down on noise and takes little space on the ground.

These panels fit into posts. Like tongue-in-groove flooring, the posts have grooves into which to slide the next panel, and the planks fit tightly together.

Precast concrete fence panels are interesting and make good replacements for high-maintenance picket fences. They require a complicated jig, but the results are attractive and unique. Use the new concrete that has been mixed with fiberglass for reinforcement.

Fences and Screens

Building structurally sound fences and screens depends on how posts are set and the bracing used to strengthen the corners and gate openings (fig. 75). The three woods used for fences and screens are redwood, treated yellow pine, and fir. Cypress is also a good choice, and California cedar is satisfactory for above-ground use but not for posts.

A basic fence frame can be used to support almost any type of fencing, from rolled snow fence to board-on-board. The frame (fig. 76) has two important bracing structure nailer blocks to add strength along the fence line. The brace should always be from the bottom of the second post to the top of the post

Basic Fence Frame

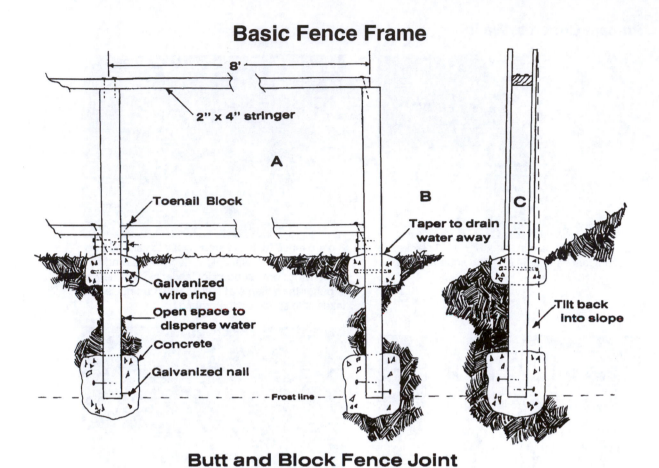

8'

2" x 4" stringer

A

B

C

Toenail Block

Taper to drain water away

Galvanized wire ring

Open space to disperse water

Concrete

Galvanized nail

Tilt back into slope

Frost line

Butt and Block Fence Joint

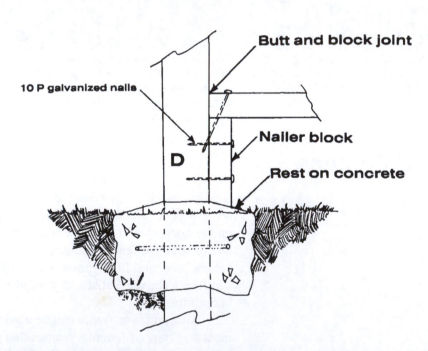

Butt and block joint

10 P galvanized nails

Nailer block

D

Rest on concrete

Figure 75. Posts and stringers should be planned in 8' lengths from the center of one post to the center of the next. There must be a galvanized wire in the top or collar of concrete because it will crack, but the wire prevents the collar from coming apart. A nailer block is important to the in-line strength and to the stability of the bottom stringer.

being braced. For example, in a corner, both braces would be to the top of the corner post. The post should be no smaller than 4 × 4″.

The fence post should be set in concrete below the frost line. It is best if the concrete is in two sections (fig. 75) in order to allow water that collects around the post to drain away without splitting the lower section of concrete. The reinforcing wire in the top section of concrete allows it to crack, but it will not separate; at the same time, the lower section will stay intact. At its top, the concrete collar should be finished with a slight slope to drain water away and provide a grass-free area around the post (fig. 75D). The large galvanized nails at the bottom of the post stop it from heaving out of the ground during the winter.

Use about 60 pounds of concrete per post for a standard 4–4½′ fence. For every foot of added height, add 20 pounds of concrete to the footing up to a 6–7′ fence. The concrete should be distributed ⅓ in the collar and ⅔ in the footing. The base can be poured dry, but the top should be moist so it can be troweled smooth to better create a waterproof surface.

Building fences on a slope causes special problems, especially if the hill is composed of fill soil. All new fences and screens will settle to some degree. To compensate, tilt the post back into the hill. Then, as the soil settles it will pack around the post. The amount of tilt depends on the soil type and the amount of settle that has occurred. Usually 2–3% tiltback into a hill is enough (fig. 75C).

When setting post for any purpose, use footing that has concrete separated in its middle. Here, the footing has been poured and a soil layer added in readiness for the collar to be poured. It is good practice to make sure that a few inches of concrete are under the post.

Place a heavy galvanized wire around the post and finish filling the hole with concrete. When the concrete cracks, the reinforcing rod will hold it around the post.

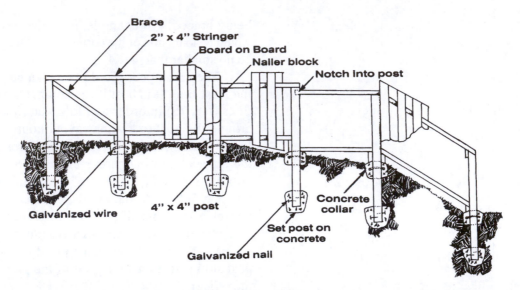

Brace
2" x 4" Stringer
Board on Board
Nailer block
Notch into post
Galvanized wire
4" x 4" post
Concrete collar
Set post on concrete
Galvanized nail

Figure 76. The post, footing, and bracing are the same for all fencing. Any cover can be applied to this basic frame.

Mound the concrete slightly in order to improve drainage away from the post. After the concrete cures and the bottom stringer has been put in place, make sure the nailer block is added.

A good view of the post, nail blocks, and stringer. It is best to stain lumber before nailing it together.

This patio screen should last a long time and be easy to mow around.

Fences and screens should be made of decay-resistant lumber on a structurally sound frame so the design or the cover will last.

Fence Built With a Ledger Plate

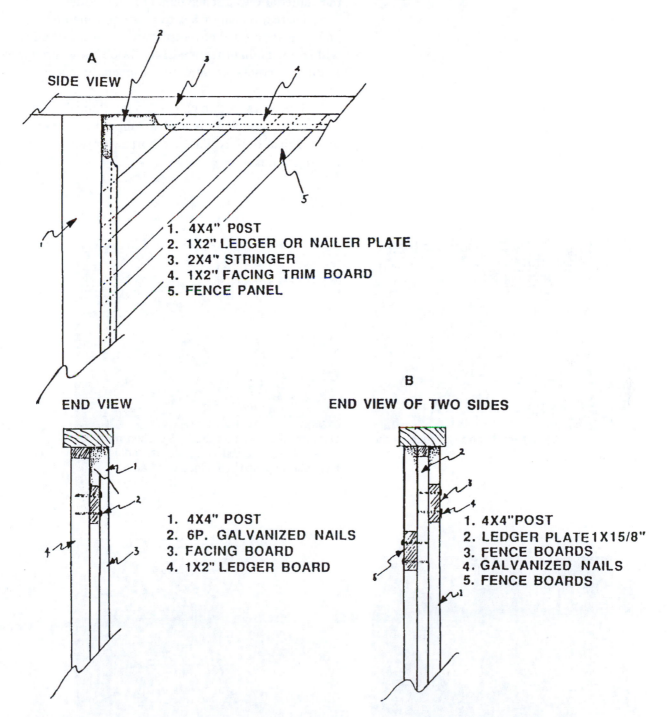

A

SIDE VIEW

1. 4X4" POST
2. 1X2" LEDGER OR NAILER PLATE
3. 2X4" STRINGER
4. 1X2" FACING TRIM BOARD
5. FENCE PANEL

END VIEW

1. 4X4" POST
2. 6P. GALVANIZED NAILS
3. FACING BOARD
4. 1X2" LEDGER BOARD

B

END VIEW OF TWO SIDES

1. 4X4"POST
2. LEDGER PLATE 1X15/8"
3. FENCE BOARDS
4. GALVANIZED NAILS
5. FENCE BOARDS

Figure 77. This fence frame is built just like the one discussed previously. The ledger or nailer plate allows insetting the fence panel to give a flush surface.

Two types of ledger plates or nailer plates are used in fence building (fig. 77). One has the ledger flush with the outside, which accommodates fence on one side only. Sometimes a narrow ledger down the center allows a fence panel on both sides.

There are many ways to preserve fencing by paint, oil stains, and cover-all stains. Cover-all stains will let the grain or texture of the wood show through. Earth-tone colors are attractive, especially in small yards.

Stretchers—often called "come-alongs"—can be used for stretching fences and moving large objects. This tool is available to borrow or rent at most fencing stores.

The fence is framed and ready to receive the panels.

Light material such as the lattice used here becomes strong when built with internal panels rather than lattice applied to the face of a frame.

Fence frames built with a nailing ledger will easily accommodate many different fence designs (fig. 77).

It is important that a screen like this be held straight and level. If not, the design is lost and the screen will need to be rebuilt.

Here, fence boards have been nailed to a ledger board, which in turn was nailed around the inside of the 4 × 8′ fence frame. The bottom stringer board follows the ground grade (fig. 76) and provides an open, airy appearance although the fence is solid and structurally sound.

A well-built frame with properly set posts will accommodate any kind of cover. In short runs or small areas, keep the fence level. The use of many vertical lines, expressed as pickets here, helps to give the impression of more space.

The rest of the fence has a step-down to keep the top looking structurally sound.

Use earth-tone stains on fences to allow them to blend with the colors and textures of shrubs and flowers.

Chain-Link Fences

Chain-link fences are often unattractive, but they help protect yards from people walking through planting beds and keep children and pets at home. They also provide a protected line from which to develop a landscape and make good neighbors.

The same chain-link fence after shrubs have matured and are in flower.

Make fencing a subdued part of a landscape rather than a distraction. In this case, removing the white strips would not only make this fence more attractive but the fence would also become part of the background rather than something that detracts from the rest of the landscape.

Coated chain-link fencing is attractive and—when used in wooded areas—almost invisible. A black fence in a wooded area provides a good security feature that would be difficult to improve upon without spending a great deal of money.

The full, overwhelming effect of the fence.

The sapwood side of fence rails should always be turned up in order to help prevent or slow sagging and warping. Sapwood is softer than hardwood and will stretch much farther.

Chain-link fencing can be purchased with a black, brown, or green plastic coating. There are also matching staves. Such a fence makes an effective plant protection screen.

The nailing ledger must be in place inside the stringer and post, ready to receive the panel no matter what its design.

This gate is well designed and attached; the gate is double-hung and the bracing meets at the latch in the middle. The matching fence is attached to the same frame (fig. 76).

Utility screens are structurally the same but vary in other factors, such as air circulation around the equipment being protected. Screening around utility entrances must hide necessary equipment and yet allow good, safe access. Leave enough space—2–3'—for servicing or making repairs. The screen can then be landscaped like the rest of the house without damaging the equipment. Do not include anything that draws attention to the area, however.

Gates

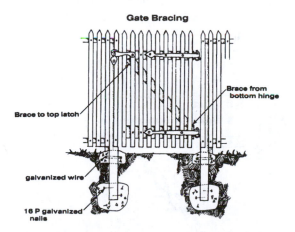

Figure 78. Gate posts and bracing are installed as is the rest of the fence. Brace from the bottom hinge to the top of the latch side.

The craft of making gates is an old one that has long been practiced in Europe. More recently, many beautiful hand wrought gates can be found in cities along the eastern seaboard and throughout the South.

It is important that gates be braced and hung, and the brace should be from the bottom hinge to the top latch so the gate will not give or fold as pressure is applied when it is opened (fig. 78).

When selecting hardware for outdoor use, make sure it is large enough to carry the necessary weight and that it will not rust shut (as small hinges and fasteners will do). Although there are many good commercial latches, nice ones can be made with strap iron, which can be attractive, functional, and also individualize a landscape.

All hardware should be heavily galvanized or weather-resistant so there is no danger of rust or freezing. A house-door hinge is not acceptable because it will rust. All nails and wire should also be heavily galvanized by a process called "hot dipped."

Strive to match all the hardware and stay within the architectural style of the structure being landscaped. Hinges, latches, braces, and hooks should be larger than it would appear necessary and thus in scale with the outdoors. Such hardware requires plenty of tolerance or space to turn freely in cold weather. Lubricate moving parts with heavy, waterproof grease that is long-lasting and will not stain.

Gate Closing Devices

The traditional chain and weight method of closing gates is still effective. A larger chain than is needed looks attractive and causes the gate to close more smoothly. Many newer gates that use this method use round weights that look like cannonballs (fig. 79). Plowshares were often used as weights in rural areas during the 1920s and 1930s.

Latches

Whale latches are one of the most common and easy styles of fasteners to use and build and work well with many styles of homes. Because it can be used with a latch string, it can be opened from either side, even if the gate is solid. Sliding bolts are also a good serviceable latches that are easy to build and use. Both of these latches (fig. 80) are simple and have a loose enough fit that rust or ice will not be a problem. Any latch should be simple, have wide tolerances, and be easy to install and use.

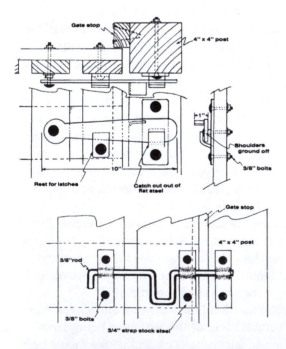

Figure 79. There are many types of gate closures. Make them as simple and durable as possible.

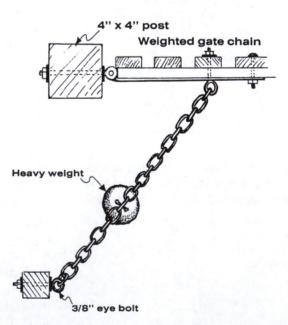

Figure 80. Select latches in keeping with the style of the fence.

This sunflower gate has been featured in many articles about landscaping; such items transcend landscape construction to become artwork.

The garden gate matches the service gate.

Moon gates, used in oriental gardens, are also latchless and swing free. This type of closure can be used on other gates.

A beautiful, handmade gate such as this can add beauty and function to a garden. The gate was individually made using square steel stock and 2½" pipe cut into rings.

This custom-built service gate meets all of the requirements for garden gates.

A similar gate made with straight, bare steel. The fence was made to match the gate.

This old gate closure system is especially good for gardens of Early American homes. It opens without the use of a latch.

This large, hand wrought hinge is ideal for outdoor use.

Coverall stain was used on this gate and does a good job of blending it and fence into the landscape.

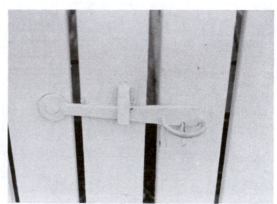

A whale latch, which will work in all kinds of weather, provides the closure for this gate.

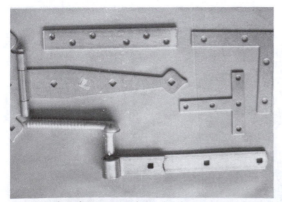

Outdoor hardware needs to be heavy-gauge and have large tolerances. Rust and ice make indoor hinges and latches inoperative outdoors.

Large wooden slide-bar latches are good choices outdoors because of their wide tolerance; bolts will slide in all kinds of weather.

Wood

Trees grow in rings of hard cellulose; the way in which these rings grow, and the way in which boards are cut, determines how easily they will warp, come apart, or decay in a landscape. Center-cut boards are the best and do not warp as easily as those cut across the grain further from the center of the tree, which warp and weather check much easier than center-cut boards (fig. 80A).

This, then, is what starts the breakdown or decay of a board. The sun shrinks and opens cracks along the hard cellulose part of the ring, then, in winter, water enters these cracks, freezes, and opens them further (fig. 80B). The cracks then collect dirt and other matter, a buildup that in conjunction with rain creates an ideal condition for decay organisms to grow and accelerate the

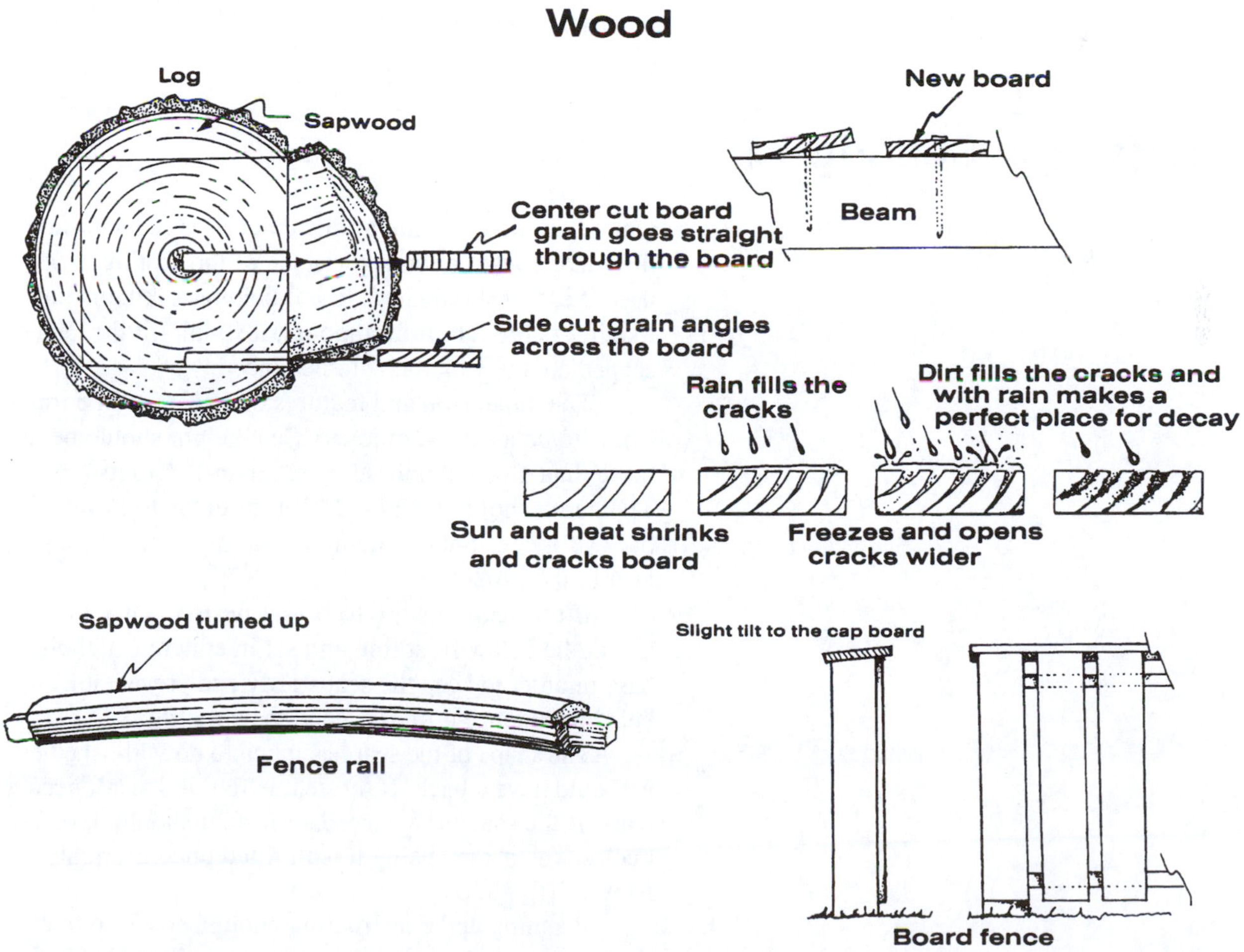

Wood

Figure 81. Examine the grain of the board to determine which side should be turned up toward the weather. The closer the board is cut from the middle of the tree, the better it will be in combatting warping and decay. Selecting the right kind and quality of wood for fencing, gates, screens, and patios is the first step in building a successful project.

breakdown of the wood. Therefore, it is important to use a soft-grain, decay-resistant wood like redwood for floors and surfaces that are exposed to the sun. It may be advisable to use a harder wood like Wolmanized fir for joists or support beams. The softer redwood nailed to these beams will then hold much longer without working loose.

Turn and sort flooring lumber before nailing it. Turn the curved grain or the side next to the sapwood (the outside of the tree) until it faces up (fig. 80C). After it is nailed it will help prevent mechanical cracking, which will help prevent the board cupping. This process only takes a few minutes and will give a long-lasting, smooth surface.

Fence rails should also be placed with their sapwood sides turned up. Sapwood sides are softer and will stretch easily, so the rails will sway quickly if turned around (fig. 80D). Post tops should be protected so the wood will not split and then decay. It is important to use a top board or flashing when building arbors or other large screens and fences (fig. 80E).

Landscape Seating

One of the first considerations that arises in landscape design or construction is the scale of the seating to be used. Seating should look like it belongs outdoors not like it was brought from indoors; it should fit the landscaped area in which it is to be placed.

The dimension and features of a seat are important if it is to be used and enjoyed. Seat height should be no more than 18" and not much less than 17" to its top. The depth should be 20–22" if the seat is to have a back. If it does not, the depth is not important as long as it is at least 20".

If the seat legs are to be set permanently they should be below frost line and set in concrete at their base in order to keep the seat steady and prevent it from heaving out during freezing and thawing (fig. 82A).

The shape of the seat has much to do with whether it should have a back. If the seat is flat, it doesn't need a back. If the seat has a curved surface, it should have a back so the person using it isn't tilted uncomfortably forward (fig. 82B).

Planning and constructing enough space so that the lower part of the leg fits under the seat is also important to individual comfort (fig. 82D).

The material of which the seat is made can add a great deal to its comfort. Wood is the most comfortable

Seating like this adds much to the design and enjoyment of a garden. Try to situate seats so they can be comfortably used for much of the day.

This patio seat is structurally sound and in scale with its surroundings. The supports are on the patio floor and do not interfere with ground cover maintenance.

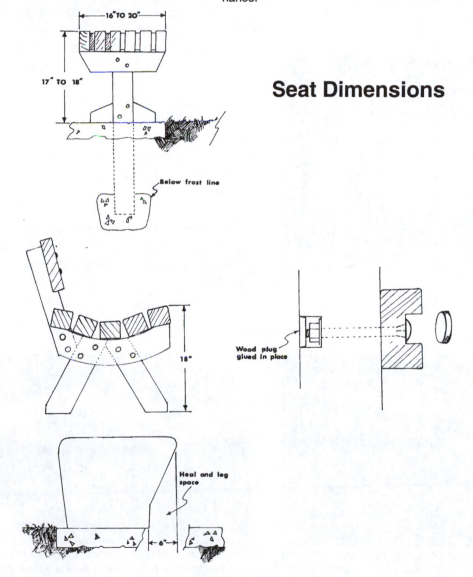

Seat Dimensions

16" TO 20"

17" TO 18"

Below frost line

18"

Wood plug glued in place

Heal and leg space

6"

Figure 82. Landscape seating must have a few basic design features: 18" to the seat, heel and leg space, and a comfortable surface.

The 2 × 4″ board seat is used often and is good as long as it is built correctly and made of weather-proof lumber.

This beautiful, well-built bench was made by Kelly Green Landscape Company. The scale and shape of the seat are both good.

outdoor material because it will retain neither heat or cold nor conduct them to the person using the seat. Because metal conducts heat rapidly, metal seats must be kept in shaded areas. Material such as concrete holds cold or heat for a longer time, but the exchange of heat or cold is much slower than is the case with metal.

The surface finish of seats can also be a comfort factor. The smoother the surface, the more rapidly heat or cold is transferred to the body. If the material is too rough, however, the seat is uncomfortable. The seat's location and the other materials in the landscape will determine what materials to use, but also keep in mind when the seating will most likely be used.

Wood meets many of the criteria for a good seat and can be shaped and finished to fit most needs. In order of preference, the best woods are redwood, California cedar, treated fir, and cypress where it is available.

All nails, screws, bolts, and other hardware should be galvanized heavily. If these metal bolts and screw heads detract from the overall appearance, countersink them and cover them with wood plugs, detail work that can be important when finishing seats or decks (fig. 82C).

If seating is to be placed on a deck, attach it through the flooring to a joist or large timbers below the floor. Seating placed on the ground-level patio edge in a lawn or landscape bed creates a maintenance problem.

Start curved seats on a straight or even end and build them with 1 × 4″ boards, one board at a time. Anchor the first board into place, nail and glue the spacers, and apply the next seat board. Continue the procedure until the seat is finished.

This seat is well-built and does an excellent job of emphasizing the patio design. Seats placed in this manner protect plant material behind them and make people on the patio more comfortable.

Gazebos and Other Lawn Shelters

Some gazebos are painted in a Victorian manner.

Gazebos are expensive and difficult to build, so either work with a construction company that employs skilled carpenters or buy a good kit—which will also require the services of a good carpenter.

In many areas of the country, insects make it difficult to use outdoor living space without the protection of screening. Outdoor screened structures must be raised high enough for protection from splashes from the ground, which will cause screens to deteriorate and stay dirty.

If a gazebo is built on a concrete or wooden floor, its life is lengthened and wet, muddy floors are eliminated. Raised floors are a good idea and keep the floor's surface dry and clean. Splashed mud can be a problem when flower beds are near a structure, particularly when it is planned for use in all weather.

The seats also function as large storage units for classroom and play equipment.

This large gazebo is used as an outdoor classroom. It is well constructed: Seats are built in and the west side features a wind screen and afternoon shade.

Here, a large gazebo in a new housing development is being used as a bus stop. A nice feature of the shelter is its double-pitch roof, the eves of which have a slight upward sweep. Detail work again provides a structure that has excellent design and construction. The floor is raised.

The roof includes two pleasing details: a slight sway and a hand-turned acorn finial.

Changeable screens and windows extend the seasonal use of a gazebo. If it is decided to do so before the gazebo is constructed, the screens can be built-in panels and interchanged with windows. Those who live in milder climates can extend the structure's use to all but three or four months of the year.

When building a gazebo from a kit, obtain a good-quality one as shown. Most quality gazebo packages are made of redwood or mahogany, often better lumber than is available locally. The unit is also fabricated with the best tools available. It will still be necessary, however, for a skilled carpenter to assemble the kit.

Outdoor living space in individual living units is quickly becoming smaller because of the lack of availability and high cost of land. The time that owners can spend caring for such a unit is also lessening. This small living area has been well designed for maximum use and easy care.

Outdoor Storage

Good-quality packaged gazebos include many nice details such as floors. Attractive matching furniture is also available.

Make outdoor storage units part of a landscape instead of isolating them. Use the same colors used in the home or the fencing and fit the unit into existing shrubbery.

Storage doors such as these are functional and easy to build, especially because of their slide-bolt latch and heavy-duty hinges.

Garden Houses

Small garden houses are becoming popular and can easily be built or commercial units can be set up in a short time. Here doors and windows are those used in house construction.

A well-made, commercially available shed that has been set into shrubbery and trees and painted the same color as the house. The hinges are on the inside of this unit, protected from the weather.

Many avid gardeners are discovering the utility and comfort of having a garden house. The structures can be designed into a landscape and be just as attractive as a gazebo and often more useful.

Gardening tools put away with soil still on them lead to dirt in a storage facility. This unit has no floor. It is raised off the ground to provide air circulation—a good feature when a unit is also used for storing or drying vegetables or flowers.

This decorative treatment on the back of a garage can be applied to any plank wall. It helps make a space more user-friendly.

Drainage Systems

Installing drain tile 2′ or less in the ground would have cured the problem of standing water in this courtyard. Although the water cannot be seen, drainage problems in planting beds are often as bad as those at this tree-planting site.

These shrubs are typical of plants suffering from too much water. The bed is covered with black plastic and rock, which does not help the situation. The yews are dwarfed, and the deciduous plants are showing fall color in June. Remove excess water from beds before starting any planting.

The four kinds of drainage tile (left to right): orange clay tile, concrete tile, rolled plastic, and ridged plastic.

Clay Tiles

Clay tiles make a drainage system that has been used for many years and is still one of the best. Lay the tile in a bed of coarse stone in order to speed drainage and lengthen the life of the system. It is a good practice to cover the top of tile joints with a tar paper or petro-mat patch to prevent sediment from entering the tile and eventually cutting off water flow (figs. 83A, 84). The ideal drop or slope in which to place these systems is 2% minimum and 4% maximum. This allows for a good deep flow in the tile and passage of any debris that might enter the line.

This slight grade helps prevent erosion into and around the tile, thereby preventing cave-ins. Use concrete tile under roads or driveways. It can also be used for an entire system, although it will add labor and expense.

This clay tile was installed under a raised bed to ensure good drainage. Such preparation is necessary because rhododendrons will be planted.

Waffle Drains

Waffle drains can be laid just below the prepared soil to guarantee good drainage in the top 12–18″, where most roots develop on most trees and shrubs. The double plastic waffle sheets provide great strength to resist crushing under walks and drives. This drain can be installed in existing beds because the installation process does not disturb root systems nearly as much as conventional tile does.

Drainage Systems

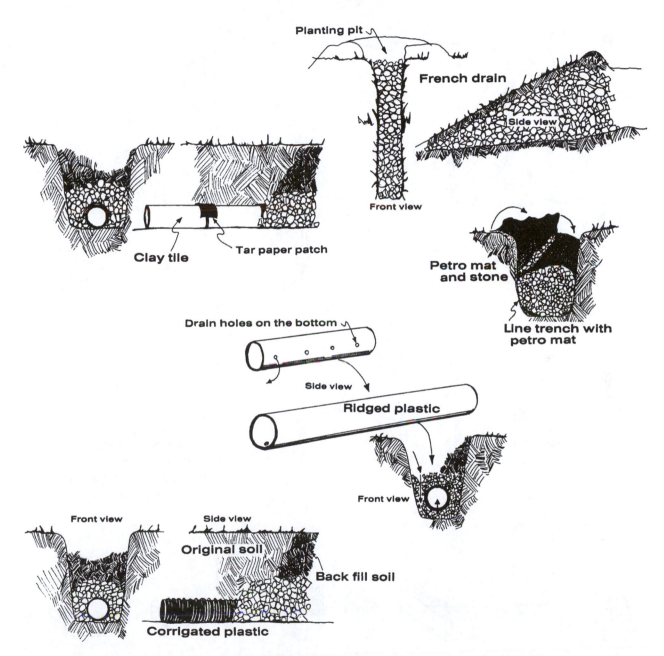

Figure 83. There are many types of drainage systems: (A) clay tile for large, flat areas; (B) french drains to use in planting pits on slopes; (C) rolled plastic, which are used in the same way as clay tile but need to be protected from freezing and thawing; and (D) ridged plastic for golf greens or any areas where near-the-surface drainage is needed. A simple ditch lined with weed barrier and filled with gravel will drain a large area with little expense (E), and manufactured metal drains (F) can be set into sod next to drives and walks to stop seeps into lawn areas.

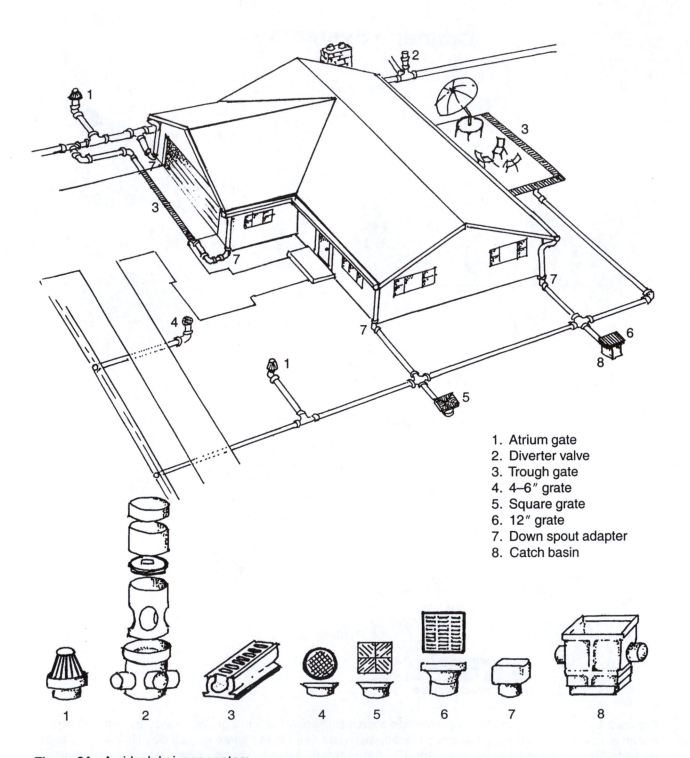

1. Atrium gate
2. Diverter valve
3. Trough gate
4. 4–6″ grate
5. Square grate
6. 12″ grate
7. Down spout adapter
8. Catch basin

Figure 84. An ideal drainage system.

Rolled plastic tile is easy to work with and does a good job of draining wet soils. It should be kept as deep in the soil as possible and covered with gravel.

Rolled drainage systems can easily be adapted to accommodate all sizes of drain pipe. In this example, a sump pump drain is fed into the tile system.

Rolled Corrugated Plastic

Rolled corrugated plastic is quick and easy to install and works well (fig. 83C). The grade for this material is also 2%, and the tube should be laid with a bed of gravel. The gravel should be laid flat so the drain tube will not have hills and valleys and the system will not retain water. This system will not last as long as the tile. Where possible, place the tile below the frost line in order to extend its life.

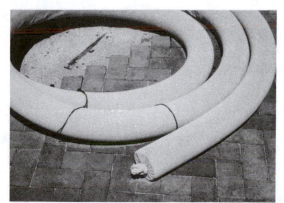

Rolled drainage tiles have nylon socks that slip over them and filter fine particles, which in time fill the fabric cover and make the tile useless. Socks work reasonably well in sandy soil but clog in silty clay and slow the flow of water quickly.

Ridged Plastic

This system is a little harder to lay and also more expensive than corrugated material (fig. 83D). It has a line of holes in a row down one side that should be placed on the bottom of the trench to allow only water to enter the pipe. The water drains down and around the pipe, leaving most of its load of silt and clay. The system is used primarily under golf greens.

Petro-Mat and Stone

This works much the same as a french drain except it will carry much more water (fig. 83E). The system works well to drain a sedimented pond. Line the trench with the mat and fill it with a foot or more of gravel, wrap the mat over the top, and cover with soil and sod. It is important to use this system at the 2–4% drop range.

Surface Drains

This large, open drainage ditch is attractive and well built. It is best to keep such drainage as shallow as possible so it will not become a hazard to mowers and cars.

Trough Drains

Trough drains can be built of any good hard material that will not absorb water. New concrete pavers are ideal for this type of construction. They will be used much more for walks and patios. New products are being introduced, and the biggest change concerns the wide range of colors that is available.

This trough drain, built in the late 1700s, feeds into a cistern. Such drainage is still used, however new concrete pavers are installed as the paving. Water from downspouts can easily be channeled out of planting beds and away from a house.

French Drains

French drains are a useful system to use in planting sites with a good slope. The system can be put in at planting time or later if problems of poor drainage develop. A french drain is a narrow trench filled with coarse stone that will allow a planting pit to drain quickly (fig. 83B). The trench can be left open at the top or, if appearance is important, it can be covered with a few inches of soil and sod. The system can be either used on one plant or joined in a network of plants.

A large, open french drain does a good job of getting rid of a large amount of water quickly. It would be better to set the stones on top by hand so they would be smooth enough to mow across.

Set in sod or in concrete drives or walks, this metal grill drain is effective (fig. 83F) and generally out of view.

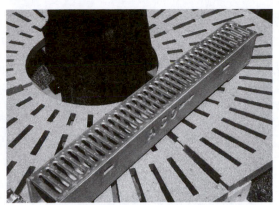

Surface floor drains are effective and fit in with all kinds of surfaces. This one collects water from a patio and driveway.

The drain is a large, strong trough covered with a metal or hard plastic grate that can be lifted for cleaning.

French drains can be connected to serve several trees or planting beds. This narrow drain, which will work for many years, was cut with a telephone trencher and filled with rock.

This small trough drain works well and looks like part of the edging.

When these planting pits were dug, french drains were built in them, ready to be backfilled. Without such drainage the trees would likely die or at least have poor growth.

Three years after planting. Without french drains the trees would likely not have lived, although they are making good growth each year.

The same planting the following year.

Diversion channels are used to collect and carry water slowly around a steep grade change and stop erosion. Runoff from a diversion channel is usually put into a morning glory tube and then dumped into a storm drain or natural stream.

Morning Glory Tubes

Morning glory tubes (fig. 85) allow water to be dropped long vertical distances without danger of erosion to the grade. This method of dropping water is out of sight for the most part, and the mechanism is not much more expensive than an open spillway. Be careful not to undersize the drainpipe used for the drop. A 4″ tile would be a minimum size and handle normal rainfall runoff from a 5,000 square-foot lawn. Areas the size of a baseball field would require a 12–14″ diameter galvanized corrugated steel pipe. Dump the water on a concrete pad in order to spread and reduce its velocity before the water hits sod or other unprotected areas.

The top of a morning glory tube. The structure is used to drop excess water down to the bottom of a steep slope without eroding or flooding surrounding property. The large pipe has a childproof grate. The concrete ring that circles the pipe about a foot below its top seals out seeping water and keeps it from eroding the ground around the pipe.

Morning Glory Tube

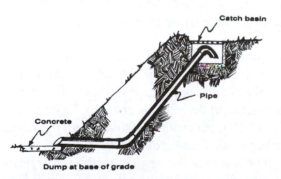

Figure 85. When building a morning glory tube, never undersize pipe. When in doubt, go larger.

The finished tube, ready to take runoff water.

The top of the tube can be funnel-shaped with a grate or a catch basin as illustrated (fig. 85). A catch basin is less likely to clog in areas that have a lot of leaves or other landscape trash.

The Catch Basin

This apparatus is the best and safest way to catch water from landscape areas (fig. 86). Such runoff will always have leaves and other trash that will clog the system, and a concrete tank catches this trash for later disposal. As the water rises, all floating trash rises above the exit pipe before the water starts to flow out. The heavy material sinks as it falls into the tank, so the remaining water that flows out does not contain enough material to clog the system. A catch basin will collect water from the surface of other drains as illustrated and can collect water from several drainpipes and drop it through one large pipe.

There are times when water needs to be collected over a large area or along the base of a slope. That can be done with a long, narrow steel grate that drops the water into a small concrete trench. This works well in large areas with slight slopes, in front of garage doors, or on the edges of patios. The long sections of this material made of heavy plastic also are useful in home landscape situations.

Catch Basin

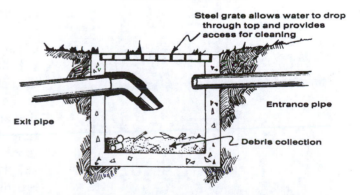

Figure 86. Dropping water from one level to another to prevent erosion will require a structure. A catchbasin is an excellent way to collect water and carry it off in a safe, nonerosive manner.

A catch basin installed in a patio. Catch basins are built to trap and hold leaves or other trash. They should be cleaned every 4 to 6 months, depending on location and potential trash accumulation.

This well-disguised catch basin collects water in a poorly drained yard and then tiles it away.

Erosion Slope Netting

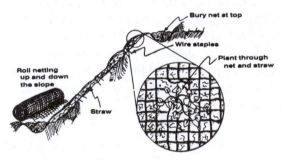

Figure 87. There are many good nets and fiber mat combinations. Lay them up and down slopes rather than across.

Always use erosion net from the top of a slope to the bottom rather than across, as shown here. This washout will eventually take out a large strip of net and ground cover.

The many kinds of netting now available to landscapers fall into two categories: those that work alone and those that must have straw or other material used with them.

All types must be laid vertically, up and down a slope (fig. 87). Bury the top of the net in a shallow trench, roll the net down, then cut it off and bury the bottom. Repeat until the slope is covered. Laying up and down the slope prevents a washout from pulling the whole netted area down; one or two sections are all that will be lost with the vertical method. Always staple the net to the ground with staples long enough to hold securely, even if the soil is wet. If the slope is to be seeded to grass, prepare the soil, seed, then apply the net. If the netting is one that is woven with paper it is necessary to top-dress it with a small amount of soil before wind hits the slope. Netting of this type will lift off the ground and form a sail, which tears the net loose from the ground. If the net is not torn it lays over the top of the grass, which hinders germination and may smother the seedlings. The grass sometimes comes up under this raised net, and then the loose net will need to be removed before the grass is smothered or the grass needs mowing. If a type of broadleaf ground cover is to be planted, cut an *x* in the net no larger than necessary to plant through and lay planking over the net to walk on. That will keep the bank smooth and prevent foot traffic from stretching or moving the net.

The paper strip woven into this net can cause a problem if it is not anchored securely. Wind lifts the net off the soil, and grass comes up under it rather than through it. The seedlings will smother and die. After the net is placed and anchored, dust its top with a small amount of soil and water the soil lightly. Then the paper in the net will stick to the soil.

A finer grade of netting that is used on roadsides. It also works well on lawn areas that have little slope.

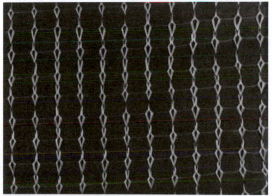

This erosion control net is woven solid with strips of paper. It is used for slope cover over grass seed.

Here, excelsior is held together with a light-green plastic fiber that breaks down in sunlight and disappears in one season. The material works well when establishing new grass.

Heavy hemp net for steep, large areas such as road embankments or ditch bottoms is strong enough to hold soil in place during large surges of water.

An excelsior mat is held together with biodegradable plastic net. This is used for cover on areas seeded with grass or ground covers can be planted through it after it is laid and staked.

A truck-mounted spray can cover a large area quickly and protect grass seedlings. Seed the area and spray on the latex and fiber solution.

The material on the ground. Not disturbing the sprayed area until the grass is ready for a first mowing is important.

One of the least expensive erosion-control methods is to apply a light layer of straw, roll it in with a disk opened to roll, not turn, the soil and cut or press the straw straight into the ground. Run the disk as near the contour as possible to catch and slow running water and help stop erosion.

Staking Sod

Sodding slopes can also be a problem. Sod should be laid across the slope and staked down with a least 5 stakes per yard of sod (fig. 88). The steeper the slope, the more stakes necessary. In extreme cases it may be necessary to net, then stake, the sod. The net should always go up and down the slope. Rapid rooting is essential in this procedure, so prepare the soil well and use good, fresh sod. Sprinkle the area with just enough water to make the soil tacky before laying the sod. Try to prevent water from running over the sod from areas above it. Water should be temporarily diverted until the sod roots down.

The soil should be prepared just as well as for seeding—if not better—for a quickly established turf that will last and cause few problems. That also applies to slopes. The quicker roots take hold, the quicker a slope will be safe from erosion.

Staking Sod

Lay across slope

Figure 88. Lay sod across the slope and overlap each strip to avoid erosion down the joint between the rolls . Use small stakes and stake sod that lies in steep areas.

Ponds, Pools, Fountains, and Streams

When building small, decorative pools keep water volume as low as possible to get the desired effect, as was done in this oriental pool. Here, cleanup will be easy.

Simple water features can be pleasant and provide water for birds and sound. This small pool has no drain; it overflows and keeps the surrounding area moist and cool. Such a pool would be nice under birch or alder trees as well as under other water-loving plants.

Simple vessels can provide sound and flow. Water flows into the vessel just fast enough to offset evaporation, and the little that runs over is unimportant.

A pool that is to contain fish and plants must be handled and designed differently than one for sound or reflection. Fish ponds need to be large enough and deep enough so that they will not freeze solid. Life in these pools slows down in winter, but fish will still need enough ice-free water (at least half of the water volume) to breathe. If a pond cannot be built deep enough to ensure ice-free water, the pool should be covered. There are many good waffle plastic blankets to spread over a pool to provide insulation. Always leave vent space between the water and the blanket; that can be done by floating sealed containers such as small barrels in the pool.

All concrete pools that are to hold fish or plants should be filled and aged, possibly for as long as a year. Such a lengthy process is unnecessary when rubber liners are used, but water will need to be aged for a few days to get rid of chlorine and other harmful gasses that can kill fish quickly. Even if all precautions have been taken it is still good practice to introduce a small number of fish and plants into the pool at a time.

Aeration, the last major problem that must be taken care of, can be done in several ways. One is to have a large surface area per fish, fountains, and waterfalls as illustrated. Movement exposes more water surface to absorb oxygen. Always place the intake and return as far apart as possible in order to keep water moving through the pool (fig. 89).

If plants like lilies are to be grown the depth of water must be held constant because they will only grow and bloom well at a proper depth. Plant shelves (fig. 89) are necessary to grow many water lilies.

Put circulation pumps out of sight and out of hearing. The location of the pump in figure 89 is underground in a large concrete pipe that creates a soundproof dry well. When selecting a pump for this type of pool, use one that moves a good volume of water with low pressure.

A good drainage system to handle overflow, keep the same water level, and drain a pool completely is necessary for drainage and cleaning. Those chores should be done annually in early spring if the pool is made of concrete in order to allow for repair of any winter damage and provide an opportunity to regulate fish numbers. A good reference on fish, plants, and pools is *Goldfish Pools, Water Lilies, and Tropical Fish* by G. L. Thomas, Jr. (distributed by T. F. H. Publications, 211 W. Sylvania Ave., P.O. Box 27, Neptune City, NJ 07753).

Fish and Plant Pool

Side view

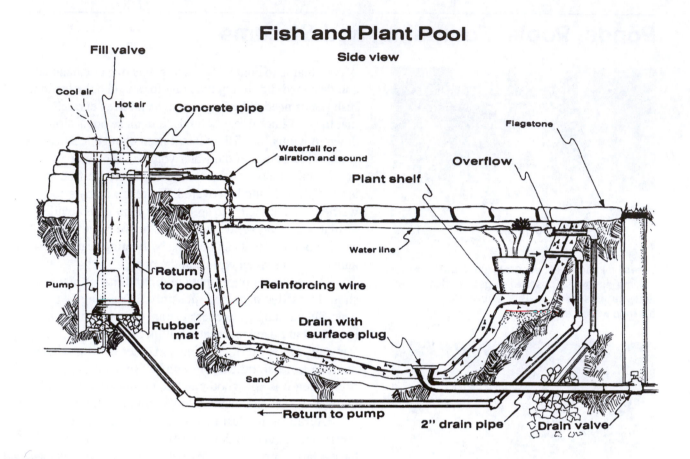

Fill valve

Cool air

Hot air

Concrete pipe

Waterfall for airation and sound

Plant shelf

Overflow

Flagstone

Water line

Return to pool

Reinforcing wire

Pump

Rubber mat

Drain with surface plug

Sand

Return to pump

2" drain pipe

Drain valve

Top view

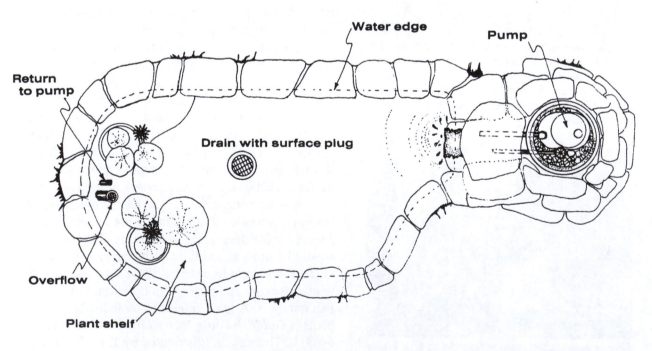

Water edge

Pump

Return to pump

Drain with surface plug

Overflow

Plant shelf

Figure 89. Pools that are to support life must have some water movement, a stable water level, and enough volume and area so they will not freeze solid in winter.

Much time and money went into this small pool and waterfall, and it should be left as the focal point of the lawn. Unfortunately, the effect was lost by using bright, distracting plants. It would have been better to use ones more complementary to the pool. Weeping juniper, for example, would come down over its top. Many bog plants are low-growing and suitable for such situations. Be sure to use the rubber liner under all water holding structures.

Aerating helps add oxygen to water, but temperature is important when trying to maintain adequate oxygen. The warmer the water the less oxygen it can hold. Most fish have a problem living in water that approaches 80 degrees F. Provide afternoon shade for as much of the pool's surface as possible. It may be necessary to add fresh water on extremely hot days. Be careful, however, not to add too much water at any one time that has not been aged. Shaded water will also produce less algae.

The pool will need to have good depth to avoid total freezing, and water should be circulated for aeration and cooling. Build the pool deep enough so it will not float out of the ground in winter and maintain a constant water level. A good low-pressure pump should be placed out of sight and hearing.

It is not easy to use rock, gravel, and boulders to make a decorative waterway. Plants and stone must be placed carefully in order to appear authentic.

The same stream at maturity

Water features do not have to contain water. Properly selected stones and logical plant placement will provide the effect of water, as is the case in this dry streambed. Grass completes the picture.

A pond at the end of the dry stream completes the picture. The stream carries some water after heavy rains.

Controlling Water in a Landscape

The first step in stabilizing a stream or drainage ditch is to grade and shape the ditch's side wall and use a farm level to make sure the streambed is steep enough to keep water moving (fig. 90). A 2–5% drop is ideal. If it must be greater, use a sudden drop or a waterfall.

After the grade is established line the ditch's wall with a rubber mat over a weed barrier landscape mat. Do so one side at a time and join the mat loosely in the middle or at the base. Concrete is then poured over the matting, stone placed over the ditch's bottom, and then more concrete added until the top of the sides are reached. The concrete needs to be dryer than most concrete so it will resist slumping as the wall is built.

Select stone that is natural-looking and uneven in size. Lay it so cleavage lines all run in the same direction and are aligned as closely as possible. As the stones are laid, keep the concrete far enough back in the space between the stones so it cannot be seen. It is

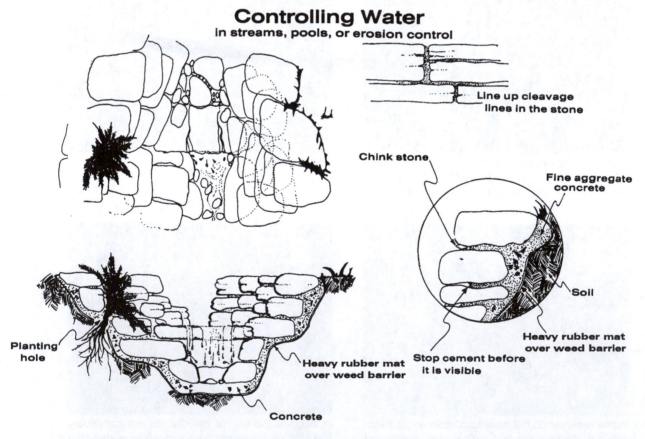

Controlling Water
in streams, pools, or erosion control

Line up cleavage lines in the stone

Chink stone

Fine aggregate concrete

Soil

Heavy rubber mat over weed barrier

Planting hole

Heavy rubber mat over weed barrier

Stop cement before it is visible

Concrete

Figure 90. Building attractive water channels can add beauty to a landscape if done properly. Check the channel, keep a 2% slope, and use a waterfall if more drop is required.

Stone does not lay like this. It must be held in place by concrete. Use at least one round stone on the bottom and flat stone on the banks.

an excellent idea to dye the concrete to match the stone being used in order to create a natural look. Readily available dyes are dark brown and dark gray. Use just enough to take away the "concrete look."

Another good practice is to put plastic over the stones already laid so they will not be splashed with fresh concrete spots that are unsightly and hard to remove.

Water features like streams need to be protected from freezing. Underground lines should be blown out to stop pipes from bursting. Pools or small ponds should be kept from freezing over if they contain fish. Float logs or cover the water surface with waffle blankets that are used in greenhouses. Keep the waffle blanket off as much of the water surface as possible because it will seal out all air. Thermostatically controlled heaters should be set around 35 to 40 degrees F.

The top or start of the stream of a large water feature. The water is received here and begins a course that leads to a lake below.

Water that is moving, falling over shallow ledges, changing directions, and running over rough surfaces is aerated, which stops larvae growth and improves conditions for fish and other aquatic life. This concrete stream is lined with natural-looking stones to create water action, and movement, in turn, helps prevent mosquitoes.

The stream can be viewed from many angles and locations. More water is added in more locations, back to the lake.

Plantings are an important part of any water feature. The way a shoreline is treated can make a project seem either natural or contrived, no matter how well the water feature was constructed.

The end of a long, man-made stream that will improve as the plants mature.

Fist-sized stones have been placed to create water action and enhance the natural look of the streambed.

Bog Gardens

Waterfalls are always popular although they are difficult to build so they operate properly. Finding the right amount of water and right width of overflow area is a matter of trial and error.

Bog gardens are often planned with a fish pond. If that is the case, be sure to enclose the bog with the same structure as the fish pond so the bog will have a constant water depth and will not lose or waste water by letting it soak into the surrounding soil (fig. 91). The same principles and requirements apply for a bog as for a fish and plant pool, of which a bog is an extension.

Bog Garden

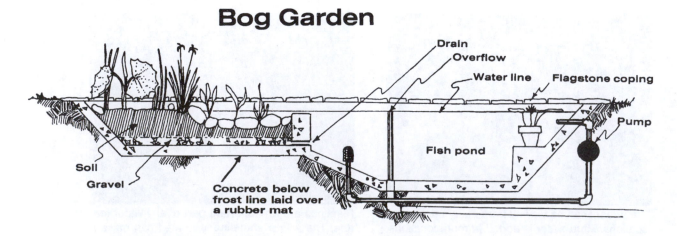

Figure 91. Bogs should be contained like an open water pond to ensure a constant water level.

Bogs should be built like a pool so water is not lost into surrounding soil.

Plants to use to create an appearance of water:
Bottlebrush grass—*Hystrix patula*
Eulalia—*Miscanthus sp.*
Tufted hair grass—*Dischampsia caespitosa*
Cord grass—*Spartenia pectinata* or 'Aureo-marginata'
Spangle grass—*Uniola latifolia*

Bog plants taller than 18″:
Siberian iris—*Iris siberica*
Yellow water iris—*Iris pseudacoruus*
Arrowhead plant—*Sagittaria japonica*
Water arum—*Peltandra*
Bog bean—*Menyanthes trifoliata*
White bullrush—*Scirpus albescens*
Variegated cattail—*Typha latifolia variegata*
Floating heart—*Nymphoides peltata*
Sweetflag—*Acorus calamus*
Pickerel rush—*Pontederia cordata*
Joe-pye weed—*Eupatorium*

Water edging plants less than 12″:
Wild ginger—*Asarum sp.* (shade)
Sedum—*Sedum sp.*
Dwarf hosta—*Hosta sp.* (shade)
Ajuga—*Ajuga sp.* (shade)
Perennial verbena—*Verbena canadensis*
Pinks—*Dianthus deltoides*

Fountain Placement

A fountain in a pool can be an aeration device and also provide a refreshing sight and restful sound. In fish ponds, use a bubbler fountain so that the view into the pool will not be disturbed.

If the fountain is used for sight and sound alone, spray can be much higher. Locate spray where prevailing winds will not blow water out of the pool. If there is to be nothing living in the pool, water should be chlorinated to protect the pump from algae and give the water more sparkle.

Pools used just for sight and sound should be filtered and skimmed to maintain clean, sparkling water. The depth of the pool in figure 92 is shallow, 1–2′ deep with a lining that is black or blue for better reflection. When designing such a filter system, consider the prevailing wind and put the skimmer where the wind will help rid the surface of dust and floating material.

Fountain Placement

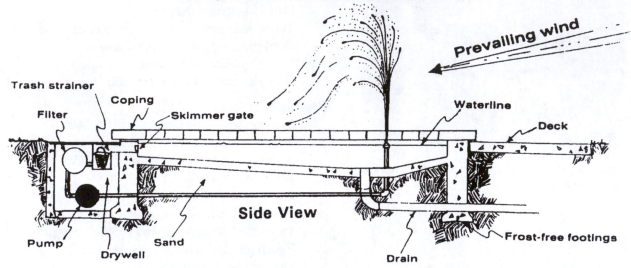

Draining Water off of Decks

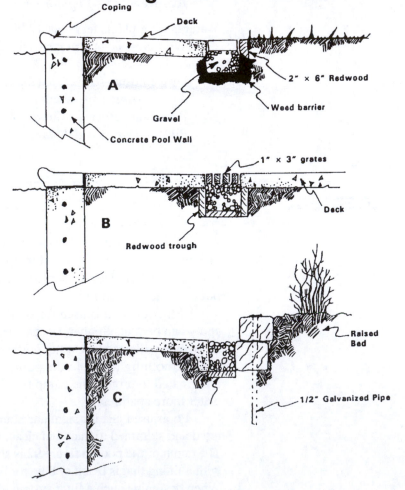

Figure 92. Place fountains so prevailing winds will not carry water out of the pool. A, B, and C illustrate how to contain and drain overspray from a pool.

Fountains on home grounds can also give a nice effect with little water. This feature was made with millstones.

Fountains with a high, fine spray will empty a pool in a short time, and fresh water will need to be added often. Doing so will change the water; it will never be properly aged and its pH will need daily correction. After the pool has matured and settled into a more balanced system it will take less care but always require regular inspection and maintenance.

The overflow, downhill from the millstone bubbler, provides small, quiet water and ends in a mushroom fountain. In this case it takes little water to provide sound and reflection and nurture plants and fish.

Well-done water features can be one of the most rewarding parts of a landscape. Like other parts of a garden, they follow the seasons. They also require regular care to stay clean and beautiful.

The Reflecting Pool

This type of pool requires many of the same construction features as fish pools, except that it does not have to be as deep and the water must be skimmed and filtered. The cleaner the pool, the better the reflection. In order to keep such pools attractive they should be treated like swimming pools, clear and algae-free.

Besides checking the skimmer and filter also check the water to keep pH near 7.0 and chlorinate regularly to eliminate algae. Be sure to place the skimmer downwind. If the design will allow, it is a good technique to round the corners of the pool so floating trash will move into the skimmer more easily and not collect in corners. Design the return-to-pool nozzles to flare and

Use as little water as possible. The more water, the greater potential for problems.

direct water to the pool's bottom to help keep the reflecting surface clean (fig. 93).

Chlorinated pools like reflecting or swimming pools that occasionally splash or overflow will need to be drained away without damaging surrounding plants or turf. A small border of gravel is easily built. If gravel causes a problem visually or structurally, it can be concealed below brick or patio stone as in figure 89.

Water lines should be drained and blown out in climates where a pool will be frozen most of the winter. Draining will not be adequate; highly compressed air will be necessary to get all water out of the lines. Then plug the lines to prevent any free water from running back into them.

Fountain spray can easily be carried out of a pool and onto walks and lawn areas where it will damage plants and make people wet. There are 3 ways to solve that problem: lower the pressure, enlarge the pool, or set the spray to the windward side of the pool. Before building a pool, study the site's soil, wind, and plants.

Cope with the spray fountain and reflection pool by draining dirty water away from the pool (fig. 92A). If the water is then caught in a hidden trough it can be drained away for safe disposal.

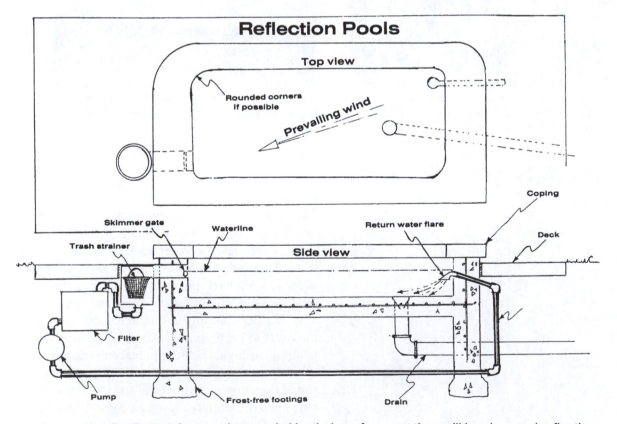

Figure 93. Keep reflecting pools very clean and skim their surfaces so they will be clear and reflective.

Garden Bridges

The simple bowed bridge is well placed and adds a great deal of charm to this oriental garden. Here there is little water but there are other elements instead.

Use large boulders to add scale and anchor the bridge. If possible, develop a dry streambed.

Garden bridges used in most home grounds tend to be somewhat contrived at best, so make every effort to place them in as natural a setting as possible. Use a design that fits the style of the home or helps carry out the theme of a garden.

Construct the bridge from good, durable woods like redwood, cedar, cypress, or treated fir. Many smaller-scale bridges can be built in a shop and moved on-site. Make sure there is a good concrete pad at each bridge approach to hold the bridge level and keep it from shifting.

If the bridge is curved or higher in the middle than at the approaches (fig. 94) make sure the approaches butt against either a concrete notch or a large stone set in concrete. That will stop sagging and allow the bridge to hold much greater weights without damage or breaking down.

10P to 16P spikes are large enough to hold the structure together, and 8P nails will be big enough for flooring. All hardware should be hot-dipped galvanized. Legscrews or stove bolts will be needed on some key points. Some rustic and Japanese bridges will require wooden pegs that should be cured, dry, hardwood (fig. 95). It is ideal to have timbers to be fastened together uncured or at least soaked so pegs will tighten in the holes as the wood cures or dries. Then, if necessary, nail these same timbers together with a hot-dipped, galvanized 16P spike.

Japanese Garden Bridge

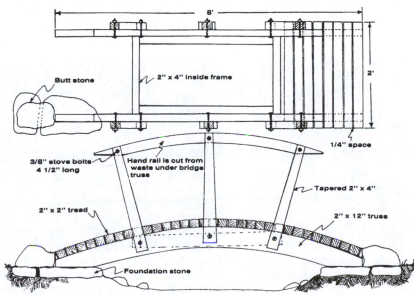

Figure 94. A Japanese bridge works well over dry streambeds as well as over water. Make the footing sound and visually in scale with the garden.

Japanese Bridge

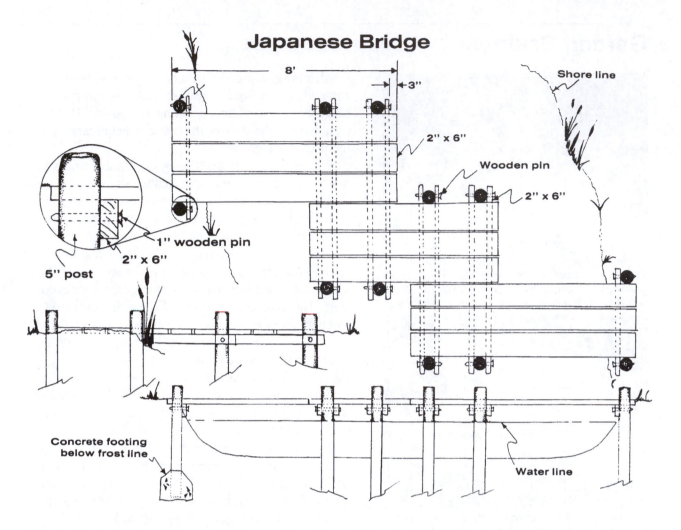

Figure 95. A Japanese zig-zag bridge provides a fine platform from which to view water plants and fish and is often used over the edge of a pond.

This zig-zag bridge is used in an oriental garden as an observation platform from which to view plants and fish.

This attractive bridge has an 1″ rise where it changes direction. The boards are laid on top of each other, just high enough to trip an unsuspecting pedestrian.

Garden Tressel Bridge

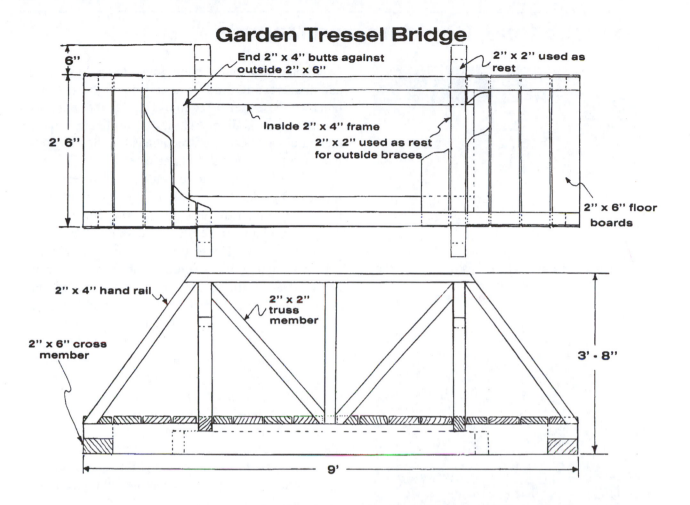

End 2" x 4" butts against outside 2" x 6"

2" x 2" used as rest

6"

2' 6"

Inside 2" x 4" frame

2" x 2" used as rest for outside braces

2" x 6" floor boards

2" x 4" hand rail

2" x 2" truss member

2" x 6" cross member

3' - 8"

9'

Figure 96. A simple tressel bridge, which has many designs, is often used. It must have good footings and should be sited where it can perform a function (or look as if it can).

Place tressel bridges in a proper setting. They usually work best when used with a planting (fig. 96).

An underwater bridge that can be crossed in dry conditions although water still runs through it. It also adds humidity for the plants.

Gravel, Stone, Boulders, and Mounds

Good use of boulders and plants has occurred in this contemplation garden.

Merrimac and Indiana creek gravel come in three grades (right to left, top to bottom): pea, B Indiana Creek and B Merrimac, and A Indiana Creek.

Landscape beds that contain gravel alone look stark and uninteresting. Add boulders and large stones to break up these areas. Try to use gravel and larger materials that look alike. Also try to duplicate nature; there are many sizes of streambeds but they all contain the same material. Indiana creek gravel, for example, grades from sand to boulders. If material is mixed and graded from small to large it can simulate a beach or another natural-looking setting (fig. 97).

Such a bed can be planted with small plants and a few specimens. The result is easy to maintain and can be attractive. For weed control, these beds can be laid over plastic or petro-mat, or a combination of herbicides can be used. The latter method is the best if large areas are involved. No matter which weed control method is used, prepare the bed ready for planting and then roll the area to smooth the surface and reduce weed seed germination. Place the boulders or large stones where needed, then lay the gravel (3″ of pea gravel or 4″ of larger grades). These depths are necessary in order to eliminate light that will reach the soil and promote weed germination and growth. After the gravel, boulders, and plants are in place, work in the smaller stone to complete the gradation from small to large.

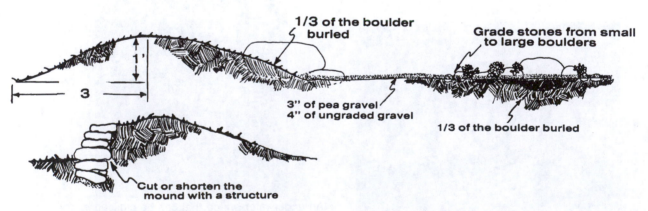

Figure 97. When boulders, stone, or soil are used to change elevation in a landscape they should appear natural and be able to support sod or plants.

Construction-grade Indiana creek gravel has stones from ½–3″ in size.

When using gravel as a landscape mulch, either put a weed barrier under the rocks or control the weeds with chemicals (which is the case in this planting).

The same bed a year after planting.

Gravel

The two most common types of gravel used for landscape mulch or decorative rock in the Midwest are Indiana creek and Merrimac River gravel. In other areas there is good, smooth-washed river gravel suitable for landscaping. Try to select gravel that is low in calcium.

As soon as the gravel, stone, and plantings are in, apply Dalpon or Dow Pon and lightly sprinkle in herbicide. This material is good because it will not move with rainwater after application—a desirable quality when working in areas surrounded by turf or near ground cover. If weeds come up later they should be spot-killed with Round-Up, which translocates to roots and kills an entire plant. Apply this material to any beginning weed growth and only to plants you intend to kill. Be extremely careful not to pull weeds or disturb the soil in the bed because weed seeds will germinate and multiply. Herbicides can also be used with petro-mat.

Granite chips or crushed stone should be the base to set larger stones in place. Without such a base large stones will be much harder to place and less likely to stay where they are put.

The same bed 4 years later.

Another example of boulders, gravel, and plants used together.

Five years later the plants and stone have blended, and the large bed of gravel and boulders appears natural.

Some ground covers require a planting bed covered with small-grade gravel to prevent diseases caused by soil splash.

Here, a mixture of various-sized stones is combined with sedum.

Plant a stone wall as it is being built. Planting afterward forces the plants into holes, and the wall will need to be stabilized with a mortar made of cement and sand.

Using one species of plant but 12 different varieties of that plant creates many different looks. Sedum was used here because the bed is located on the west of the building, a location that attracts heat.

These large slab rocks are beautifully placed and the cleavage lines are perfectly matched.

Created through thousands of years of weathering, these large boulders were taken from a stream bank. They should be put back just as they came from the bank. The well-built bank provides an excellent grade change.

Although this boulder is on top of the ground, it appears to be anchored in bedrock. Striation marks are visible, an important consideration when many boulders are placed. Align the marks as they appear in nature.

Sometimes boulders break off and slide down a slope or into a streambed. When attempting this effect, set the boulders nearly level and then, starting at the bottom, break them off one at a time, let them drop down, and slide them into place. Work from bottom to top. This rock garden looks as though the boulders have broken away and slid into the streambed as the bank eroded.

This beautiful stone work covers a high concrete foundation that stair-steps back into the hill. Stones set in this way seem to have always been in place, waiting to be exposed when the house was built. All of the sedimentary layers run parallel, just as in nature. Pay attention to these lines when setting sedimentary stones.

These huge stones in London's Kew Garden were all brought onto the site and placed by manpower and small machines.

A year after the stones were laid. People who do this type of work are artists, especially considering the damage that stones of this size could have done to surrounding gardens.

Most crushed gravel contains calcium.

Field lime is used to lay concrete pavers. It makes a good base, but the leach that comes through it must be drained away because it will raise soil pH above 7.0 and cause damage to plants.

Combing crushed gravel gives the bed the appearance of water. Here, the gravel forms a homogeneous, even surface.

Road Pack and Crushed Stone

This material is the most commonly used in making concrete. Its other primary use in the landscape industry is for road base, which is larger rock, ¾–2″+ in diameter. Road pack is only ¾″ to almost dust and often contains clay and soil. It packs hard and can easily be graded smooth, proving an ideal surface for covering with concrete or asphalt. If necessary, road pack alone makes a satisfactory surface.

Finely ground limestone is made to apply to field crops to lower pH. It is sometimes used under brick or flagstone but doing so can lead to serious problems for some plants. Limestone makes an excellent base, but it is best to use granite or torpedo sand to avoid pH problems. Finely crushed limestone can raise pH to 8.0 or greater.

Mounds are often used with stone or boulders and should be constructed to look as natural as possible rather than contrived and out of place. Soils that contain a lot of clay, especially soil that has been compacted during construction, must be built at a lower angle. In heavy soil it is better to use a set ratio—a run of 3′ and a rise of 1′. Mounds built steeper will not absorb enough moisture to support turf or other plant life. Steeper slopes that have grass on them are difficult to mow without scalping and making ruts with the mower. If irrigation is provided absorption is so slow that the water will need to be run several times for a few minutes at a time. The bulk of a mound should be made of good topsoil all the way through or at least 1′ of good soil over other well-drained soil. If that ratio cannot be maintained because of space, cut the mound off with a group of boulders or a small retaining wall (fig. 97B). No matter how the angle of the slope is determined, avoid having the mound look like a grave.

Beach pebbles are expensive and difficult to find, so reserve them for specific purposes. To provide good cover and use fewer stones, either lay them on a hard, stable base such as packed granite or press them into wet concrete that has been dyed gray or brown.

These well-proportioned mounds add to and strengthen the design. They also screen and cut down noise.

Artificial boulders may be the answer when natural boulders are unavailable, although it takes skill to shape them. They can either be attractive and appear real or, when poorly built, look like lumps of concrete. They are built on a shell of steel reinforcing rods and chicken wire. Texture is applied with burlap bags, plastic garbage bags, and sponges.

Mounds and berms are more effective if they are planted with appropriate plants placed properly. Tall ground covers give mounds more elevation, and pines add to the sight barrier.

Too many mounds serve no purpose and detract from a home.

Erosion can be prevented on steep banks or mounds by staking erosion netting over straw or some other material and planting through the mat. Space plants closely so they will grow together more quickly.

Sharp corners and sharp, pointed crests are maintenance problems that should be avoided.

Landscape Containers

This well-built, attractive landscape container is concrete and has a copper-insulated liner. The planting was installed without enough soil to compensate for shrinkage, which robs the tree of root-growth space and is unattractive.

Large, permanent outdoor landscape plant containers that are to be used in cold climates (–20 degrees Fahrenheit in winter and 90 degrees + in summer) need to be designed and built for extreme changes in temperature.

The construction materials used should be able to withstand great pressures over a long period of time. Because these containers are used as part of landscapes, they should suit the location and be attractive. The best materials for such construction are wood and concrete. Plastic and fiberglass are also used, but should be of a heavy gauge to withstand stress and accommodate extra insulation. Metal is sometimes used, but metal conducts heat and cold rapidly. Metal containers also require continual maintenance in order to prevent rust stains on floors. Containers such as aluminum and stainless steel are expensive and are usually used indoors.

Once in containers, soil mixes will shrink, so overfill slightly and make a mound when planting. If the soil settles, the plant will need to be removed and the planter refilled and replanted. If the plant is not lifted up it will probably die because it will smother like plants that have been planted too deep.

It is difficult for many people to determine whether containers need to be watered. Indicator plants such as petunias, vinca, marigolds, and wax begonias wilt in deep shade. It is clear that when a flower wilts it need water, but often trees can drop every leaf before their problem is diagnosed as lack of water. Some people also believe that plants will survive as long in a container as in the ground. Those who install the container

Overfill containers to compensate for shrinkage and not slight plants of much-needed growing space. This container was not filled correctly, and insulation is exposed. Use as large a piece of insulation as possible to prevent heaving out during winter freezing and thawing.

should protect themselves in two ways. First, tell the container owner that the plant's life is shortened because of its small, isolated space. Second, impress upon the owner that the length of life of any container plant is in direct proportion to the amount of good, regular care it receives. If a container is forgotten for a week everything in it will be lost, even if the best of care has been given for years.

In cold areas, if at all possible, store containers in a protected lathe house out of direct sun and drying winds. Containers that are too large to move should be all right if they are insulated (fig. 98).

Fertilizing container plants can be a problem if it is not done on a strict schedule and in closely metered amounts. With too much fertility plants outgrow their space, require more watering, and become root-bound. For the best results use just enough fertilizer to maintain good color and healthy appearance. Doing so will require some experimenting and some trial and error for a specific plant in a specific container.

A major maintenance problem concerns how to handle water that runs through a container after watering. Hopefully, drains were supplied during construction of the site. If not, drains or drain pans that can be removed after each watering (to remove all free water) need to be installed (fig. 98).

Small drain holes 1″ in diameter should be placed every few inches. Holes smaller than this will clog quickly. A layer of coarse gravel should be at the bottom of most large containers to provide lateral movement of free water. Do not use a layer of more than 4″ unless the container is larger than 6′ across and 4′ deep. This layer and the perched water table just above the stone cuts out 6–8″ of usable growing area. "Perched water table" refers to a saturated layer of soil at the bottom of the soil column. Whether it is on the bottom of the container or on the gravel, the layer is always present. Because it must be subtracted from the growing area for roots it should be kept to a minimum.

In most containers it is a good idea to place a porous plastic fabric mat over the stones to separate the soil from the stone and provide better drainage over a longer time. Because the mat will collect fine sediment, it will eventually clog, but that should not be a problem for the life of most containers and container plants.

All landscape containers should be lined with an insulation material such as styrofoam or fiberboard to slow freezing and thawing, prevent root damage, and stop the container from cracking because the insulation

Landscape Container

Side view

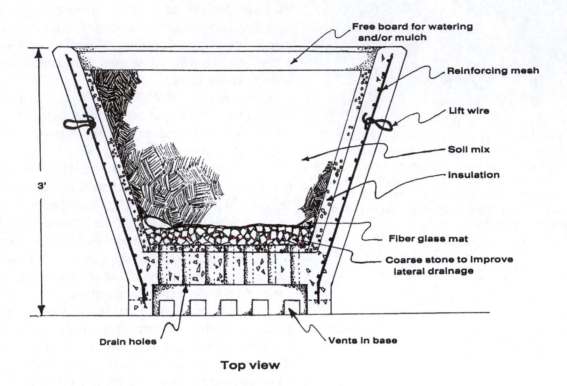

- Free board for watering and/or mulch
- Reinforcing mesh
- Lift wire
- Soil mix
- Insulation
- Fiber glass mat
- Coarse stone to improve lateral drainage
- Drain holes
- Vents in base

3'

Top view

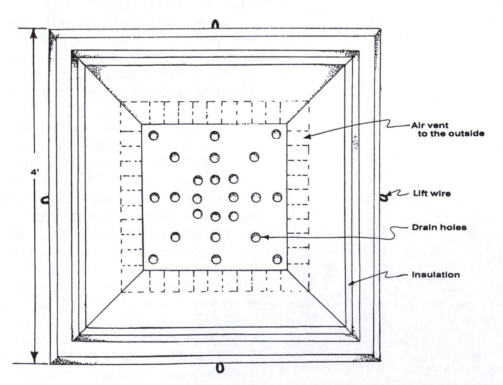

- Air vent to the outside
- Lift wire
- Drain holes
- Insulation

4'

Figure 98. Landscape containers must be designed to support plant life and also remain intact through all kinds of weather.

The larger plant in this well-built and planted container is planted a little higher to allow for settling.

When planting trees or large evergreens in containers, cover the soil with plants for a natural look and for cooler soil during the summer. If flowers are used, their appearance may alert a maintenance person to the fact that the tree is in need of water.

Plants in large containers require more water and care as they grow. Water should drain out the holes in the container's bottom. That will indicate how well the container is draining and remove salts and extra water.

will give under pressure and protect the wall of the container. These components are extremely important for the life of the plants in containers and the length of time the container will be usable. Many large containers have a copper lining that leaves an open space around the walls, dead-air space that provides satisfactory insulation.

All containers should have sides that slant so the container top is larger than its bottom. This feature works with insulation to prevent cracking of the container. As soil freezes it heaves up and out rather than applies direct pressure to a container's sides. It does not matter what the container's outside shape is as long as its inside walls slant out at the top.

When selecting a landscape container, make sure that it is well constructed. If it is fiberglass or plastic, make sure the walls are thick, corners are reinforced, and that it will accommodate insulation. It should be strong enough to allow relocation or turning to expose all sides to better light. If the container is to be made of concrete, be sure it is reinforced with wire mesh. Build in lift handles to provide easier moving when turning or loading the container. Also ensure some way to let out water from below so the floor underneath the container remains dry.

Container soil should be open and porous to permit good, rapid drainage. One of the best soil mixes is ⅓ soil, ⅓ composted hardwood bark, and ⅓ vermiculite. That mix will hold enough moisture and is light in weight. When adding sand to the mix, use more than 50% by volume. Any mix that contains less sand will become hard and drain poorly, adding extra weight to the mix. Overloading can be a costly and dangerous problem if a container is in a roof garden.

The containers should be filled and planted with the plant already in place. If the plant needs soil underneath it to raise it to the proper height, fill the container to that point, place the plant, and then continue to fill.

All container plantings will settle and the soil mix will compress. Compensate for this shrinkage by planting a little higher and overfilling the container slightly. If that is not done root space is lost and the insulation around the sides is exposed, which is unsightly. It is better to overfill and then remove soil later if necessary. It is detrimental to add more soil later because the plant's root system will be smothered. If containers are used in large, urban centers or other locations where vandalism and theft is possible, loops like the lift handles can be left inside so the plants can be cabled into place.

Terra-cotta or other fragile containers should not be allowed to remain outdoors in freezing weather. In very mild climates where few nights are colder than 30 degrees, an insulation blanket can be wrapped around the container. Moving plants into protected areas will also provide time for extra care and rejuvenation.

Plants in shallow, dish containers need water at least once a day in hot, windy sites. Evergreens seem to take such use more readily than flowers and other shrubs.

There should always be some free board left to provide for good water holding capacity. Large woody plants react slowly to dry conditions in a container, so it is a good idea to add an indicator plant to cover the soil. Annuals or deciduous ground covers wilt quickly and alert caretakers to the need for water.

If a container is well designed and the soil is properly formulated and mixed, the next consideration is what to put in the container that will live a reasonable length of time and also be attractive. Some species should never be used in containers, some can be adapted for containers, some will work well for a limited time, and some plants seem to adapt well to containers.

A regular maintenance program is the final and most important factor for a successful container planting, and a watering schedule is a key to success. It must be done regularly, regardless of rainfall. Fertilizing should be done regularly in small amounts rather than in a heavy application given once or twice. It is best to give small amounts of a water-soluble, balanced fertilizer once or twice a month during the growing season. In addition to the water and fertility program, a plant will need to be pruned often to balance root and top growth. A small amount of pruning done evenly over the year is good because it reduces the shock and keeps the plant attractive and even in appearance all season.

Among plants that will grow successfully in outdoor containers are:

Container Plants

1. Sumac (*Rhus*): All types are good, however they are not a long-lived plant.
2. Witch hazel (*Hamamelis* sp.): A good plant, it lasts a long time and provides flowers when nothing else is in bloom. It is little trouble to prune it into a small tree shape.
3. Hawthorn (*Crataegus*): Cockspur and Washington hawthorn are the best. The problem with this plant is its susceptibility to hawthorn rust, which can cause the plant to be messy and unattractive in some years.
4. Crab apple (*Malus*): Newer, disease-resistant varieties are good, especially smaller types

Container plants can withstand a lot if they are cared for regularly and correctly. This planting is on the twenty-first floor of a Chicago high-rise.

If plant security is required, attach a light cable to a disk or board laid in the bottom of the container and fill the container with the planting mix. After planting, use 2 U-bolts to secure a cable around the trunk.

Plants in large containers that have a great deal of surface but are not very deep tend to dry out quickly. It is best to use those with a shallow root system, and even they need to be watered frequently. This birch tree has adapted nicely.

such as Coral Burst, Selkirk, Red Jade, and Prairie Fire.

5. Birch (*Betula* sp.): All birch are good. If white-bark birches are used, yearly treatment for bronze birch borer will be necessary.

6. Junipers (*Juniperus* sp.): All are good, but some are better because of size and disease resistance. Canart and Keteler junipers are good upright forms. Sargents and Bar Harbor are good creeping forms, and the Blue Rug is an excellent low-creeping form often used for weeping over the sides of containers.

7. Pine (*Pinus* sp.): Scotch pine is most widely used as an upright form. It is quick-growing and will adapt well to containers. The Mugho pine is good for a lower form.

8. Maple (*Acer* sp.): Amur maple is the best because of its size. Japanese maples are good where the temperature does not drop below zero and if the container is out of the wind.

9. Chokeberry (*Aronia* sp.): Both the red- and black-fruited forms are good and do well in heavily polluted areas.

10. Spirea (*Spireae* sp.): Anthony Waters and Snow Mound are two of the best; the others will thrive but tend to be too woody.

A similar planting, only the soil has been mounded to give more root space.

English watering troughs or tubs are idea for miniature plantings such as dwarf evergreens.

Containers such as this, although beautiful, should be left to serious gardeners. It will take almost daily care, much like bonsai.

An alpine tub planting makes an attractive patio ornament in a cool, bright spot.

A simple clay-tray pot is an attractive and inexpensive container

Containers that have been built into decks, if well constructed, are a good way to bring interest and beauty near a house. Make the container of heavy, pressure-treated lumber. Line the inside with a heavy plastic film or the newer poured liner material. Then apply a veneer of decorative wood to the outside.

Landscape Lighting

Three different voltage ratings can be used in the landscape: 110-volts, 12-volts, and 6-volts. The 110-volt system is still the most versatile, and it produces enough light to handle large areas an advantage over the 12- and 6-volt systems. The disadvantages of the 110-volt system are that it is much more expensive to install and operate, and it can be dangerous if not installed properly or if the wires get damaged, especially around water.

Because the 12-volt system was developed especially for landscape use, there is a wide selection of different types of fixtures. One disadvantage, however, is that the fixture, as a general rule, is not strong and must be placed in a protected place (fig. 99A). It is best to install any system in this manner; none of them will withstand lawn mowers and pedestrian traffic.

A 12-volt system has many advantages when used in home landscapes. It is inexpensive to operate, safe, requires little installation skill, and uses any 110-volt outdoor outlet (fig. 99E) as a power source. Just mount the transformer time clock and plug it in. Although the light produced by a 12-volt system is much less, it is adequate for most landscape situations and provides a soft light that enhances flower colors and water features.

The 6-volt system is not very satisfactory in that it is not bright enough except in small, closed areas and has all the disadvantages of a 12-volt system. Although its use is limited, it may have advantages for a small, closed area.

It is important to understand how light affects an object that is being lit. Figure 99B shows how shadows can change the shape and "mood" of an object. When light is directed from four directions it can help raise or define the object. It is important to select the right direction to locate the light source. For most objects, especially lettering, direction markers, and building markers, light should be on an angle (fig. 99C). When an object is lit from directly behind it is turned into a shadow (fig. 100). Sometimes that may be desirable, but in most cases it is objectionable. When light is cast from the direction in which the object is viewed, the object fades, or at best lessens, its importance in the lit area.

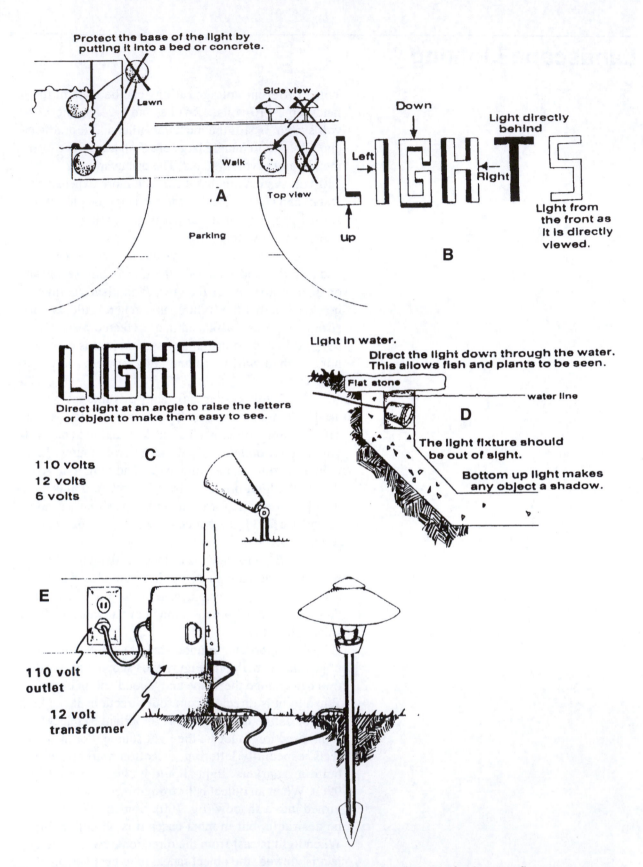

Protect the base of the light by putting it into a bed or concrete.

Lawn

Side view

Walk

A

Top view

Parking

Down

Left

Light directly behind

Right

Up

Light from the front as it is directly viewed.

B

LIGHT

Direct light at an angle to raise the letters or object to make them easy to see.

C

110 volts
12 volts
6 volts

Light in water.

Direct the light down through the water. This allows fish and plants to be seen.

Flat stone

water line

D

The light fixture should be out of sight.

Bottom up light makes any object a shadow.

E

110 volt outlet

12 volt transformer

Figure 99. Landscape lighting placement is far more important than issues of voltage or fixture appearance. Place the fixture where it is out of sight or at least out of the way of mowers and foot traffic.

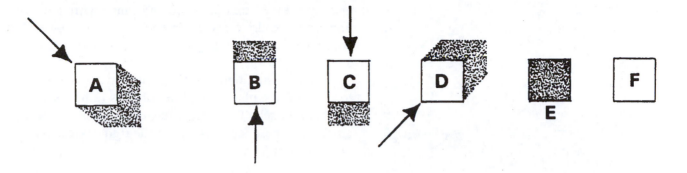

Figure 100. The blocks labelled A-D have an indirect source of light, casting a shadow in that direction and making them stand out. Light comes from directly behind square E and directly in front of F.

Landscape lighting should be protected from traffic and lawn mowers. This small extension at the end of a walk will work nicely.

All lighting systems or fixtures must provide protection for light bulbs so that when rain strikes a hot bulb the bulb will not explode. Wet grass clippings will also make a hot bulb explode. At best, the rapid change in temperature will shorten the life of a bulb.

Lighting companies all provide good specification charts on the layout and installation of equipment. Read these charts carefully, especially if you are inexperienced. When lights are installed, wires should be run under walks or other locations where soil preparation edging tools could cut the wire. Where the wire goes under a walk, drive, or patio, cover the wire with a redwood board or a piece of angle iron.

When installing any of these systems, the 12-volt in particular, it is best to use ridged conduit with a light riser set in concrete. The plastic riser that comes with the lights is weak and brittle in cold weather. Place the underground wires out of the way

Good and poor placement of yard lights on or near a mound. A light on top of a mound (left) will look like a watch tower. Place it off to one side. Never place a yard light so it is behind the person arriving at, or standing at, the front door. With that alignment, all that is seen is a visitor's shadow.

A small pad of concrete will protect the lamppost and eliminate the need for hand-edging.

and lay a 2 × 6″ treated board any time a wire goes under a walk, driveway, or bed edge where a power edger would be used. Lay the board over the wire at a depth of 6–8″.

When using lights in all landscape areas, do so to show off the plants and other objects rather than the fixture itself. There are a few exceptions (for example, Japanese lanterns) when the light fixture is also an art object.

Lights like this must be placed out of harm's way. They will be bumped each time someone passes or when the lawn is mowed.

Up-lighting is effective, but the fixture must be placed on a high spot so water will drain away from it. This light is too low and exposed to be effective. The plants will cover it, but they will be badly burned. Use a stone or a square wooden frame to hide and protect the bulb. A light placed in the ground still needs to be protected from standing water. Loose soil in a bed might cover or dull a light.

These wooden fixtures are attractive, but their ventilation is poor. Overheating is a serious problem in 110-volt systems; a 12-volt system would do the job nicely and not overheat.

The right fixture for either home or business should match or complement the structure. This palm tree has a hard time fitting into its location in the Upper Midwest.

Water lighting is difficult to do well, and best results are achieved when it has been planned carefully. Here, the light is under the pile of rocks at the center of the pool and provides harsh rays that silhouette everything. If a collection of expensive Koi were in the pool, they would all look black. Hide the light under the ledge on the side from which the pool will be viewed and fishes' true colors will be illuminated.

Water Lighting

Light fixtures are usually not desirable or planned to be seen; the feature wanted is the light itself. The fixture is often unattractive, mechanical, and harsh at its source—not the desired feeling in a nightscape in or out of water.

Lighting a water feature can be effective if done properly. It is the light that is important rather than the light fixture. If plants and fish are to be featured, hide the fixture under a rock overhang (fig. 99D) around the rim of the pool so that the light is cast downward and what is in the water can be seen. Place the light and point it away from the viewer. If light comes from a pool's bottom, all of the impurities in the water will be visible and fish and plants will be shadows. A 12-volt lighting system works well in water gardens and is safer than a 110-volt system.

Statuary

Yard ornaments like this do not add to a landscape.

This attractive piece of small statuary, well done and one of a kind, was once the top of a cornice of a building that has been torn down.

Statuary and other yard ornaments are difficult to use in a landscape for several reasons: They usually are not great pieces of art, they all need to have a suitable place planned for them, and they should reflect the style or type of garden in which they are placed. Finally, all pieces need to be placed on structurally sound bases.

Most small garden ornaments are made of stone or concrete and need to be treated or aged so they do not appear to have been mass-manufactured. Rather than painting such items, allow them to age and weather with time or treat them with a mild acid wash (1 part muriatic acid to 10 parts water). It may be necessary to make the acid mix stronger, depending on the concrete. When acid washing a piece, treat the surfaces that will be exposed to light and leave the inside of folds or shaded areas smooth to give light and shadow more emphasis. Acid will quickly erode the finish of concrete made of marble dust, so test the mix on an inconspicuous place before you begin.

Try to find an unusual piece of statuary or age the piece to give it some character. Place the statue where it can be the focal point in a garden or where it will add to a particular planting.

Large pieces will need bases deep enough to go below frost line. The base will need to weigh as much or more than the object being set on it. If the concrete or base extends above the ground-line, that weight will need to be estimated and a like amount added to the underground base.

Try to make statuary like this look as natural as possible. The statue on the left is weathered; the one on the right was painted and will peel.

Statuary that is made and copied thousands of times such as a Japanese lantern can be individualized by assembling individual parts. Be aware of the scale of each piece and then use an acid treatment to weather and age them, thereby helping them blend with surrounding plant material.

A statue's background and surroundings are important, so include it with the overall landscape design. There are two ways to approach the problem. Either create a setting or a "stage set" to make the statue a focal point or blend it into the landscape. The second method is the best alternative with weathered concrete, which—set in a shady, quiet spot in a bed of ground cover—will become more attractive as time passes. Create an original, or at least an individual, piece of art and then provide it with a specific setting.

This collection has aged naturally, and the surface has a texture that defines shadow more clearly than would be the case using an applied finish.

Sometimes it is difficult to tell real from man-made.

Figures like this can be interesting and useful.

Japanese lanterns are made in sections and in many sizes. Pick the pieces that suit you, and the light will be your choice.

One combination using 2 light chambers.

The same wide base with the 6-sided light chamber.

A 3-piece combination that has good balance and is very low.

The same light chamber with the smaller base.

The same as the preceding, only on a large base.

This large, beautiful lantern is well placed and in scale with the surrounding area.

Mailboxes

Mailboxes are another landscape item that presents problems in how they look and function. The box must be placed in a prominent location because of postal regulations. By law, it becomes one of the first things seen upon approaching the home.

Follow two rules when installing a mailbox: Strive for simple, clean lines that do not attract attention and install the box in a structurally sound manner. Nothing looks worse than a leaning or ill-kept mailbox. The box should be located out of view as much as possible. If it is painted, use the color that was used on the home. If it is metal, make it as simple as possible. All posts, regardless of their construction, should be set at least 36″ in the ground or below frost line, whichever is deeper. Set the post as discussed for fences and screens.

Keep mailboxes simple and functional. Their sole purpose to collect the mail, and they should not attract attention away from the home.

Mailboxes do not need to provide visual clutter. In this case, 4 neighbors could have gotten together and built one community holder that would be easier for the mail carrier to use and for them to maintain. Decoration on a mailbox distracts from the home behind it. The eye is drawn to the box rather than to the home.

Where it is necessary to have several boxes in one location, keep them together and as uniform as possible. Although this is a good solution, it could be less massive if used in front of a home.

Boat Docks

Floating Docks

A floating boat dock can be built in sections and assembled on-site. This type of construction is durable and provides a constant height above water line so that boats can be tied up and changes in water height will

This dock is floated on styrofoam blocks. Fifty-five-gallon oil barrels are also used in this way, but they rust and the dock slowly sinks.

Floating docks must be attached to the shore securely. If you are worried that the dock is not being held fast enough, then it likely isn't. In cases where a lot of wave action from wind or boat wakes occurs, attach the dock to a frost-free concrete footing that has about twice the weight as the dock.

This small floating dock can be moved to different locations and even taken out of the water for winter storage. It can also be widened and anchored in deeper water and then used as a base for swimming.

have no effect as the dock moves with the boat. Side panels and extensions longer than 16′ will need to be anchored to the shore in order to take some of the stress from the base hinge.

All lumber used in a dock should be rough-sawn cypress, treated California cedar, or fir. Put the lumber together with zinc galvanized straps, nails, and bolts. Bolt a small bar of zinc to each side of the metal hinges in order to keep them coated with zinc for many years. This method will also work on galvanized steel cables used to anchor the dock. When putting down the deck, be sure to leave ½″ cracks between the boards for quick drainage and to lengthen the life of the board.

A large concrete base is needed to keep docks stable against wind and wave action. The base of this concrete block must be below frost line or at least 36″ in depth on the water side. It can be poured like a concrete box with 8″ thick walls. Fill the "box" with rock. Pour it solid or leave openings in the back of the box so trapped water can soak away.

It may be necessary to cover or pad the hinges in the boat slip area with a thick rubber fabric such as an old conveyer belt or a section from a nylon tire.

A dock made like this is easy to maintain. Just disconnect it, drag it up on the shore, and turn it over if work on its underside is necessary.

Placement of flotation blocks is important for a more stable dock. Blocks should be placed as near the dock edge as possible, and heavy timbers should be added if the dock still is not stable. The timbers add weight to hold the dock in the water and stabilize movement.

The paraffin treatment given pine and fir is ideal for this use. It will not waterlog, and it will last a long time. When the dock is placed into the water it must be anchored to the shore by cables that are as long as possible. Anchor both sides to a dead-man or pilings. The anchorage must be able to hold sideways currents, waves, winds, and high water during storms (fig. 101).

Solid Boat Docks

Sharpen the 4 × 6″ posts and drive them as deep as possible, using a post mall, and then tamp stone around the posts until their tops stop moving. A large amount of stone may be necessary in soft clay. At times the posts may drift one way or another, and side supports or joists

Floating Boat Dock

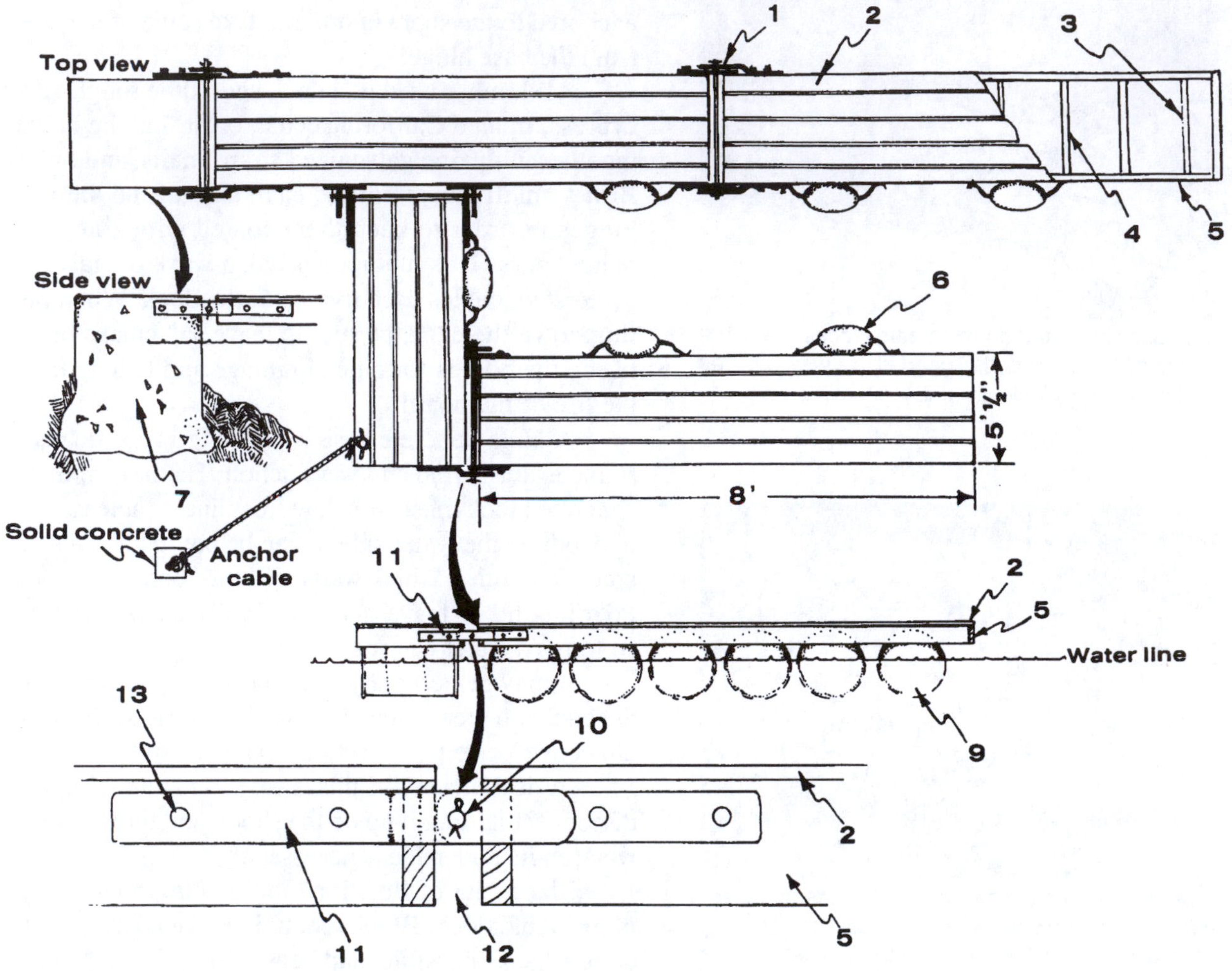

Figure 101. A floating dock and how it is anchored to the shore:

1. Overlapping metal hinges allow the dock to move up and down with wave action, keeping it a constant height above water.
2. Deck boards should be cypress, treated fir, or California cedar. It is best if the lumber is rough-sawn.
3. The frame or box under the deck should be made of 2 × 8″ cypress, treated fir, or California cedar. The first cross-member should be 2 × 8″ placed 12″ from the end board to reinforce the hinge area of the dock section.
4. The other cross-members should be on 24″ centers.
5. Outside the box, use 2 × 8″ lumber.
6. Soft, padded bumpers protect boat hulls.
7. Solid concrete shore base to hold the dock in place.
8. As the dock becomes wider it will be necessary to anchor it to keep it in line with the shore. It may be necessary to install another concrete shore base.
9. Although empty oil barrels can be used as floats, commercially prepared styrofoam floats are better.
10. Half-inch steel rod to hinge the dock sections. Secure the rod with a cotter pin.
11. A 3″ wide, ½″ thick, 30″ long piece of strap iron for the outside strap and 21″ long piece for the straight inside strap.
12. Leave about 3″ between sections.
13. Use ⅝″ carriage bolts 2¾″ long. Use large washers or back up with another strap of metal on the inside.

This strong, solid dock is being built almost entirely ashore; the outer piles had to be driven in water, however.

A dock of this type can be constructed in 2 ways, either on shore or by getting wet. Final squaring of the posts is done with shims before the deck floor is applied.

Dig the soil out of the slip area before the deck is laid because the job can be muddy if done with a backhoe. For a small job like the one pictured, hand-digging may be the best alternative.

will need to be shimmed to keep the floor supports square. Posts set in the a dry area can be set like fence posts but below frost line. Also keep stone or concrete well below frost line, well below the post's footing.

The finished dock is attractive and safe and will remain in good condition for a long time.

Details are important when finishing a job. At the front, under the dock, boulders cover the bare soil to make it attractive and stop soil erosion. The board in the front was made by curfing the board, soaking it overnight, and then bending it into shape. The soil bank that meets the lawn will be graded down to the dock floor and sodded.

This large deck structure is built in the same way as the preceding dock.

A lower dock that will be used for a canoe. Getting out of a canoe is much easier if the dock is nearly the same height as the canoe.

In addition to the fact that it is built to last, this completed deck and dock combination has many good features: storage is provided as well as lighting, a large patio area, and a small boat dock.

Playgrounds

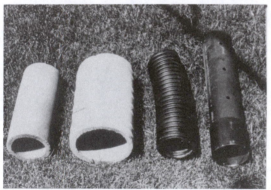

The most common drainage pipes (from left) are clay tile, the oldest type of tile and still the best for many uses; concrete tile, excellent in high-traffic areas; rolled plastic pipe, often seen in agricultural use; and golf green drainage pipe, which has a row of holes that should be installed on the bottom.

Before these play structures were installed, plans should have been made for draining the playground.

Playgrounds should provide a good clean surface that is well drained. Provide areas for adults and children so each will have individual space

Drainage. Play areas must be a good surface, well drained and quick to dry. If play areas are on flat ground or situated where water runs into a location or across it, field tile must be installed to give needed quick drainage.

Play Movement. Set play equipment to encourage movement and allow children to go from one object to another. A play object can have movement within it; the tricycle path illustrated is a good example of internal movement. Select playground surfaces that will not harm children and will drain and stay clean.

Car Tires. Starting from the bottom in terms of desirability, ground tires have proven to be more of a mess than any other surface material. They smell and stain clothes. The stains are hard to remove, and the smell stays on a child all day.

Ground Corncobs run through a ¾" screen make a good cover but mold and break down quickly. This characteristic is bad for people with asthma or other breathing problems.

Wood bark is used, but it deteriorates rapidly and needs to be augmented every year. Bark makes clothes dirty and can be smelly. It also creates a problem for people who have breathing problems.

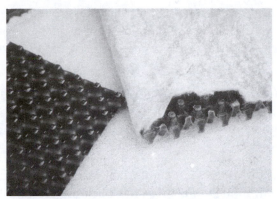

Flat drain systems made with spunbond weed barrier are becoming popular in the landscape industry and rightly so. Useful in shallow or narrow beds, the drain is a waffle-shaped strip of plastic covered with a layer of the barrier.

Four materials used to cover playgrounds (left to right): torpedo sand, ground corncobs, hardwood bark, and ground-up tires.

The top view of a good play structure incorporating movement, change, living plants, and a chance to use the imagination.

A hard, cold place to play.

A side view of the structure.

A large sand-play area.

Irrigated, lawn-type tall fescue is a stiff grass that does well in high-traffic areas.

This playground has separation of space and provides a good feeling of enclosure. The ground is covered with wood chips and pea gravel.

A nice shade arbor made of large California cedar timbers--a good place to put a seat swing.

Pea gravel has been used on some playgrounds. It drains well, is clean, and dries fast, but it can be thrown and kicked. It is also too coarse for play areas in most cases.

Torpedo sand is one of the most common and probably the best all-around play-area surface. It drains well, dries quickly, and does not stain clothes. It is also a play object itself.

Grass is by far the most comfortable and pleasant play surface. Kentucky bluegrass has been the grass of choice in the northern parts of the United States, and Bermuda grass is used throughout the South and Southwest. A large selection of lawn-type tall fescues is available for use in the Midwest from USDA Zones 5-8. This turf wears far better than bluegrass. Fescues can be used alone or mixed with blue or rye grass. Over seed in early fall with a silt seeder. Grass in any form and in any amount improves play areas.

A Separate Place for Children

Play areas must be for children alone and should be separated from areas for adults or supervisors. Objects in these areas should be safe but challenging enough to hold interest and keep children growing physically and mentally. Arrange play equipment or objects so traffic flows from one object to another. Plan play areas for different age groups and stretch the abilities of each. It is best to separate ages by grouping objects.

Planting and Play Structures. Shade is the first priority. Use overhead arbors in small areas, start trees as soon as possible, and use the largest trees available. Trees in high-traffic areas need to be carefully protected. (See the section on the 3-stake method.) Introduce as many living elements into a play area as are practical. Trees and grasses have been recommended, and do not overlook flowering trees and small shrubs. Where possible, introduce beds where small children are allowed to pick flowers. That is easily done by using irises, daisies, and bulbs for spring (spring flowers are a nice bonus) and gladiolus, verbena, and chrysanthemums for fall. The six listed will be in bloom when school is in session.

There are also many shrubs that are good to use because of their ability to bloom and recover quickly from rough treatment. Shrubs used in and around play-

Telephone poles, railroad ties, and other timber used in playgrounds need to be smoothed.

A concrete-block house and ladder.

Any kind of planning can result in a better play area than this.

A pretend train made of block and concrete pipe.

grounds need to be soft to cushion children who might fall into them and can separate areas to stop traffic in front of swings and slides. Some of the best shrubs to plant are Anthony Waters spirea (used in sun to 50% shade) and potentilla (used in sun to 50% shade). Amelancher and witch hazel grow a little taller but are also good to use.

Wooden playground structures must be free of splinters and wood preservatives. They should be sanded, have rounded, shaped corners, and be sealed with one of the many good wood sealers. If a high gloss is desired, use a polymer floor seal. If the wood tends to crack, rub it well in late fall with linseed oil. Telephone poles have been used in many playgrounds, but they need some work before they are played upon. To prepare the top of telephone poles for use in a playground, use a portable grinder with an abrasive wheel and then polish with medium-grit sandpaper. All poles need to be rounded and smoothed.

Concrete in a playground should be finished smooth and/or painted. Prefabricated items such as concrete pipes and blocks need to be treated with a cement paint and then painted with a latex paint; never use lead-based paint. After the play project has been built, paint it inside and outside with cement paint (a mixture of cement, a color pigment, and a fine sand filler). After the cement paint has had two or three days of good drying weather, give the object two coats of latex paint. This treatment helps prevent scrapes and saves a great deal of wear on children's clothes.

When building telephone pole play areas like mazes or tricycle paths, never make children feel cut off or trapped. Leave sections low enough so they can see out and exit easily.

The pole maze is extensive but children will still not feel trapped.

Water used where children will be playing is a safety concern. One way to help allay fears is to keep the depth to only a few inches and have the area supervised. The pirate lagoon shown is only 3–4″ deep and can be drained quickly when supervision is unavailable. The bottom of the pool is painted black to make the water look much deeper.

Water used as a play object is always exciting and cooling on a hot summer day. Fine-mist head sprays are great fun and also safe, and fountains at ground level are inviting and add beauty.

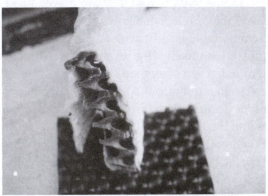

Pirate ships are a great idea, and one sailing in water is more than one can hope for. This one seems to be ready to set sail. The water in the play area is only 4–5″ deep; the bottom of the pool is covered with a black pool membrane.

Some high-pressure sprays emit water particles small enough that children who play in the spray will dry in just a few minutes, even when fully dressed.

This swinging bridge built over the same body of water drops slightly too low when someone is on the bridge. The slide-for-life tire and cable over the water make good use of the area.

Fountains that spring from the ground are wonderful to run through on hot days. A good filter system will be necessary to remove the leaves and plastic bags that can seal an intake line and burn out a pump in a matter of minutes. Chlorinate the water and send it through a sand filter large enough to supply a sufficient volume to handle the pump. Chlorinate the water as well.

Irrigation Installation and Maintenance

A quick-coupling valve being used to cool and water dry spots on a golf green.

There will be no attempt here to go into system design, but this discussion will focus on problems encountered in building a durable, trouble-free irrigation system. For example, every company that manufactures irrigation equipment has its own recommendations about pipe size and pressure and makes charts of step-by-step procedures available. Use these engineering charts and other support materials that dealers provide. Manufacturers design heads and other equipment to work as a unit at a specified pressure. It is also important to understand how soil, water, and plants interact and depend upon each other in an irrigated landscape.

Water Sources

Most homes in urban areas are supplied by a ¾–1″ water line from a community water source, usually delivered into homes at or near 40 psi, in some cases, 60 psi. Pressure can drop much lower during times of peak load in the early mornings and evenings; the drop will also become more serious during hot weather, when both personal water use and the need for irrigation increase. Irrigate when water pressure is high enough to operate the system properly.

Water for large areas may come from wells, ponds, or streams. Moving water usually does not have an algae problem, but if a pond is used there will be algae to control. The best method is to keep the water slightly cloudy and the shore drop-off steep, to a depth of 18″, which will stop weed growth. If possible, prevent shallow, warm-water areas that accelerate algae growth. Because sun and warm water mean trouble, keep water deep and cool and cut out as much sun as possible by shading the water with shoreline trees and protecting it with afternoon shade. Catfish and carp are useful for creating cloudy water because they are bottom-feeders and stir up mud. (Livestock that are allowed to wade in the shallow areas of tributaries do the same thing.) Most algicides on the market contain copper sulfate. Be cautious about using them because this material will cause spotting, dieback, and kill plants if the chemical is used repeatedly. Copper sulfate will also eliminate fish, especially fingerlings, if too much is applied at once.

Keep a close check on pond water pH, especially if the pond is sometimes charged by a well. If the water is high in iron it can stain foliage, especially broadleaf evergreens. Iron in the water will stain foliage a dull brown, and calcium will turn leaves gray or leave white deposits.

If water drains from a farm field into a holding pond, check it often to ensure against chemical runoff. If the water is often muddy or contains other sediments, channel it through a settling pond before allowing it to enter the irrigation pond.

Wells usually provide good clean water but can be high in iron and calcium. The filters and purification procedures to remove these chemicals are expensive, and you could be trading one problem for another. Aeration devices help a great deal with pond water quality.

When designing a residential irrigation system, make sure its supply line is large enough to deliver the water needed. If the water supply is not present, it will be necessary either to enlarge the supply line or install a large supply tank. If pressure cannot be maintained at or near 40 psi, a booster pump will be needed. Pressure can cause drastically different soak patterns in the irrigated area around a spray head. Low pressure forms a doughnut-shaped soak pattern (figs. 102-105). High pressure gives a lopsided, uneven soak. Sprinkler heads that are properly set and have the proper water pressure will show a wedge-shaped soak area. When large, open areas of lawns are to be irrigated, overlap spray patterns to even out the soak pattern, which can be a serious problem in heavy clay (fig. 105).

Figure 102. This soak pattern is due to low pressure that forms a doughnut shape.

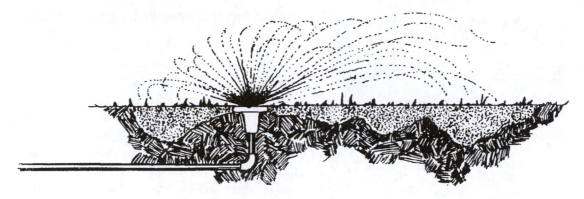

Figure 103. A soak pattern that is uneven and one-sided.

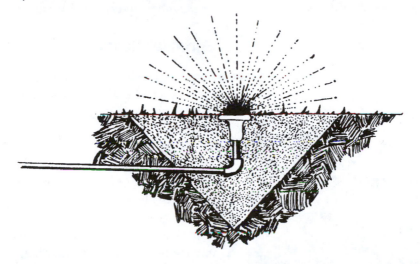

Figure 104. When pressure is correct and the heads are properly placed, this is the expected soak pattern.

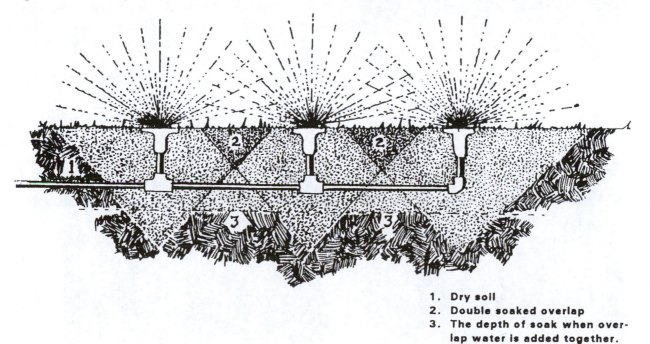

1. **Dry soil**
2. **Double soaked overlap**
3. **The depth of soak when overlap water is added together.**

Figure 105. The average of several heads provides an even soak.

One commonly used type of plastic head for ground cover beds will pop up about 18″ while in use and retract out of sight when turned off.

Housing, strainer, motor case, motor lock cap, motor, positive retract spring, setting ring, housing cap, nozzle.

A brass head and riser without a break-free riser. The head is destroyed.

Selecting the Proper Irrigation Head

The right head—whether brass, plastic, neoprene, or a combination—for the job is critical to a system's operation. Motor-operated lawn heads have neoprene gears and bearings. As a general rule, brass is best used in large heads, and valves and plastic heads are best for small lawns and shrub beds. High-impact plastics are much better in public areas and where large mowers are used; brass can also be used for bubblers in shrub beds and for sprinklers for large turf areas (with some high-impact plastic parts). Gears in large turf-head motors are brass with neoprene bearings and cast metal housings.

Sprinkler Heads

Sprinkler heads come in several kinds: basic heads are cast brass and static (no moving parts). Pop-up spray nozzles have only one action and operate the same as a static head; water pressure causes them to pop up. There are also pop-up, motor-driven, and impact-driven nozzles that have positive-retract nozzles and are made of high-impact plastic. A turf pop-up head rises just enough to clear the grass. Some pop-up heads rise 18″ to clear ground covers and small shrubs. Positive-retract heads have a strong spring that snaps the nozzle back into the body of the sprinkler housing to keep it safe from mowers and other traffic.

Pop-up static heads rely on gravity to return the nozzle. Small bits of material like algae, sand, or blades of grass will prevent the return and the mower will destroy the head.

Irrigate shrub beds with bubblers to avoid spray on foliage, prevent discoloration if the water is hard, and stop diseases caused by wet leaves. Bubblers allow

A collection of nozzles for different sprinkler uses.

Many types of risers have been used, and all have proven to be much less satisfactory than ones that swing or break free risers.

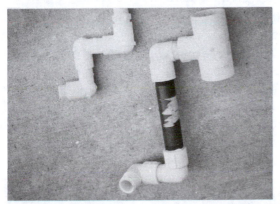

Both of these risers are good, but the manufactured riser, which costs slightly more than the homemade one, will not leak. Every sprinkler and ground-level water supply should have one. The length of pipe after the first elbow should rise at 30 or 40 degrees.

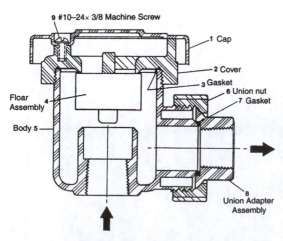

9 #10–24× 3/8 Machine Screw
1 Cap
2 Cover
3 Gasket
6 Union nut
7 Gasket
Float Assembly 4
Body 5
8 Union Adapter Assembly

Figure 106. The back-flow is a safety device to protect water on the source side of a system. This valve is used when the system is shut down.

for good soaking without losing a lot of water to runoff. Steep slopes, however, will need spray because of the difficulty of holding water on a slope. The best head for residential use has a high-impact plastic body, neoprene gears and motor, and a positive-retract spring. It is ideal if the head has a flow-control screw on its nozzle.

Any riser that can move is better than a straight-ridged pipe. A swing-free riser will cost more to install but will cost much less over the life of the system in maintenance and replacement than a straight pipe. Mixing galvanized steel, plastic, and brass when laying pipe and risers for a system will cause weak spots where a hard material meets a softer one.

Valves

Valves are used for more than turning on a system. A backflow valve, for example, is not only a good thing to install for drinking water protection but also required in many urban areas (fig. 106). The valve allows for water in the system to drain away and not back into the water source and so provides protection from disease, chemicals and fertilizer. Place the valve in front of the manual cut-off valve.

Negative-pressure Drain Valves. Negative-pressure valves open and drain a line as soon as water pressure is turned off. In all systems, place valves in areas where freezing is a problem. Install them at all low points in lines and back-fill around them with sand to allow faster drainage.

The ends of trunk lines should have plugs that can be opened so a high-pressure air tank can blow out water in the lines, especially in cold climates. Plugs should be opened and water allowed to flow through lines after every repair in order to clear away bits of soil that could get into the head and cause damage.

A negative-pressure drain valve should be used in all low spots in a line.

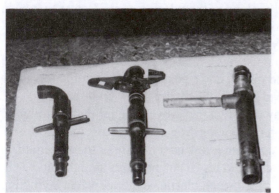

Quick-coupling valves are usually underground and out of sight. This riser needs one more elbow near the quick-coupling to make it truly a swing-free riser.

Quick-coupling nozzles used in the quick-couple valve.

Quick-coupling Valves. This valve is usually installed at or below ground level and can be used to snap in a hose bib or an impact sprinkler. All irrigation systems will need some of these valves to provide the capacity to water dry spots and wash walks. Quick-coupling valves are also useful temporarily if an automatic head is damaged; they are never seen until they are needed.

Valve Operation. There are three types of valve operation: positive, or manual; hydraulic, or water-activated; and electric (operated by a thermal valve or an electric magnet). Manual valves are controlled by hand and are useful in a fully automatic system at the supply source; quick-coupling valves should be placed out in the system of emergency use.

Either automatic system should have a control panel indoors, out of the weather and away from anyone that might tamper with the setting. Hydraulic controls use small tubes from the valve to the control panel. The system is hard to repair and run smoothly because of breakdowns, leaks in the control tube, and algae and grit buildup. It is difficult to locate and repair leaks in such small tubes. Electric-operated valves have no such problems, therefore an electric-control valve system and a solid-state control panel would be the best choice at present unless the purchase of a hydraulic system is much less. Installation or labor costs are nearly the same.

Cutaway view of the quick-couple valve.

The small tubes are the water control source.

Electric valves are plumbed in just as hydraulic valves are. They are much more dependable, however, and it is easier to set and use a solid-state time clock. When the control wire is damaged or cut it is also much easier to trace the wire than small water tubes.

Valves are located in different places in an irrigation system, for example, in-head or in-line. They can be any of those just discussed. An in-head valve controls just the head, and an in-line valve controls one set of several heads. The in-head type often is used in large areas so water can be placed more carefully. Most residences have in-line valves with electric controls. Solid-state controls are much less trouble to operate, require little repair, and settings for running time can be determined more exactly.

Valve in head operates only that head.

Valve in line operates several heads in a line.

Pipe

Pipe used in an irrigation system will vary with respect to kind of pipe, price, municipal regulations, frequency of use, soil, and local climate. The colder the area the heavier the use, and greater use should indicate the need for a stronger, more durable system.

Galvanized pipe is still the most permanent and structurally sound material available, but because of the cost of labor it is no longer an option in most areas. Many systems now installed are composed of ridged plastic (PVC). In areas in which lawns are irrigated and cut frequently, a more ridged pipe might be needed. Make sure you consider the use of the system and the area it serves. If there is a choice, always select the stronger, more durable material.

PVC pipe is popular and works well if used and installed properly. Rolled or flexible PVC lacks a lot of these good traits. PVC has made installation of irrigation systems much less expensive as well as quicker and easier. Ridged pipe must be cut and fitted like steel pipe and if

The top row is galvanized pipe designed for high-pressure water (40 psi); the bottom row is black pipe to be used for gas only.

Rolled plastic being installed.

installed correctly it is the next best material to steel. Considering the cost difference in installation, plastic pipe would be less expensive and adequate for most residences.

Rolled or soft PVC does have problems, however. It is difficult to roll out a section, especially in cold weather, and have it lay flat in a ditch without being weighing it down. The pipe is not perfectly round and its walls are thinner than ridged pipe. The oval shape causes problems at connections during cold weather. Another weakness of soft PVC occurs when a fitting and the pipe are joined with screw clamps, which rust in a short time. Rusting causes small leaks in the system, and the riser joint will not tolerate movement such as a lawn mower hit. When making these joints in cold weather do not use a torch to soften the pipe so it will accept the compression fitting more easily. The pipe will be weakened where the heat stopped, which is usually right at the fitting end where most stress is applied.

Weight is needed to hold rolled pipe in the trench.

Ridged PVC is straight and must be fitted around corners with pipe fittings. Softer, rolled PVC is usually egg-shaped because of the way it is handled in large rolls. The small pipe on the right is for use when pressure is very high.

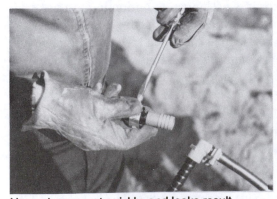
Hose clamps rust quickly, and leaks result.

Do not heat PVC pipe with a torch.

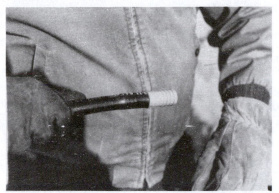

After the fitting is placed into the pipe, it stretches out of shape and the PVC hardens, which makes it easy to break.

Rolled pipe is too easy to bend. Bending around a corner without an elbow is not a good practice because the pipe will slowly flatten, which will restrict flow, or the pipe will crack and cause an underground leak.

Pipe Installation

It is no problem to install steel and soft PVC pipe. Good manuals are available. Soft PVC is simpler than steel. Cut it to lengths and assemble it with radiator clamps.

Installing ridged PVC, however, requires cleaning both the pipe and the fitting by sanding them lightly with a fine sandpaper. Clean the outside of the pipe about 2" back from the end. The inside should be reamed to eliminate the burrs and curls of material created when the pipe was cut. Make sure the pipe and fittings are wiped clean with a tacky rag dampened with acetone (glue). File or cut a bevel around the pipe's end to allow for glue (rolled up) on the inside of the fitting as the pipe is inserted into the fitting (fig. 107). After painting glue on the pipe and the inside of the fitting, butt the two back together as quickly as possible in one motion. All cutting and fitting must be done before any glue is applied because it sets up quickly.

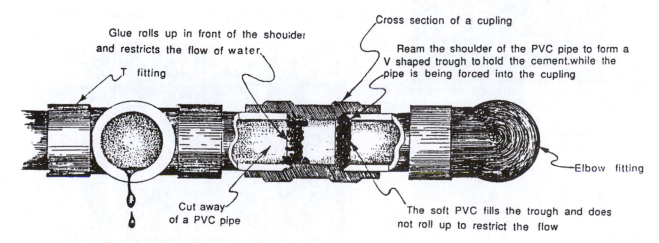

Glue rolls up in front of the shoulder and restricts the flow of water.

T fitting

Cut away of a PVC pipe

Cross section of a cupling

Ream the shoulder of the PVC pipe to form a V shaped trough to hold the cement.while the pipe is being forced into the cupling

Elbow fitting

The soft PVC fills the trough and does not roll up to restrict the flow

Figure 107. Glue rolls up when PVC is inserted into a fitting.

Using a trenching machines gives the best results when laying pipe. The floor of the trench can be kept level, risers can be set more easily, and the entire system can be checked for leaks before the trench is backfilled.

The vibrating machine knifes into the soil and pulls the pipe into the ground. The method is quick and easy but has two disadvantages: It cannot be used to run lines next to a wall, and sprinkler heads must be dug in after trenching.

Mixing Pipe Material

Never mix pipes in an irrigation system. If steel is used, it will put most stress directly onto the weaker plastic. When the same material is used it spreads the stress over a much larger area. Breaks and leaks are harder to repair in a mixed system, and more equipment will be needed. PVC is easily repaired, however, with a can of glue, a piece of sandpaper, and a knife or hacksaw.

Do not mix kinds of pipe within a system.

Using the System

Using an irrigation system involves more than turning on a valve or switching on a clock. The first consideration is the soil. Sandy, well-drained soil does not present too much of a problem, but clay soils with poor internal drainage do and will need water applied in a completely different manner. To determine the maximum time that a set should run, run it until water starts to run off the bed or lawn. If the water runs off in 5 minutes, if it soaks in 2″, and the desired soak is 6″, then the set will need to run 3 sets of 5 minutes each. The last two sets should have 15–30 minutes before the set runs again. If the soil is light or mostly clay it may be necessary to lengthen

The mark left by the machine; the pipe is too far from the wall to set the heads.

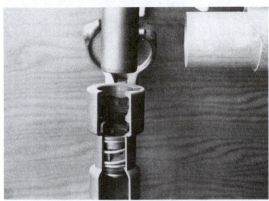

Head number 1 is the quick-tach, manually operated valve. The sprinkler head is forced down into the valve chamber, given a quick turn to the right, and the water is on. This valve is also used to quick-couple a hose bib as well as a sprinkler head.

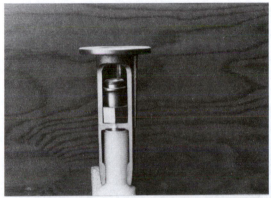

Head number 2 is a spray that pops up under water pressure; gravity drops the spray nozzle back into the head.

Head number 3 is a simple plastic pop-up with a positive-retract spring that ensures that the spray nozzle will snap back out of harm's way.

the time between water runs to allow all water to soak down and the soil to be ready to take more.

Water will run off rough, hilly ground quickly and be wasted, so time this kind of area as well. The number of inches of water to be applied can be determined by placing a straight-sided container in the spray pattern and measuring the depth to which it fills. That depth, however, may not be as important as the soak pattern. Check the runoff time and then determine the length of runoff and the number of runs to get the depth of soak desired. The amount of water caught in the container can be measured on flat areas and will likely be a good indicator of how much goes into the soil. A soil test probe is also a good tool for checking soak depth. Always irrigate enough to hold plants for a few days; wetting the surface harms them more than it helps. Shallow irrigation tends to produce grass and plants that are shallow-rooted, which makes those plants dependent on regular irrigation, causing roots that can be heat-damaged and plants that are disease-prone.

Time of day is also an important consideration when planning an irrigation schedule. Always irrigate when the temperature is on the rise, normally in the morning, to give plants time to dry before darkness, when disease grows the fastest. Irrigating at a peak water-use period can cause a drop in water pressure, and there may not be enough pressure to operate the sprinkler properly. The best time to use the sprinklers at a typical suburban residence is from 10 A.M. to 1 P.M. Irrigation systems on golf courses and other public areas can be started before dawn. Monitor any irrigation system, automatic or manual. The closer the watch kept on the system, the fewer the problems encountered and the better results will be. There is no such thing as a completely automatic system, because automatic systems cannot determine wind speed, water pressure, soil type, season, slope or grade, area use, the type of plants being grown, and natural rainfall. Automatic systems can measure and allow for some of the variables but not all.

Water shortages in many areas are moving the industry to develop more water-economical systems. In time, most water used on lawns, parks, and golf courses will be recycled from sewage plants. That is already the case in many urban areas where clean water for human use is in short supply. Most waste water is difficult to treat. When it is treated, it is put back into rivers and evaporation ponds—not a good use of a valuable irrigation resource.

Good irrigation systems are part of a well-designed landscape in which irrigation construction has been considered in order to accommodate irrigation heads suitable for the plants that are present.

Head number 4, which is impact-driven, pops up under water pressure, and the head's spray nozzle turns by impact. Water pressure from the nozzle hits one end of the hammer and makes it snap around. That causes the hammer to strike the nozzle and the nozzle to rotate.

Good irrigation installations are built with ridged pipe and glued fittings. The small extra cost of installation will soon be recovered in repair of a cheaper, rolled-plastic system. Another advantage of a ridged system is that it is easier to repair and adjust. Swing-free risers can be used. Here, a reinforced valve box contains cut-off valves and controls that allow easy access.

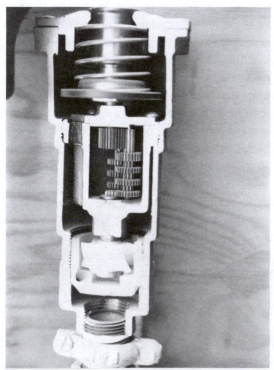

Head number 5 is the best type to use for a home lawn. It is motor-driven and has a positive retract. Water pressure drives the hydraulic motor and therefore regulates the speed with which the spray head turns.

A design for an irrigation system should first be done on paper. Then stake out the plan and check the directional head to see whether assigned areas are covered correctly. Advice on how to size the pipe to handle an area and the type of head to use is available in a number of good reference books. Factory representatives of many manufacturers will also assist at the planning stages of clients' irrigation systems.

Narrow chain trenchers are useful for laying pipe at an even depth and have less effect on a lawn or final grade.

After trenching, lay out the pipe and cut it to fit before any gluing is done. Once a connection is made it cannot be taken apart, and the fitting must be cut. First make a dry fit. Then, if that fits, raise the pipe out of the trench and prepare it and the connection by reaming the inside of the pipe to remove the burrs that cutting caused. Clean the outside and apply glue. File or cut a small chamfer to provide space for the glue to collect as the pipe is pushed together.

Three types of plastic or PVC (polyvinyl chloride) pipe are available, but soft-rolled is used most frequently. It is, however, the least durable and the least serviceable. It is also harder to install. Rigid PVC pipe is by far the best.

Make sure the valves are clean and in place before gluing. Always dry-fit first to make sure it all works— then go back and apply the glue.

After the pipe is placed in the trench, it will have enough flex to compensate for the rest of the angle.

There is a head available for every purpose. This in-ground valve box contains just a small sample of those available.

There are several electrically controlled valves to suit any need. Electric solenoid valves provide the best, most trouble-free operation. The wires that control the valve are much easier to find if it is cut or disconnected and do not clog with algae or sand, as do the small tubes that control the hydraulic system.

Placing sprinkler heads next to a walk or next to driveways is important to ensure that each head is protected and the grass along the walk is watered. This sprinkler head has been installed with an elbow, which makes it hard to keep the head straight and level and against a driveway or walk. Use one of the swing-free risers described earlier.

Here, a t-shaped fitting was used to get the head closer to the driveway, but it still can be damaged if hit by car tires or lawn mowers.

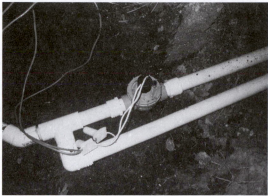

Install in-line valves as close to the start of the run or the head the valves will control. This one controls several heads. In-line valves are used for large heads, such as those used on golf courses.

Several electrical in-line valves are being placed in this single location and will be put in the ground-level box for easy maintenance.

If irrigation pipe will cross under a concrete slab such as a walk or drive, lay pipe about twice the size of the irrigation pipe, preferably before the concrete is poured. Doing so will enable you to pull pipe and control wires under the concrete. It will also save time and money because the walk or drive will not have to be cut or disturbed. If the irrigation installation is begun after the concrete, push the larger pipe under the walks. A water-jet tool will likely be needed. In the case of parking lots, cut the concrete's surface--an expensive process that leaves a patch.

It may be hard to plant and have good livability without using a temporary irrigation system in an area of large trees or plants. This row of large pines was moved in August and the picture was taken in mid-September. They were irrigated by a flexible pipe and drip tubes at each tree and are growing well under that system.

A close-up of the watering system used on the large pines. The main ½" feeder lines were laid down both sides of the trees and a ⅛" tube with a lead diffuser was put at the exit end. This was then inserted into the feeder line. These were laid in place and covered with mulch to keep the diffuser heads from moving and slow moisture loss. There is a new feeder line for every 6 trees. Water was turned on and allowed to run 12 to 14 hours a day until a freeze was predicted. Then the line was blown free of water, ready to use in the next growing season.

Underground leaky pipe irrigation is a good temporary system. In nurseries, the pipe is dug with the plant, and a new pipe is placed in the ground before the next planting. The system would be excellent insurance for the survivability of trees and shrubs at a large landscape site and could be abandoned when no longer needed.

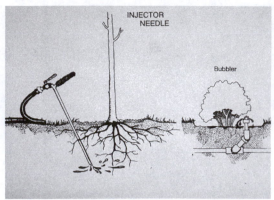

The needle should be used as shown. Also shown (right) is how bubblers should be installed. At planting time, place them just above the soil or mulch and at the location of the plant's root zone.

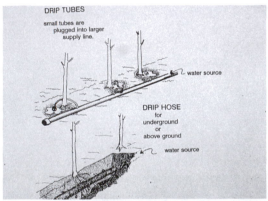

How above- and below-ground systems are installed.

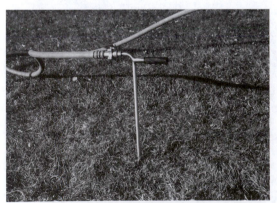

A commercial needle-injection tool can apply water directly to the root zone or the root ball of a newly planted tree. Use the needle at low water pressure and in 3 to 4 locations around the plant.

Freeze-proof Hydrants

Freeze-proof hydrants are used in landscapes where supplemental water is needed to syringe water off golf greens and to water dry spots.

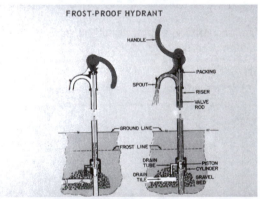

Freeze-proof hydrants are useful around a landscape area and provide the ability to water new plantings or to add extra water during hot, dry periods.

APPENDIXES

Appendix A   Tables

A-1. AMOUNTS OF FLOWERS OF SULFUR NECESSARY TO LOWER SOIL pH

original soil pH	Amount of flowers of sulfur needed tolower soil pH to 5.0 (ounces per 100 square feet)		Amount of flowers of sulfur needed to lower soil pH to 4.5 (ounces per 100 square feet)	
	dark-colored loams	light-colored loams	dark-colored loams	light-colored loams
6.4	74	52	112	75
6.2	66	44	104	69
6.0	59	39	97	65
5.8	53	35	91	61
5.6	46	31	85	56
5.4	34	22	72	48
5.2	21	14	59	39
5.0	—	—	38	25

   The correct amount of flowers of sulfur to be added for various pHs and types of soil; pH is determined by soil testing. Additional soil tests are not required unless the plants do not grow properly (discolored leaves, slow growth, etc.).

A-2. CHARACTERISTICS AND SUITABILITY OF VARIOUS TYPES OF MULCH

	Holds moisture	Maintains temperature	Controls weeds	Controls erosion	Supplies nutrient	Attractiveness	Comments
Hardwood bark	E	E	E	F	P	F	Needs to be replaced each year. Need to add 6 lbs. nitrogen per cubic yard before use as a mulch. Will raise the soil pH if used in large quantities. Allow to compost 90 days.
Pine bark	E	E	E	F	P	F	Same as above.
Manure	E	E	E	P	E	P	Supplies the most nutrients of all the mulches. Different animal waste will provide different amounts. Manures like chicken and sheep should be mixed with cobs or straw. Manures contain weed seed so it should be well compacted before use.
Mushroom	E	E	F	P	P	P	This material is very fine and light, it will blow around in windy areas. High soluble salts content.
Hulls, shells process residue	F	G	F	P	P	F	Rodents and birds scatter the material and some blow around. They do not last long as an effective mulch. Bad odor when wet.
Cobs	E	E	E	F	P	F	This is one of the best. It does not change the soil nutrient level. It will mold and turn gray quickly. Good soil additive.
Leaf mold	E	E	F	P	F	F	Does not last long as a mulch. Good soil conditioner.
Straw	F	F	F	G	P	P	Used in turf erosion control. Should be chopped and composted for bed mulching.

E — Excellent; G — Good; F — Fair; P — Poor; N — None

Continued

A-2. CHARACTERISTICS AND SUITABILITY OF VARIOUS TYPES OF MULCH (*Continued*)

	Holds moisture	Maintains temperature	Controls weeds	Controls erosion	Supplies nutrient	Attractiveness	Comments
Straw & asphalt	F	F	F	E	P	P	Controls erosion nd large steep turf areas.
Black plastic	E	P	F	F	N	P	Holds moisture too well. Smothers plants. Tem perature builds under the black plastic. Cracks in cold weather, allowing weeds to come through. Apply to smooth surface.
Rubberized spray	P	P	P	G	N	F	Erosion in turf and ground cover bed. Very difficult to apply. Can be mixed with straw or seed and applied together.
Fabric weed barriers	F	P	F	E	N	P	Weeds tend to germinate on top of this material. Weeds like quackgrass will penetrate.
Leaves & lawn clippings	E	G	F	P	F	P	These materials are good but do not last long. Be careful of herbicides on lawn clippings. First cuttings after application should not be used.
Peat moss	E	F	F	P	P	F	Blows away in windy areas, pH varies greatly. Acid peat can aid in lowering pH.

E — Excellent; G — Good; F — Fair; P — Poor; N — None

Continued

A-2. CHARACTERISTICS AND SUITABILITY OF VARIOUS TYPES OF MULCH *(Continued)*

	Holds moisture	Maintains temperature	Controls weeds	Controls erosion	Supplies nutrient	Attractiveness	Comments
Wood chips	G	G	E	E	P	F	Breaks down slower than bark and has a very coarse texture. It lasts a long time.
Creek gravel (Merrimac river gravel; Indiana creek gravel)	F	P	F	P	N	E	Good color combinations and a smooth surface.
Crushed stone	F	F	F	P	P	P	Most crushed stone is calcium. This can raise the pH much too high for good plant growth. Look for granite as a non-calcium stone. All crushed stone compacts badly. See Figure 2.
Sawdust	E	E	F	P	P	F	Needs to be well composted before use. Six lbs. nitrogen per cubic yard of sawdust. Allow to compost as least 90 days before use. Six month old sawdust or older will require less nitrogen.

E — Excellent; G — Good; F — Fair; P — Poor; N — None

A-3. CHEMICAL ANALYSIS OF VARIOUS TYPES OF MULCH

Fertilizer	Analysis in Percent			Pounds per 100 sq. ft.	Remarks
	N	P	K		
Manure					Although manures in general are
Cattle	0.5	0.3	0.5		low in fertilizer, when used in
Chicken	0.9	0.5	0.8		relatively large amounts to improve
Horse	0.6	0.3	0.6		soil structure, damage may occur
Sheep	0.9	0.5	0.8		because of too much fertilizer,
Swine	0.6	0.5	0.4		particularly after steaming.
Mushroom manure					Chicken manure and sheep manure
(spent)	1	1	1	5	can burn plants if used in large amounts and too near to plants.
Oyster shells	0.2	0.3	0	5	Because of their alkalinity these are best used for raising pH rather than as a fertilizer.
Peat (reed or sedge)	2	0.3	0.3	5	Best used as a soil condi tioner rather than as a fertilizer. Breaks down too rapidly.
Rice hulls (ground)	0.5	0.2	0.5	5	
Sludge	2	1	1	5	Examples of activated sludge are
Sweage					Milorganite (Milwaukee, Wisc.),
Sewage, activated					Hu-Actinite (Houston, Tex.),
(special macro-					Chicagrow (Chicago, Ill.) and
organisms added)	6	5	0	3 to 4	Nitroganic (Pasadena, Calif.)
Tankage	4	1.5	2	5	An excellent organic material high in potash. Has an alkaline reaction.
Wood ashes	0	2	6	5	Quite alkaline.

A-4. POUNDS OF ACTUAL NUTRIENT IN A BAG OF FERTILIZER

Percent Nutrient	10-lb. bag	15-lb. bag	20-lb. bag	25-lb. bag	30-lb. bag	40-lb. bag	50-lb. bag
1	0.10	0.15	0.20	0.25	0.30	0.40	0.50
2	0.20	0.30	0.40	0.50	0.60	0.80	1.00
3	0.30	0.45	0.60	0.75	0.90	1.20	1.50
4	0.40	0.60	0.80	1.00	1.20	1.60	2.00
5	0.50	0.75	1.00	1.25	1.50	2.00	2.50
6	0.60	0.90	1.20	1.50	1.80	2.40	3.00
7	0.70	1.05	1.40	1.75	2.10	2.80	3.50
8	0.80	1.20	1.60	2.00	2.40	3.20	4.00
9	0.90	1.35	1.80	2.25	2.70	3.60	4.50
10	1.00	1.50	2.00	2.50	3.00	4.00	5.00
11	1.10	1.65	2.20	2.75	3.30	4.40	5.50
12	1.20	1.80	2.40	3.00	3.60	4.80	6.00
13	1.30	1.95	2.60	3.25	3.90	5.20	6.50
14	1.40	2.10	2.80	3.50	4.20	5.60	7.00
15	1.50	2.25	3.00	3.75	4.50	6.00	7.50
16	1.60	2.40	3.20	4.00	4.80	6.40	8.00
17	1.70	2.55	3.40	4.25	5.10	6.80	8.50
18	1.80	2.70	3.60	4.50	5.40	7.20	9.00
19	1.90	2.85	3.80	4.75	5.70	7.60	9.50
20	2.00	3.00	4.00	5.00	6.00	8.00	10.00
21	2.10	3.15	4.20	5.25	6.30	8.40	10.50
22	2.20	3.30	4.40	5.50	6.60	8.80	11.00
23	2.30	3.45	4.60	5.75	6.90	9.20	11.50
24	2.40	3.60	4.80	6.00	7.20	9.60	12.00
25	2.50	3.75	5.00	6.25	7.50	10.00	12.50
26	2.60	3.90	5.20	6.50	7.80	10.40	13.00
27	2.70	4.05	5.40	6.75	8.10	10.80	13.50
28	2.80	4.20	5.60	7.00	8.40	11.20	14.00
29	2.90	4.35	5.80	7.25	8.70	11.60	14.50
30	3.00	4.50	6.00	7.50	9.00	12.00	15.00
31	3.10	4.65	6.20	7.75	9.30	12.40	15.50
32	3.20	4.80	6.40	8.00	9.60	12.80	16.00
33	3.30	4.95	6.60	8.25	9.90	13.20	16.50
34	3.40	5.10	6.80	8.50	10.20	13.60	17.00
35	3.50	5.25	7.00	8.75	10.50	14.00	17.50
36	3.60	5.40	7.20	9.00	10.80	14.40	18.00
37	3.70	5.55	7.40	9.25	11.10	14.80	18.50
38	3.80	5.70	7.60	9.50	11.40	15.20	19.00
39	3.90	5.85	7.80	9.75	11.70	15.60	19.50
40	4.00	6.00	8.00	10.00	12.00	16.00	20.00
41	4.10	6.15	8.20	10.25	12.30	16.40	20.50
42	4.20	6.30	8.40	10.50	12.60	16.80	21.00
43	4.30	6.45	8.60	10.75	12.90	17.20	21.50
44	4.40	6.60	8.80	11.00	13.20	17.60	22.00
45	4.50	6.75	9.00	11.25	13.50	18.00	22.50
46	4.60	6.90	9.20	11.50	13.80	18.40	23.00
47	4.70	7.05	9.40	11.75	14.10	18.80	23.50
48	4.80	7.20	9.60	12.00	14.40	19.20	24.00
49	4.90	7.35	9.80	12.25	14.70	19.60	24.50
50	5.00	7.50	10.00	12.50	15.00	20.00	25.00

A-5. NUTRIENT APPLICATION AND YEARS EFFECTIVE

Nutrient	Rate lbs/100 sq. ft.	How to Apply	Years Effective
Nitrogen	4-6 lbs.	Surface	1-3
Phospohorus	2-8 lbs.	Incorporate	3-5
Potassium	4-30 lbs.	Incorporate	5-10
Calcium ($CaSO_4$)	80-300 lbs.	Incorporate	5-10
Magnesium ($MgSO_4$)	24-100 lbs. 1/2 as much as Ca	Incorporate	5-7
Sulfur	10-24 lbs.	Incorporate	5-7
Boron (Borax)	0.4-2 lbs.	Surface	5-7
Iron Chelate	0.4-1 lb.	On surface	1-3
$FeSO_4$	24-36 lbs.	Incorporate	3-5
Manganese ($MnSO_4$)	4-20	Incorporate	1-5
Molybdenum [Na_2MoO_4 or $(NH_4)_2MoO_4$]	4-40	Surface	3-7
Zinc Chelate	2 when soil pH < 6.0 4 when soil pH > 6.0	Incorporate	1-3

An application of a blend of micronutrienst will normally be sufficient every 5 years for all of the micro-nutrients except for iron on high pH soils. It is difficult to provide a long lasting solution to acid loving plants that are growing on soils with pHs above 7.0.

A-6. COVERATE FOR MULCHES AND COMPOST

1 cubic yard will cover:	324 sq. ft.	1" deep
	162 sq. ft.	2" deep
	108 sq. ft.	3" deep
	81 sq. ft.	4" deep
1.5 cubic foot bags will cover:	18 sq. ft.	1" deep
	9 sq. ft.	2" deep
	4.5 sq. ft.	4" deep
2.0 cubic foot bags will cover:	24 sq. ft.	1" deep
	12 sq. ft.	2" deep
	6 sq. ft.	4" deep
3.0 cubic foot bags will cover:	36 sq. ft.	1" deep
	18 sq. ft.	2" deep
	9 sq. ft.	4" deep

A-7. PLANTS NEEDED TO COVER A SQUARE FOOT (ROUND BED)

Diameter/Feet	Equals Square Feet	Planted 3" Apart	Planted 4" Apart	Planted 5" Apart	Planted 6" Apart	Planted 8" Apart	Planted 10" Apart
8	50.25	800	450	300	200	100	70
9	63.5	1000	600	350	250	125	90
10	78.5	1250	700	450	300	150	100
12	113	1800	1000	650	450	250	150
14	154	2450	1400	900	600	350	200
16	201	3200	1800	1150	800	450	300
18	254	4050	2300	1450	1000	570	350
20	314	5000	2800	1800	1250	700	450
22	380	6100	3400	2200	1500	850	550
24	452	7250	4050	2600	1800	1000	650
26	531	8500	4800	3050	2100	1200	750
28	615	9850	5550	3550	2450	1400	850
30	707	11300	6350	4050	2800	1600	1000
32	804	12900	7250	4650	3200	1800	1150
34	907	14500	8150	5200	3600	2050	1300
36	1017	16250	9150	5850	4050	2250	1450

A-8. PLANTS NEEDED TO COVER A RECTANGULAR BED

Amount Square Feet	Planted 3" Apart	Planted 4" Apart	Planted 5" Apart	Planted 6" Apart	Planted 8" Apart	Planted 10" Apart
100	1600	900	600	400	225	150
110	1750	1000	650	450	250	160
120	1900	1100	700	500	275	170
130	2100	1150	750	500	300	190
140	2250	1250	800	550	325	200
150	2400	1350	850	600	350	220
175	2800	1600	1000	700	400	250
200	3200	1800	1150	850	450	290
250	4000	2250	1450	1000	550	360
300	4800	2700	1700	1200	675	430
350	5600	3150	2000	1400	800	500
400	6400	3600	2300	1600	900	580
450	7200	4050	2600	1800	1000	650
500	8000	4500	2900	2000	1125	720
600	9600	5400	3500	2400	1350	860
700	11200	6300	4050	2800	1575	1010
800	12800	7200	4600	3200	1800	1150
900	14400	8100	5200	3600	2025	1300
1000	16000	9000	5750	4000	2250	1440

A-9. SOME COMMERCIALLY AVAILABLE ANTITRANSPIRANTS

Trade Name	Antitranspirant Ingredient	Manufacturer/Distributor	Type
All-Safe	latex	Certified Laboratories, Inc. P.O. Box 237 Irving, Texas 75060	film-forming
Clear Spray	latex	W. A. Cleary Corp. P.O. Box 749 New Brunswick, NJ 08903	film-forming
Foli-Gard	acrylic copolymer	E-Z-Flo Chemical Company 2011 N. High Street P.O. Box 808 Lansing, MI 84906	film-forming
Keykote	plastic-wax	Key Chemicals, Inc. Box 37 Anacortes, CA 98221	film-forming
Mobileaf	wax	Mobil Research & Development, Inc. Paulsboro, NJ 08066	film-forming
Needle Fast	latex and phenylmercuric acetate	W. A. Cleary Corp	film-forming & stomata-closing
Protecto	wax	Kerr-McGee Chemical Corp. Kerr-McGee Building Oklahoma City, OK 73102	film-forming
Spruce Seal	phenylmercuric	W. A. Cleary Corp	stomata-closing
Stoma Seal	phenylmecuric	Aquatrols Corp. of America 217 Atlantic Avenue Camden, NJ 08100	stomata-closing
Sun Guard	hydrated lime	Sun Guard Chemical Company 1269 E. Copper Avenue Fresno, CA 93726	reflecting tree trunks
Sunoco Folicote	wax	Sun Oil Company, Sunoco Division P.O. Box 426 Marcus Hook, PA 19061	film-forming
Tre-Co-White	hydrated lime	Mapco Products Michel & Pelton Co. 5743 Landregan Street Emeryville, CA 94608	reflecting tree trunks
Vapor Guard	polyterpene	Miller Chemical & Fertilizer Corp. Box 311, WHVR Road Hanover, PA 17331	film-forming
Wilt Pruf	polyvinyl chloride	Nursery Specialty Products, Inc. 410 Greenwich Avenue Greenwich, CT 06830	film-forming

A-10. NECESSARY PIPE REPAIR MATERIALS

Galvanized Steel	Rigid PVC	Soft PVC
pipe vise	1 pipe vise	hacksaw
pipe compound or tape	hacksaw	knife
cutting oil	knife	pipe clamps
two adjustable pipe wrenches	glue with swabe	shovels
one crescent wrench	sandpaper	tile spade
onepipe reamer	shovels	screwdrivers
tape and die set	tile spade	heavy hammer
rake	crescent wrench	rags
hacksaw	heavy hammer	
rollerpipe cutter	rags	
screwdrivers	file	
shovels		
tile spade		
heavy hammer		

For many survey jobs, pacing off distances will be accurate enough. It is a good idea to take measurements of your stride. Do this measuring several times in order to get a good average distance. Try stepping off 100′ to see how many paces there are.

Measuring distances with a wheel or rolotape (a wheel attached to a meter, like the odometer on a car) is a good idea if the terrain is smooth enough so the wheel will not lose contact with the ground by vibration.

The best method for figuring distance is the steel tape or chain. Use a 100′ steel tape if at all possible. Fabric tapes stretch and are easily damaged. All tapes need to be used carefully so they do not kink and break. Pull the tape tight and keep it as straight as possible when taking a reading. Do not leave it lying out in the sun. Dry the tape before returning it to its case. Steel tapes should be dried and wiped with a lightly oiled rag.

The following examples will provide the means to figure areas of all shapes that you might see in the landscape or in structures in that landscape.

Area of a Square or Rectangle

$$AREA = \frac{Width\ (feet) \times length\ (feet)}{43560}$$

$$AREA = \frac{350 \times 1150}{43560}$$

$$AREA = \frac{402500}{43560} = 9.24$$

AREA = 9.2 acres rounded to the nearest tenth

Area of Triangles

$$AREA = \frac{Base\ (feet) \times height\ (feet)}{2 \times 43560}$$

$$AREA = \frac{1150 \times 320}{2 \times 43560}$$

$$AREA = \frac{368000}{87120} = 4.22$$

AREA = 4.2 acres rounded to the nearest tenth

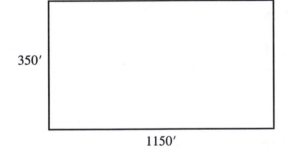

350′

1150′

320′

1150′

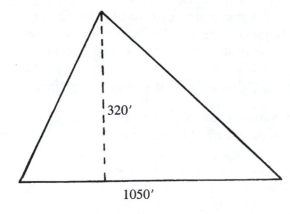

$$AREA = \frac{Baseline \times Height\ of\ triangle}{2 \times 43560}$$

$$AREA = \frac{1050 \times 320}{2 \times 43560}$$

$$AREA = \frac{336000}{87120} = 3.85$$

AREA = 3.9 acres rounded to the nearest tenth

Area of a Trapezoid

$$AREA = \frac{\frac{1}{2}\ the\ sum\ of\ the\ 2\ parallel\ sides \times Height}{2 \times 43560}$$

$$AREA = \frac{\frac{1}{2}(800 + 1,150) \times 230}{2 \times 43560}$$

$$AREA = \frac{975 \times 230}{2 \times 43560}$$

$$AREA = \frac{224250}{87120} = 2.56$$

AREA = 2.6 acres rounded to the nearest tenth

Area of Curved Boundaries

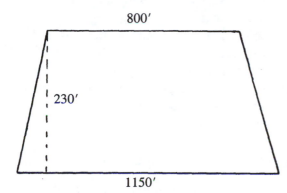

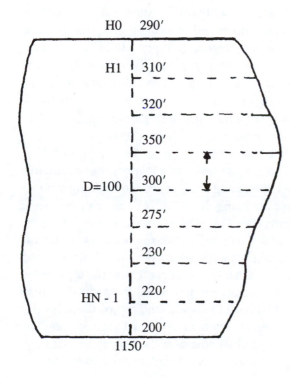

$$AREA = (\frac{HO}{2} + sum\ h_1\ to\ H_n - 1 + \frac{HN}{2} \times D)$$

$$AREA = (\frac{290}{2} + 310 + 320 + 350 + 300 + 275$$

$$+ 230 + 220 + \frac{200}{2}) \times \frac{100}{43560}$$

$$AREA = \frac{290}{2} + 2005 + \frac{200}{2} \times \frac{100}{43560} = ?$$

$$AREA = 145 + 2005 + 100 \times \frac{100}{43560} = 5.165$$

$$AREA = 2250 \times \frac{100}{43564} = 5.17$$

AREA = 5.2 acres rounded to the nearest tenth

Figure 108

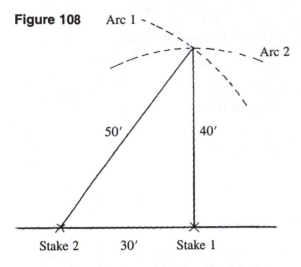

Arc 1

Arc 2

50' 40'

Stake 2   30'   Stake 1

Figure 109

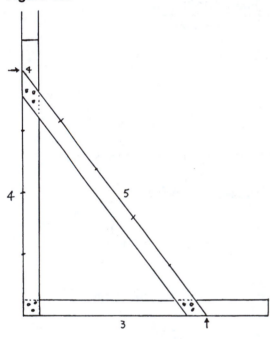

4

5

4

3

Figure 110

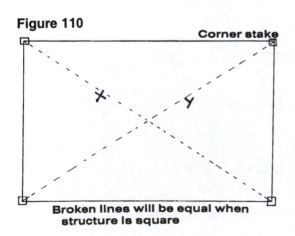

Corner stake

X   Y

Broken lines will be equal when
structure is square

To find the area of the other side, repeat the process. This formula is useful in finding the area of lakes, riverfront property and other irregular-shaped areas.

Squaring a Corner with the 3-4-5 Method

The 3-4-5 method is often used when laying out a square or a rectangle of a lot or the corner of a building. Using a steel tape, lay out a base line parallel to another building or with a direction such as an east-west line. Drive a stake at the intersection. This will be the 90-degree angle. Measure along the base line 30' and set another stake.

At this stake, extend the tape to 50' and swing an arc. Return to the first stake and swing an arc of 40'. The 2 arcs cross at the top of the 2 legs (fig. 108).

You can build a large wooden square by using two 1 × 4" boards 10' long and one 5' long. Nail the two 10' boards together at the ends as square as you can judge. Then, with the steel tape, measure off the hypotenuse of 5' and the base leg of 3' and a leg of 4' and nail them together (fig. 109).

Staking Out and Squaring a Building

Determine one wall or line as it will relate to other buildings or objects such as trees and streams. Establish the length of the structure. The other two corners can be set approximately by measuring off the distance to the opposite corner and marking it temporarily. Use the 3-4-5 squaring method in figure 108. Do the same at the other corner. Now measure the diagonals X-Y and adjust the two pins until the diagonal distance is the same (fig. 110). The structure then should be square. When laying out a building in this manner, mark an X on top of the stakes and measure exactly.

If a building is to be built on the site, it must be built both square and level, in a manner that maintains the square corners and the level of the building while the footings are being dug. This is done with the use of batten boards (fig. 111). Drive a stake about 2-3' back from the corner; then drive a stake about 3-4' down the wall and parallel to the wall in both directions. Drive such a stake in at all four corners. Level the tops of the stakes as they are driven in; leave them about 2-3' high. Nail a 1 × 4" board flush with the top of these level stakes and then check them afterward to make sure they stay level. Tie a chalk line over the boards so that they cross exactly over the X on the corner stake. This is

Batter Boards

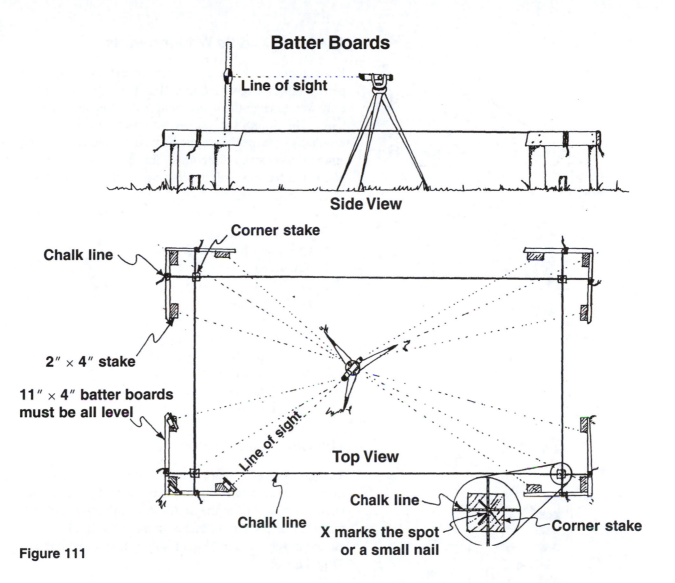

Line of sight

Side View

Corner stake

Chalk line

2" × 4" stake

11" × 4" batter boards
must be all level

Line of sight

Top View

Chalk line

Chalk line

X marks the spot
or a small nail

Corner stake

Figure 111

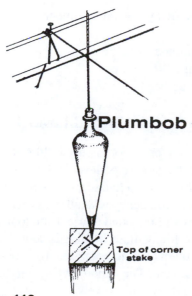

Plumbob

Top of corner
stake

Figure 112

done with a plumb bob dropped at the corner and the lines adjusted until they touch the plumb bob line (fig. 112). With a small nail, mark where the string goes over the board. A saw can be used to mark this location as well. Cut a groove for the chalk line to fit into after the lines are all squared. This is done so the lines can be taken down while digging is in progress. The lines can then be put back up quickly and easily to mark the corners even after the corner stake is dug up. Be sure to check the level of these boards before using them to set corners, foundations, or level floors.

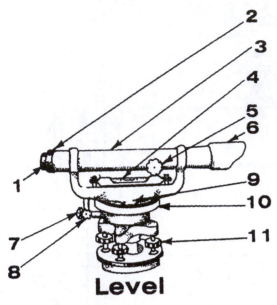

Figure 113

The Level and Its Working Parts

It is important to learn the instrument and how to quickly perform the various functions (fig. 113). Practice is the only way to level the instrument and focus the cross hairs. The thumb screws seem to present the most problems because they must be turned exactly the same amount in opposite directions. This procedure is explained in section 5 of "Becoming Proficient with the Tripod Level."

1. Eye-piece and cap
2. Cross-hair focus ring
3. Telescope
4. Level vial
5. Focusing knob
6. Sun shield
7. Horizontal setting clamp screw
8. Fine horizontal setting made with the tangent screw
9. Telescope yolk
10. Horizontal vernier
11. Leveling screws

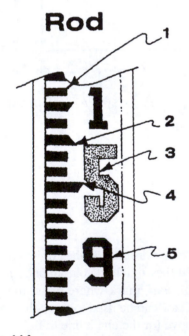

Figure 114

The Self-Reading Rod

The red number 5' mark is easily seen, and the red 5' mark is repeated halfway to the 6' mark (fig. 114). This small red 5 will be at the 5/10 mark to the right side of the rod. The proper use and reading of the rod is discussed in section 8 of "Becoming Proficient with the Tripod Level."

1. Top of black always an even number
2. 5/10 mark
3. Foot mark number
4. Foot reading 5.00
5. 9/10 black number

Landscape Use of the Tripod Level

Structures of any size or importance should never be started without the use of a tripod level. This instrument is one of the most useful tools a landscaper can have if it is used properly. Once proficiency with a level is achieved, many opportunities will be found to use it and to improve the quality of work. Many times leveling is done "by eye" or "guess," which often leads to poor drainage, no drainage, or reverse drainage. The tripod level is very useful when laying out and leveling driveways.

Survey Notes

There are a few universal procedures and symbols used in taking survey notes. Carefully record all data in a notebook as it is taken. Always use a pencil, not a ballpoint pen. There will be too many numbers to keep track of and to keep in order to rely on memory or sloppy notes.

The survey party consists of the level operator, who is represented in the notebook as 𝝠. The rod man is indicated by the symbol Ø and the note-taker with ㎝.

Many letters or abbreviations are used in the notebook. The first is *BM-1* (benchmark): This starting point should be a solid or immovable object like a sidewalk or driveway. Be sure to mark the point on the drive or walk. This point is given an assumed height of 100.00.

The next abbreviation is *BS* (back sight). The back sight is a reading taken on an object of known elevation, such as the first reading on the bench mark which was assigned the assumed height of 100.00.

The height of instrument (*HI*) is calculated height of the cross hairs in the level. This is done by placing the rod on the bench mark with the elevation of 100.00 and adding the reading to the elevation of the BM. If the reading on the rod is 5.50, the *HI* would be 5.50 + 100.00 = 105.50.

The next item would be the foresight, *FS*. This reading is taken on an unknown elevation. The rod man will place the rod on a spot where the elevation is needed. Then this reading is subtracted from *HI* and this will be the elevation of the unknown spot. Take the height of the instrument, 105.50, and subtract the foresight reading, which we will say is 4.50. 105.50 − 4.50 = 101.00. This then is the elevation of the new sight in relation to the *BM:* 1′ higher (fig. 117).

When the numbers on the rod increase in size, say 5.50 to 6.50, it means that the terrain is dropping or getting lower. When the numbers go from 6.50 to 4.50, the terrain is rising.

The turning point (*TP-1*), is the spot where a *FS* is taken before the instrument is moved. Therefore, the spot where the rod is placed needs to be solid and held constant with as little movement as possible while the level is moved and reset. When the *BS* reading has been taken on this *TP,* then the rod can be moved. If the rod is moved before the *BS* is taken, the reference back to the starting point or *BM* is lost. If that happens, start over.

Becoming Proficient with the Tripod Level

Practice using the tripod level until you feel comfortable with it.

1. Set up the tripod and plant one of its legs firmly in the soil.
2. Take the second tripod leg and close it in until the top of the tripod is high enough so you can look through the scope comfortably; plant this leg firmly.
3. Move the third leg from side to side until the top of the tripod plate is level across the two set legs. Then bring the third leg in toward the center of the tripod until it pushes the plate above level just enough to compensate for the height lost as this leg is set firmly into the soil.
4. Remove the level from the case and screw it onto the tripod plate. Turn it until it firms up but don't wrench it down hard or it will often stick. If this happens, the level could be damaged by the force needed to remove the level from the tripod when it is put away.
5. Place the scope over two of the brass thumb screws. While standing directly in front of these screws, grasp them between thumb and forefinger. You must always turn these screws keeping the same firm tension as you adjust the level bubble. This is done by turning the screws the same distance in opposite directions. This is easily done by pushing the thumbs into the center or pulling them out while pushing the forefinger in. The level bubble will follow the direction of the left thumb, so move the bubble to the level position.
6. Now move the scope over the other two screws and repeat the process.
7. At this point rotate the scope 360 degrees slowly; it should stay level throughout the 360-degree turn. If it does not, start over by making sure that all of the thumb screws are firm and repeat the thumbscrew procedure.

   The scope lens should be protected from the direct sun. If the lens gets dusty or spotted, clean it with a soft cloth or lens paper. It is good to keep the lens shade on during use. This protects the lens from being touched or scraped as well as deflecting the sun's rays.
8. The rod is an important part of the survey equipment. The rod and the person holding the rod are the key to a fast, accurate job. It is marked off into feet, tenths, and hundreds. Survey rods are divided into tenths, not 12 inches. The self-reading rod lets you read the rod through the scope without the help of the rod man or a target. The large red figures mark the feet. The smaller black numbers mark the tenths. The black and white marks or space on the left side of the rod marks the 1/100 marks, the width of the white and black spacing. Start with the top of the black mark that indicates the foot mark which is 0. Then from the top of the black mark or 0 to the bottom of the black spaces are all even numbers (fig. 113).
9. The rod man must hold the rod steady and as vertical as possible. The rod should be placed on a stake or on firm soil. Stand directly behind the rod and hold it with both hands.
10. Set up the instrument several times until you are comfortable with all of the adjustments.

Testing the Instrument for Accuracy

From time to time it may be advisable to test the survey instrument for level. The 2-stake method is simple and can be a good practice exercise to help you master the level. Set up the level in an open, nearly flat area. Measure 100′ in one direction and drive a stake. Read the height and set the target. Measure the same distance in the opposite direction and drive another stake a little higher if you can judge; drive the stake slowly until it reaches the same height as the first stake. If it is too low, drive another stake until it levels with the first stake. Move the level to just one side of the stakes and set the level. The reading back to the two stakes should be level, the same as was the case for the original two readings. No matter where the level is set up, the reading on the two outside stakes will be the same (fig. 115). If you should find the scope is not level, do not try to adjust it; send it back to the manufacturer.

Leveling the Instrument

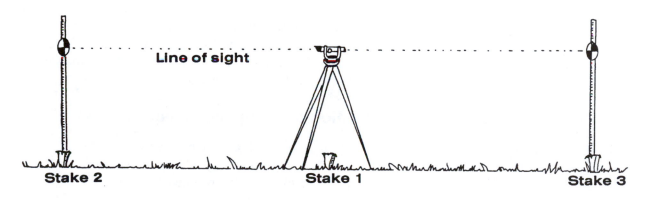

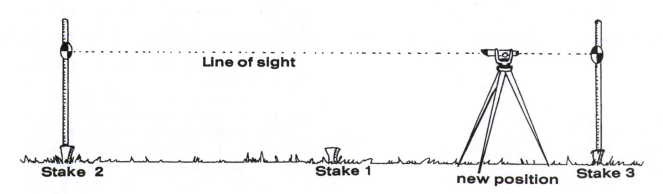

Figure 115

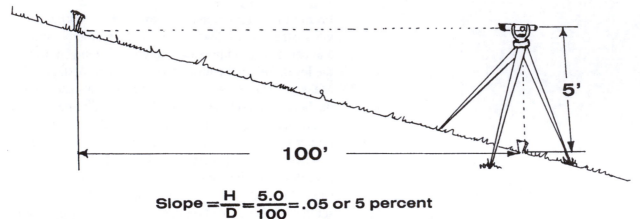

$$\text{Slope} = \frac{H}{D} = \frac{5.0}{100} = .05 \text{ or 5 percent}$$

Figure 116

Figuring Percent Slope

Percent slope is easily figured by setting up and leveling the instrument. Measure the height of the scope and then sight through the scope and find where the line of sight intersects the ground. Use the formula *slope = H/D*. If the height of the scope is 5.0 and the distance from directly below the scope to where the level line of sight is 100', *slope* = 5.0/100, or .05, or 5 percent slope (fig. 116). The percent slope can be figured with the hand level but it is not as accurate.

How to Set Up the Notebook

1. First reading is the backsight.
2. Complete this by adding the elevation to the backsight. This will give you the height of the instrument.
3. The second reading is on the rod at turning point number one.
4. This elevation at the bench mark is arbitrarily at 100.00
5. This elevation at *TP-1* is computed by subtracting the foresight at turning point number one from height of instrument.
6. The distance is measured by pacing or steel tape. One other abbreviation that will appear in the upper lefthand corner of the page of the notebook is *Sta* (Station). This is the column down the left side of the page of the place where readings were taken and *TP* were made. These then are the computations that will need to be done (fig. 117):

Benchmark (*BM*) = 100.00

Backsight (*BS*) = reading on the *BM* (5.50)

Height of instrument (*HI*) = *BS* - *Elev* (5.50 – 100 = 105.50)

Foresight (*FS*) = reading on an unknown sight (4.50)

Elevation of the instrument (*Elev*): = *HI* - *FS* (105.50 – 4.50 = 101.00)

Use these formulas to find *Elev* and *HI*: *HI* – *FS* = *Elev* and *BS* – *Elev* = *HI*.

This typical notebook will consist of a page to keep the level readings and graph paper to plot the work done and location of readings (figs. 117-118).

When acting as a note taker, always print neatly and clearly and always use a pencil, because you will need to erase. Always use the standard form for recording this data.

Record readings so the decimal points will be in line down the column. Record these readings as 4.50, not 4.5. Always use the 00. Above all, be consistent; don't record 4.5 one time and 4.50 the next. Use all of the pages needed to record without crowding. Draw the sketch of the job in proportion as carefully as possible with a ruler or straight edge (fig. 119).

Notebook Setup

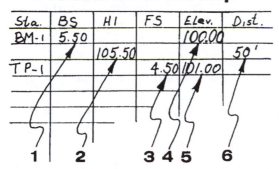

Sta.	BS	HI	FS	Elev.	Dist.
BM-1	5.50			100.00	
		105.50			50'
TP-1			4.50	101.00	

1 2   3 4 5   6

Figure 117. This is the proper way to set up the field notebook for differential leveling problems.

Notes

Sta.	BS	HI	FS	Elev.	Dist.
BM-1	4.10			100.00	
		104.10			100'
TP-1	4.80		5.20	98.90	
		103.70			100'
TP-2	6.10		4.50	99.20	
		105.30			90'
TP-3	6.50		5.60	99.70	
		106.20			110'
TP-4	5.10		4.55	101.65	
		106.75			70'
BM-1			6.70	100.05	

Figure 118

Map

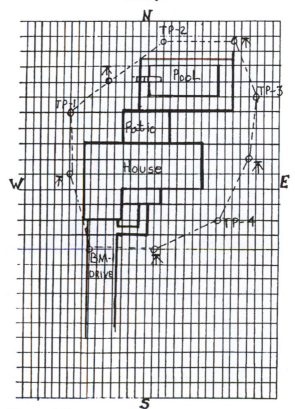

Figure 119

Differential Leveling

This procedure is done to find the relative elevation of points that are a good distance apart or points hidden behind structure or terrain.

Begin this exercise with the BM having the arbitrary elevation of 100.00. Set up your book as shown and follow the steps listed in figure 119.

1. Set up the level and decide who will do the different jobs.
2. The rod man Ø should extend the rod and place it on the *BM* selected or made by driving a stake at a point where you would like to start.
3. The level operator ⊼ should take a reading on the rod and read it aloud so the note keeper can record it. This is back sight (*BS*).
4. Now the rod man Ø moves the rod to the next point where you wish to find the relative elevation. This is a foresight (*FS*).
5. The level operator will again read the rod, and the note keeper will record the number of this *FS* (figs. 117–118).
6. This point where the *FS* reading was taken now becomes the turning point (*TP-1*). The rod man should take particular care in holding the exact spot while the level is moved.
7. This procedure is repeated for all points where elevation readings are needed. Then make your last foresight reading, it will be back on the beginning point *BM-1* (fig. 117).

As you can see by looking at the elevations at the *TP*, the slope or drainage direction is from the middle of the area from *TP-4* and the last instrument set up. The water will drain from this area to the area left of *TP-2* around both sides of the house. In this example, it would be important to protect the pool from surface drainage. A swale should be cut around the northeast corner of the pool starting east of the patio at patio grade. Drop from this point to 1′ at *TP-2*. The water on the west of the house should drain well to the northwest corner of the property.

It is also evident in this example that the drive may have a problem of water running across it and toward the garage door. It may be necessary to put a drain under the drive or raise the grade to the right of the drive in order to divert water to the right of the house.

The notes in the figures 117 and 118 examples show a typical set of readings. The map in figure 119 shows where the readings were taken. This type of information may be all that is needed. If more information is necessary, then a topography map will be needed.

Appendix C

Figure C-1. Equipment to use for soil sampling.

Figure C-2. Taking the soil slice from a hole.

Figure C-3. Collecting and mixing the samples.

Use a clean bucket or other suitable container in which to collect soil samples and mix them. The tool used can be any of the following: a soil probe, a soil auger, a trowel, or a garden spade (fig. C-1).

Proper sampling is essential for the accuracy of results. Samples can be taken any time during the warmer months, but late summer or fall are best. It is desirable to take them before soil temperatures drop below 50 degrees F. If the soil is too wet to spade, roto-till, or hoe, it is too wet to sample.

If the garden or test area as a uniform soil type, take several samples over the area at randomly selected and evenly spaced intervals. If there is a variation of soil types or if there are disturbed areas where fill soil has been added (such as clay from a basement hole), each of these areas should be handled as individual sampling units, keeping their composite soil samples separate. These different areas may need special care or extra treatments.

How to Take a Soil Sample

1. Within an area selected for sampling, take a sample as indicated and use a oil probe or auger. If you use a trowel or spade, dig a hole and then cut a thin slice down one side (fig. C-2). When placing the sample in the container, do not include roots or debris. The depth to which the sample should be taken depends on what plants are growing there now or what ones will be planted. Take samples in sodded areas 3 or 4″ deep; for shrubs and trees, 12″; and for flower and vegetable crops, 6–8″.

2. Repeat this procedure in at least 8 well-scattered spots within a garden or selected sampling area approximately 100′ square or the equivalent. Place each slice in a bucket along with those taken previously.

3. Thoroughly mix the slices of soil you have placed in the bucket (fig. C-3). The more samples taken and mixed, the better the test results will be. Do not include large pieces or organic matter such as roots, stalks, and leaves.

4. Spread the composite soil sample thinly on clean paper and air-dry at room temperature. Do not heat to dry, for example, in an oven or over a radiator.

5. Send in only about half a pint of soil from the total mix for testing.

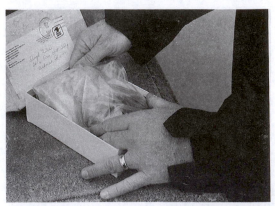

Figure C-4. Packing the soil sample for mailing.

Packing and Mailing the Sample

1. Pack the half-pint sample, thoroughly air-dried, in a plastic bag. Then place the sample in a strong box, carton, or can (fig. C-4). Flimsy containers may break open or draw moisture during shipment.

2. Label each sample with your name and address. When sending more than one, label each sample with a number, so you will know from which area they were taken. Mark each sample with the following information: "flower garden," "vegetable garden," "shrub border," "orchard," "lawn," and so on.

3. Include information describing what was grown in the garden (lawn, special trouble area, or place) last year and what has been done to the soil, such as adding manure or other organic matter.

4. Also include information about the use you intend to make of the sampling area.

How to Use the Soil Test Results

Take the results you receive to your county extension adviser and discuss the best treatment for your soil. Frequently, that involves much more than just which fertilizer to use.

Some laboratories read and interpret the results for you, but it is still best to have someone familiar with local conditions recommend treatments. Many variables can affect soil fertility and plant grown, such as rainfall or irrigation, tillage practices, soil type, slope of the land, and past use of the soil.

Interpreting Soil Test Results

The following ranges for soil tests will provide an idea of how yours compares to the average:

P1 readings lbs/acre:

0-22 lbs/acre	low	100 lbs of P_2O_5/acre
23-59 lbs/acre	medium	50-75 lbs of P_2O_5/acre
60+ lbs/acre	high	0 lbs of P_2O_5/acre

It takes 9 pounds of P_2O_5 to raise a soil test reading 1 lb/acre

Potash readings lbs/acre:

0-66 lbs/acre	low	200-250 lbs of K_2O
67-158 lbs/acre	medium	100-200 K_2O
159+ lbs/acre	high	0-100 K_2O

Lime and sulfur recommendations to alter pH should be based on information in this book. (Table A-1.)

Organic Matter and Humus in Garden Soils

Incorporating organic matter is a frequently overlooked necessity in the preparation of garden soils. Humus, the product of organic matter breaking down, is usually associated with the dark color in topsoils. It is needed to maintain a loose, well-drained soil that does not compact easily. Soil containing good quantities of humus will cultivate easily and promote good root growth.

Humus is also useful in supplying nutrients to plants, particularly nitrogen. Keep adding partially composted plant material to the garden each season in order to improve tilth and fertility. Good materials to use include compost, well-rotted manure, and peatmoss.

Index